bi

bi

Bisexual, Pansexual, Fluid, and Nonbinary Youth

Ritch C. Savin-Williams

NEW YORK UNIVERSITY PRESS *New York*

NEW YORK UNIVERSITY PRESS
New York
www.nyupress.org

References to Internet websites (URLs) were accurate at the time of writing. Neither the author nor New York University Press is responsible for URLs that may have expired or changed since the manuscript was prepared.

Library of Congress Cataloging-in-Publication Data
Names: Savin-Williams, Ritch C., author.
Title: Bi : bisexual, pansexual, fluid, and nonbinary youth / Ritch C. Savin-Williams.
Description: New York : New York University Press, [2021] |
Includes bibliographical references and index.
Identifiers: LCCN 2021011915 | ISBN 9781479811434 (hardback ; alk. paper) |
ISBN 9781479825875 (paperback ; alk. paper) |ISBN 9781479811465 (ebook)
| ISBN 9781479811472 (ebook other)
Subjects: LCSH: Bisexual youth. | Bisexuality. | Sexual minority youth.
Classification: LCC HQ74 .S28 2021 | DDC 306.76/50835—dc23
LC record available at https://lccn.loc.gov/2021011915

New York University Press books are printed on acid-free paper, and their binding materials are chosen for strength and durability. We strive to use environmentally responsible suppliers and materials to the greatest extent possible in publishing our books.

Manufactured in the United States of America

10 9 8 7 6 5 4 3 2

Also available as an ebook

To the love of my life, Kenneth Miles Cohen

CONTENTS

Nearly four decades ago, an influential psychiatrist suggested that bisexuality does not exist. By denying individuals can have attractions to more than one sex, he was not alone then or now. Just over a decade ago, the most famous sex therapist in the United States, Dr. Ruth, concurred: Bisexuality is "an in-between stage," and "there really is no such thing as being bisexual." Subsequent scientists, clinical practitioners, educators, and the general public appeared to agree, creating in their wake a dilemma for those who thought otherwise, those living lives that were neither straight nor gay but *something else*. Were they merely in transition to their ultimate gay or lesbian identity, or when they meet the perfect woman or man, they will become straight? Other supposed truisms also confused them: sexual orientation is an either/or category, not a continuum with gradation marks; knowledge about deviant sexuality can be gleaned from a small number of clinical patients; and, if one identifies as bisexual, then they suffer from psychological and emotional conflicts such as having a split personality, manifesting a self-destructive rage directed at the self, and displaying a crushing dependency on others. In other words, they were either straight or gay, and thus there is no need for a book on bisexuality—except in courses on clinical psychology, sociology of deviance, and public health.[1]

These beliefs would now shock many Millennials and Zoomers (Gen Zers) who are living a life inconsistent with these caricatures. The documented clinical and scientific "truths" do not resemble their lives, and as a result, many bisexual, pansexual, fluid, and nonbinary activists challenge these very ideas. In their wake, they have created a bisexuality that defies traditional views, disputes false notions, and reimagines sexuality, with regard to both practice and identity. Broadly speaking, many young people experience a complex, nuanced existence with multiple sexual and romantic attractions and gender expressions, which are seldom static but fluctuate over their life. I support their vision.

I began the process of challenging perceived wisdom about the lives of sexual-minority youth with earlier books, including *The New Gay Teenager*. I reviewed nearly everything I knew about nonstraight youths, including bisexuals, but the available information was primarily about bisexual women and not men. This was because, consistent with mainstream gay/lesbian psychology, it was "difficult to view bisexuality [among males] as anything other than a transitional identity or a state of identity confusion." Realizing this gap—as well as others, such as the intersection between sexual orientation, romantic orientation, and gender expression and identity—I interviewed in-depth over 300 young men and women. They led me to radically revise what I thought I knew about young adults who are neither gay nor lesbian. My first effort was writing about those who identified as "mostly straight" or "mostly gay"— the sexual identities I knew the least about. As they talked to me, I was struck by the realization that these individuals are bisexual because they have sexual and romantic attractions to multiple sexes. This fact should qualify them as legit bisexuals, and yet in our surveys and popular literature, they disappeared, evaporated, and, as we now call it, were canceled. I then went on a three-year odyssey of reading everything I could find on bisexuality—and now, the present moment.[2]

This book is a testament to the lives of the young adults who shared their stories with me.

Introduction

We are to varying degrees bisexual and some so little that
they're completely straight. Everyone has subconscious fantasies that indicate otherwise.
—Toby, age 20, white, part-time waiter

During the past few years, innovative ideas about both sexuality and
gender have exploded, driven primarily by young people, not by science.
Yet, there is a limited core of social and behavioral scientists who are
listening to young people express their substantially complicated understandings of their sexual, romantic, and gender selves. This book focuses
on bisexuality, which I believe necessarily includes sexual, romantic, and
gender fluidity; pansexuality; and nonbinary identities; and a host of
other ways of experiencing and describing sexual, romantic, and gender
aspects of the self. These perspectives might appall us or thrill us—but
they are real, and we need to understand them. Closets for sexual and
gender minorities still exist, but now there are far more ways to emerge
from them with authenticity and pride.

Although most developmental and sexual scientists, clinicians, educators, and parents now theoretically believe in the existence of bisexuality, they are not always prepared to believe youths who come out to them
as bisexual—especially if it is their own subject, client, student, or child.
When 19-year-old celebrity model Woody Cook disclosed to his mother,
"Her first reaction was: 'You can't be, you like girls?'"[1] Yes, most bisexuals like girls—and boys. Woody's mother is highly educated, and yet, she
heard "gay" when her son said "bisexual." This will be a common theme
running through the book—bisexual stereotypes are pervasive and difficult to dislodge. True, some bisexuals are psychologically confused (or

worse)—but no more so than straights and gays. Most simply go about their daily lives, similar to their friends and comrades.

Who Is Bisexual?

Possible answers to this question include those who have a bisexual identity, a bisexual "lifestyle," or a mix of sexual and romantic desires, attractions, and behaviors. Is it sufficient to ask someone whether they identify as bisexual, or should we pursue biological proof? Is it merely the sex or gender of those whom they have sex with or fall in love with? Does one method have priority over another? These questions assume we know who a bisexual is—and historically we have blundered because we only thought in narrow, simplistic terms. Now consider the many other sexual and gender terms that have gained currency: pansexual, queer, plurisexual, fluid, asexual, nonbinary, androgynesexual, multisexual, polysexual, omnisexual, and bi-romantic. What do they mean? I will revisit some of these terms in this book, but for now I use "bisexual" to refer to individuals who are, to varying degrees, sexually and/or romantically attracted to multiple genders or sexes. Even if the word "bisexual" is an inadequate namesake, it has currency with the public. Over time we will develop better language.

For this book, I listened to the voices of 69 young adults who participated in one of three studies that focused on the spectrum of sexualities and genders. All agreed to an in-depth interview about their sexual and romantic development from their first memories to the present and to their projected futures. The interview process followed the historian and broadcaster Stud Terkel's advice to throw out the intransigent protocol and ask open-ended questions, not as an inquisition but as an explanation: "Then, what happened?" Topics covered were broad, and then I followed where the youths took me.

What the youths frequently shared was having an assortment of sexual and romantic attractions, a mixture of sex and romance that did not always correspond to their attractions, and a search for an identity that made sense—maybe bisexual, trysexual, pansexual, fluid, unsure, queer, asexual, questioning, or unlabeled. Most were in college at the time of the interview, though not necessarily at the school where I teach. Nearly three-quarters reported they are white and grew up in middle- or upper-middle-class homes in small or medium-sized towns throughout the United States; rural and urban areas were also represented. Their academic majors spanned the full range of disciplines. Even though I interviewed only a few multiattracted young adults of color, I highlight in separate chapters the developmental trajectories of particular African American, Latino, and Asian American young adults as they considered the unique interactions of their communities with their sexuality (see appendix).

The interviewees' revelations about their sexual and romantic histories were astonishing, entertaining, and enlightening. As to their motives that prompted their participation, I'm not sure, but at the end of the interview, many *thanked me* for the opportunity to talk about their sexual development. As to why, a common response was, "No one has ever asked me these types of questions!" This sentiment is not an unusual one, as others who attend to self-narratives, such as the psychologists Niobe Way and Deborah Tolman, have told me. They discovered in their interviews with youths details about their intimate friendships, sexualities, and relationships that were novel, even unexpected. For example, because Niobe Way listened to adolescent boys, who are "most heavily stereotyped as stoic and only interested in one thing (i.e., sex)," she learned that they wanted, maybe even needed—or else they "would go 'wacko'"—to talk about their social and emotional intimacies. The boys could openly express "their love for their friends and emphasized that sharing 'deep' secrets was the most important aspect of their closest male friendships. . . . These patterns among boys have been ignored by the larger culture because such expressions are considered by this culture as girlish and gay."[2] With regard to girls, the writer and actress Lena Dunham's review of S. E. Hinton's classic young-adult novel *The Outsiders* suggests that what we thought we knew about adolescent girls and boys is terribly naïve: "Teenage girls are hard-pressed to find a safe vessel for the wild lust that gives them a fever but can just as quickly scare them straight." In support of Niobe Way, the book is also "pulsing with teenage boys whose primary value is friendship and whose secondary interest is romance."[3] Young people want to tell us their stories, their secrets, and all we have to do is to want to listen.

Questions for This Book

This book is a blend of scientific research on bisexuality and beyond with excerpts I recorded from the life stories of young adults I interviewed who have, to varying degrees, fervent, passionate, and deep-seated attraction to multiple sexes/genders. Their stories complicate simplistic research as to the nature and expression of bisexuality, pansexuality, fluidity, and nonbinary identities; their lives are far more nuanced and, at times, contradictory to what we think we know. As applied to bisexuality, they raise fundamental questions addressed in this book:

1. Why do more individuals have bisexual feelings or behavior than identify as bisexual?
2. How much attraction or sex with each sex is necessary to be bisexual?
3. Is a straight woman or man with occasional sex or crushes on the same sex bisexual?
4. Can one have bisexual sex but not bisexual romance, or vice versa?
5. Is bisexuality advantageous from an evolutionary perspective?
6. Does bisexuality differ depending on race, ethnicity, social class, and geography?
7. Are there different types of bisexuals, some more distressed or healthier than others?
8. If one is bisexual now, does that mean one will be bisexual in the future?
9. Are we entering a postidentity era?

The young people I interviewed with attractions to multiple sexes and/or genders who generously shared their histories with me ranged from mild to strong preferences for one sex over others; are sexually and romantically attracted to varying degrees of body and personality types; are happy, distressed, or blasé about their sexual and romantic lives; and have stayed solidly bisexual or have become more or less fluid, nonbinary, or pansexual over time. Some will stay where they are, and others will drift in their sexual, romantic, and gender preferences. Though some may have once hoped they might be slated to become exclusively straight, gay, or lesbian, most have given that up.

Bisexual Resources

Another critical reason, other than familiarity, to maintain the "bisexual" word and our generic understanding of what it means is the visibility provided to those who might be questionably or negatively besieged by their sexual or romantic life. Several online organizations have evolved to help individuals cope with personal struggles by providing educational and supportive resources and advocating for their civic and personal rights. Robyn Ochs, one of the nation's foremost advocates for the birthrights of individuals regardless of their orientation, sexuality, and gender to live safely and openly with full access and opportunity, has educated many regarding bisexual, pansexual, and nonbinary issues. Her work is liberally used by many online resources, such as the following national bisexual sites:

Bisexual.org: "A project designed to introduce our community to the world. With this site, we hope to bring faces and voices of the bi community to the world, share accurate information, answer questions, and provide resources for further learning."

Bi Resource Center: "Envisions a world where love is celebrated, regardless of sexual orientation or gender expression. Because bisexuals today are still misunderstood, marginalized and discriminated against, the BRC is com-

mitted to providing support to the bisexual community and raising public
awareness about bisexuality and bisexual people."

Bisexual Organizing Project: "We are committed to building the bisexual,
pansexual, fluid, queer, and unlabeled (bi+) community through regular
events and the yearly national BECAUSE conference. BOP is welcoming
and inclusive of everyone, including but not limited to people of all gender
identities, sexual orientations, sexes, relationship orientations, ethnicities,
abilities, religions, and political affiliations."

Unfortunately, these organizations did not—and perhaps could not—
help most of the young adults I interviewed, largely because the youths
did not consider themselves bisexual in a traditional understanding of
the term. Jacob watches gay porn and falls in love with women; Laura's
Asian American culture cannot fathom bisexuality; and Malachi does
not care which biological equipment the love of his life has. Plus, there
are so many other options other than being bisexual. Millennial celebrities such as the Olympic diver Tom Daley and the actors Anna Akana,
Brigette Lundy-Paine, Cory Michael Smith, and others have recently
come out—not as bisexual but as queer, fluid, pansexual, or something
else.[4]

PART I

Understanding Bisexuality

1

Bisexuality Now

Everyone likes to think that you are one thing or the other.
—Juan, age 20, Chilean American, student

While working on a college play, 23-year-old Dave fell really hard for a fellow male actor. When he told friends about his romantic feelings toward Smith, they accused him of being "bi or lying" because he hadn't ever been with a guy sexually.

> I was attracted to Smith but not thinking about it or that it was a priority, not looking for him or considered that I had attractions. I met Smith and hung out a lot and had a huge crush on him, stronger than half of those I had with girls—just hung out, and I would have dated him. I told him because he asked me to move to his apartment with friends, but I didn't think that was right under the circumstances. He didn't like me in "that way."

Was this a thwarted romance? Was sex going to happen if they moved in together?

First semester freshman year, Eden enrolled in a popular writing course on women and discovered her heretofore passionate friendships with women might mean something beyond the friendships all girls have with other girls. In high school, Eden tried to impress guys and get them to date her.

> For four months I realized that my attractions were to females but not physically but romantically. Then I realized that I could combine them. I am bisexual through an intellectual process for me. Before [this] course,

I thought of females, but I never opened myself up to the possibility of being romantically involved with females. Did lots of thinking and diary writing, and the more I thought, the more I realized I could date females.

As a thought experiment, if we adopt the position that the world is organized around bisexuality rather than heterosexuality and homosexuality, we would group people into two groups: bisexual and the non-bisexual ("monosexuals," consisting of straights and gays). Scientists would then search for genes that make us unable to love or have sex with multiple sexes, or as one interviewee wondered, Why are individuals so limited in their sexual and romantic lives that they only focus on one sex? One could argue that having sexual and romantic attractions to multiple sexes is the most "natural" state—and I will later make this argument in the "Evolution of Love" section in chapter 7.

Women are less likely than men to be disbelieved if they say they're bisexual. In the straight world, if a young woman identifies as bisexual, has sex with more than one gender, or has crushes on girls and boys, few people blink or doubt her word. Her sexuality is considered to be more susceptible than male sexuality to environmental influences because he is supposedly hardwired to be either straight or gay, not something else. She either is not hardwired either way or is wired for fluidity and thus is granted the liberty to express a range of sexual and gender selves without being categorized as odd. The developmental psychologist Lisa Diamond suggests several reasons why a woman is given this greater freedom: a greater propensity for bisexual attractions; a greater sensitivity to social factors that give her choices to express multiple aspects of her sexuality; or a greater tendency to change her sexuality over time (fluidity) and thus to have less internal conflict with sexual discrepancies in her life.[1]

Although these are potentially spot-on observations, I have several questions. Foremost, what is the source of this female "propensity"? Is it because of her biology, the way a girl is socialized, or some degree of both? If all individuals have a biological predisposition to be sexually and romantically fluid over time and given the right context, then existing differences among the sexes could be ameliorated and equality achieved—that is, equal numbers of bisexuals regardless of biological sex. Even if we say bisexuality is influenced by both biology and socialization—in which nature affects nurture, which in turn affects nature ad infinitum, to paraphrase the biologist Anne Fausto-Sterling—that would be difficult to untangle.[2] The reality, however, is that the young women I interviewed seldom spent much time thinking about why they are attracted to multiple sexes or are fluid in their sexuality.

That was not so true with the young men. Several had their personal, dare I say, even bizarre theories about the origins of their sexual attractions. As a college junior, Roberto, who was born in Puerto Rico, attributed his bisexuality to his weight: "I was a chubby guy, and girls never really paid any attention to me. So, I kind of went the other way. I guess my biggest regret is not losing weight earlier." He began working out and developed a sculptured body, but it's worth noting that Roberto did not become any more heterosexual—but it did bring more guys (and sex with men) into his orbit.

There is a lot we don't know about male bisexuality that we know about female bisexuality. Why so little? In a special issue of the *Journal of Bisexuality* devoted to male bisexuality, the scholars Erick Steinman and Brett Beemyn conclude that there is a general hostility and stigmatization "of all expressions of male-male emotional, sensual, and sexual intimacy, [that] continue to warp and distort the self-images of men who identify as bisexual."[3] We like our boys simple. They are to be attracted to either girls or boys, love girls or boys, and have sex with girls or boys—not both. Straight boys are not to touch other boys intimately, only superficially and briefly. As young adults, they have their bro culture of sports apparel, fraternity parties, and red plastic cups as they bark, "What's up!"

Even if the biology were equal for the sexes with regard to the capacity to motivate loving all sexes, is the force of socialization so powerful as to enhance a woman's bisexuality even as it overrides a man's bisexuality? Can we shift gears to be as accepting of bisexual boys as we are of bisexual girls, even if that task requires countering standard male messages? That is, can we conquer toxic masculinity in male bodies even as we reverse toxic femininity in female bodies? If so, perhaps we can close the gender gap or, possibly, eradicate it. This is an enormously optimistic scenario because in reality, we know so little about bisexuality, such as the origins of multiple romantic and sexual attractions. If a boy has child or adolescent sex with girls and boys, does that affect his sexuality for life? Can we fathom what bisexuality insinuates for his future? How does a bisexual boy experience his sexual and romantic worlds? By neglecting critical aspects of his life, we contribute not only to distorting that life but also to not fully appreciating all boys or, I would guess, liking or supporting boys.

Signs of hope are the celebration in *Teen Vogue* magazine of the new bisexual "chic" and in the Pulitzer Prize–winning writer Laura Sessions Stepp's *Washington Post* article "Bisexuality Goes Trendy," but these were more for teenage girls than boys because supposedly girls and not boys can easily express physical and emotional affection with each other. A girl can kiss another girl out of curiosity, "the taste of her cherry chap stick," and because it's "human nature," as Katy Perry's "I Kissed a Girl" anthem cheers on female bisexuality. The male parody, by Cobra Starship, is not so redeeming:

> I kissed a boy and they liked it
> Got all the honeys in the club excited
> I kissed a boy just to start shit
> And homeboy was not about it
> I know it's wrong, but I don't mind
> I'm going to start shit tonight[4]

On a more hopeful note, boys and young men now have alternatives, allowing them to be metrosexual, similar to the manner in which girls and young women have their passionate friendships with each other. Within bromances and passionate friendships, same-sex pairs can spend considerable time together, share personal information, and reveal their feelings to and for each other. Are we to wonder whether these supposedly nonsexual relationships might be romantic or, worse yet, fraught with secretive desire for sex? Are they only to love each other as brothers or sisters? Are we encouraging girls to experience their romantic orientation but not their sexual orientation, and boys, their sexual but not their romantic orientation? Are we telling Dave he can't love or have sex with Smith? Are we telling Eden to forget what her women's studies writing course taught her?

We know so little about bisexuality because we expect—maybe want—youths to know so little about their own sexual and romantic proclivities. If bisexual youths exist, then they are to be "gay-lite." Yet, bisexual young people are not a monolithic group because with this identity we join together the lives of individuals who are incredibly diverse, with experiences so distinctive that the singular concept of bisexuality is suspect, though it still has community and political significance. The lives of bisexual youths are a black hole we dare not enter—or, at least, so we believe.

To rectify these gaffs, I turn to *the source*—talking with young adults who are not exclusive in their sexual or romantic attractions. They are the spine of this book because they provide the substance and soul of what it means to reimagine being young and bisexual, pansexual, fluid, or nonbinary. Their narratives reveal seven essential steps that should be adopted:

1. Recognize the multitude of ways in which individuals are bisexual in their sexual and romantic profiles, developmental pathways, and life experiences.
2. Calculate the prevalence of bisexuality on the basis not of a single domain but of multiple domains that include behavior, attraction, and identity.
3. Expand the bounds of sexual orientation to include romantic components such as crushes, romantic fantasies, dating, love, attachment, and romantic relationships.

4. Assume a continuous, feminine if you will, perspective toward sexual and romantic lives, a perspective that runs counter to traditional masculine views of sexual categories.
5. Alter ill-informed, disparaging attitudes and stereotypes that hinder individuals from identifying as bisexual.
6. Examine assumptions that bisexuals have a high rate of physical and mental health complications.
7. Celebrate the many assets possessed by bisexuals.

Our inquiries into these developmental changes should begin during childhood and extend through young adulthood. These are times when sex, love, and gender ascend, some people say soar, in importance, to be continued at a somewhat less theatrical fashion throughout life. The surge in sexual and romantic interest between the ages of 6 and 11 begins adrenarche. According to the biopsychologist Martha McClintock and the anthropologist Gilbert Herdt, with the rise in sex steroids from the maturing adrenal glands, "Adrenarche is clinically recognized primarily by the onset of pubic hair, but it also includes a growth spurt, increased oil on the skin, changes in the external genitalia, and the development of body odor."[5] The angst and flurry of middle school might be due in part to these adrenal hormones.

With the following gonadarche, adolescence proper begins, and sexual, gender, and romantic variety and experimentation expand. According to the developmental neuroscientist Ahna Suleiman and colleagues, puberty activates "neurobiological changes that are critical for the social, emotional, and cognitive maturation necessary for reproductive success."[6] Even though adolescents might exit into young adulthood with the same gender, sex, and romantic selves they had during late childhood, how they got there can vary enormously. Thus, developmental milestones resolved during this time influence health and well-being not only during adolescence but throughout the life course.[7]

As scientists, educators, health-care providers, and family members, we have a checkered knowledge base about sex and love, especially during the critical evolution from childhood to young adulthood. The blame must at least partially fall on parents, who seldom provide accurate and relevant information, and schools, which fail to teach an unbiased, value-free sex-education curriculum.[8] When parents do communicate with their adolescent child about sex, it is primarily about sexual risk (sexual diseases, pregnancy, abstinence, safe sex) rather than sex-positive topics (sex variety, masturbation, pleasing a partner, sexual satisfaction), especially with daughters. Youths list their most frequent (and usually best) sources as friends, social media, and pornography.[9] We might consider whether this is ideal—but, again, this is beyond the scope of this book.

2

Men

Stories across the Bisexual Continuum

Miss Curry was with the *Rocky Horror* theater group, a drag
queen on Broadway. . . . I invited him to my bed. Was obvious what I was going to do.
—Donovan, age 21, white, student

Donovan was one of the first to volunteer for the interview—and it
turned into one of the longest, extending beyond two hours. At times,
Donovan "spaced out" (his words). Tall, almost gaunt, Donovan sported
a wrinkled, half-buttoned shirt, frayed jeans, and an assortment of
leather bracelets. He was barefoot and had a three-day-old scruffy beard;
blue hair becoming blond completed the look. Donovan described himself as "creative," "deep thinker," "colorful," "attractive," and "excitable"
and rated himself considerably above average in self-acceptance, life satisfaction, purpose in life, and positive relations with others.

Donovan grew up on a Vermont farm to self-identified hippie parents, and the family lived in an ecological commune with shared community resources. For population-control reasons, Donovan was an
only child—a sincere gesture by his parents to combat the world's food
shortage, enhance sustainability, and eliminate environmental squalor.
In the commune, he was known as a quirky, gifted boy who did not join
other boys in their toned-down version of touch football. Rather, Donovan cultivated imaginary games, pretending to be *Star Wars* characters
shooting things with his Nerf gun; this was something his parents at-
tempted to dissuade because it was, after all, a gun. School was a difficult
space, beginning the first day of kindergarten when his vegan food in a
pink pony lunch box didn't go over well. By first grade, Donovan real-

ized he was not meeting peer standards with his sweatpants, "the red kind with elastic"; his rat tail ("which Mom still has"); and his heartfelt efforts to find someone to be his best friend. His saving grace was his parents' aphorism to become "self-actualized and, if different, fine."

Girl crushes, evident throughout Donovan's life, always overshadowed his ambiguous boy infatuations. His first sexual memory was a sleepover romp with five commune boys during fourth grade. They jumped into a sleeping bag naked and masturbated each other with mouths and hands. "One of these guys had started puberty early, and it was very interesting that he could have an orgasm and see him masturbate and have something come out. Why can't I have one?" Equally memorable was his own pubertal development in sixth grade: "I was showering, and Mom was talking to me and she said, 'Oh, you have pubic hair!'" Masturbatory fantasies, with the assistance of internet videos and lingerie ads, were female oriented. He had advice to share with the world.

> Children are sexual from a much younger age than our society as a whole embraces, and ignoring that fact only has negative consequences on childhood development. Teaching children about sex will not make them promiscuous now or later. It will only help them become better-adjusted people once they start to have sexual experiences of their own later on.

Donovan's parents were concerned their son's "exceptionality" was not going over well, so they transferred him to a gifted high school program, where he flourished with a "creepy sense of humor" and a knack for theater-set construction. He blossomed and for the first time had a male best friend who liked him in return. A year later as a sophomore, Donovan met his first girlfriend, Sasha, a *West Side Story* Jet (in drag). After two weeks, they had sex.

> Sasha was a virgin but very sexual, and me, I'd not been with a girl. She said while we were making out, "You know you can touch them," and I was thrilled. Heavy sex then, and next day, oral sex. Several months later, both of us virgins, and we were very nervous. She was small. . . . Awe-

some! Nervous, excited about it. . . . Probably told Mom because talk to her about everything. She would have said, "Tee-hee-hee," nudging me, saying it was cool, trying to embarrass me.

Once Donovan was in college, temptations multiplied. Freshman year, Donovan's dorm suite became *the* place to gather until the early-morning hours for Pony Box, his punk band. Donovan enrolled in a masculinity course and joined the drama club—both of which colluded to net Donovan his first adult gay encounter. The boys-to-men course inspired Donovan to reexamine his "toxic masculine assumptions" and to shave his legs for four months. Through class discussions and writing projects, Donovan could not find a reason why not to have sex with a guy. "Sex can be a pure physical act, and I had never done it, so maybe try it."

He [Miss Curry] came down to do our local ensemble's makeup and tips on directing. . . . Was infatuated with her because he is taller and bulky, played rugby, and went to *Rocky Horror*. I had an emotional craving, an emotional equivalent of a hug from a guy, to be satisfied with being picked up and held. I'm over six feet, and I like to be picked up as representing my feeling of being small and feminine. It led me to conclude what I wanted, and he did this, biting my stomach, which he did all the time to others. Was I infatuated with him or for the craving of being picked up? . . . It was okay because this was stretching me. He bit my stomach and threw me up and caught me. I came onto him, rubbing his back. . . . He went down on me. I was nervous so did not do him. I had an orgasm. Very different completely than other orgasms. . . .

I thought long and hard and felt with it within a context of social views of gender, sexual construction, that I wrote my research paper on it: "Why I thought that bisexuality did exist." . . . I concluded that I'm a bit bi and understand what it means to me. I'm not gay, straight, or lying. Possible to be bisexual and was against the study that says bisexuality does not exist. . . . Even if one like me is in a romantic relationship with a girl and can still have sex with guys and girls.

In college, Donovan had intercourse with more than 20 women, but none evolved into a long-term committed relationship. Freed from previous constraints, Donovan's sexual and romantic fluidity expanded, and he now identifies as "bisexual leaning straight": "with the caveat that I like girls mostly." He enjoys sex and infatuations with all sexes and has no desire to change or hide this sexuality. For Donovan, bisexuality also refers to bi-gender. "Boys will be girls just as much as boys will be boys, and this should be considered more normative than it is now." More advice for the world.

A year later, Donovan emailed an update: he is now a metaphysics philosophy graduate student in California, lives in a graduate student co-op, DJs for a local punk radio station, has a new best friend (Jimi), and identifies as "bisexual/fluid." He said that a few women serve as "friends-with-benefits type things, nothing significant," adding a smiley emoji. Jimi is a fellow DJ, and they talk about difficult "personal stuff" they've each gone through: "We have a similar mind-set about the meaning of life, or distinct lack thereof. We're both very aware that life is what you make of it, and sometimes that thought is overwhelming." They spend considerable time together, and the passion in Donovan's writing led me to wonder if Jimi is a bromance or more. There is certainly a connection between them, and it might be an infatuation.

Casey

I've had interactions with dick, and yet I really, really love, love vaginas. It is awesome and primal. I was born straight and happened to have homosexual urges.
—Casey, age 23, white, returning student

Growing up as an only child in rural Oregon, Casey hung out with boys who called him "faggot," not because of his sexuality but because he didn't totally act like one of them. Casey was, however, into masculine things such as mechanics, cars, and technology; rode dirt bikes; had no filter on his mouth; squatted 400 pounds; played in a rock band; and drank lots of beer (he named his favorite brands). But he also had a feminine side, which bothered the boys. "I'm a vegetarian. I'm a huge liberal. I don't fight. I can allow people to walk over me." Being more masculine would be nice, but then he'd have to be less fat, give up beer, and exercise more. He wants "a bigger dick," though he's received "no complaints about it being short."

Casey's first sexual memory was fooling around with a girl his mother babysat. "I didn't know what I wanted to do to her, but I knew it was something. We were in my room, and we said, 'If you show me yours, I'll show you mine.' So, we pulled down our pants and poked each other here and there." They kissed in the closet and said one day they'd marry. His mother said it was cute puppy love and took pictures. The girl moved away and is now married—to someone else.

With pubertal onset, Casey and his guy friends engaged in a variety of sexual activities—which wasn't homosexual to them. Although these activities stopped at age 13 for the other boys, Casey subsequently engaged the twins Joan and Sloan. He was puzzled about how a girl masturbates and proceeded to show Joan how boys did it. To her it was "gross and funny" when he ejaculated. Casey asked Joan, "show me your boobs."

> Joan pulled down her pants, and I touched her vagina. The boobs weren't much to see or feel. I knew there was a hole down there but didn't stick my finger in because knew about the hymen and didn't want to break it. . . . We did other acts, never going further than kissing, playing with her breasts, and general frottage. . . . Excited, freakin' cool, four total times over the course of a year.

He refrained from "sticking it into her because God hates premarital sex."

Joan's brother Sloan took more maintenance. Before telling me this story, Casey prefaced it with, "I'm not ashamed of it because I've heard that it's normal for children to have homoerotic relations."

Oral sex on each other . . . until 14 or 15, about a year and a half. At the time, it [*points to his groin*] wanted something, and it wanted to find out. Curious. Wanted to feel it and take it in. More pleasurable doing things with him than with his sister. She said, "Gross!" and he didn't. I tried anal with Sloan, but we didn't know about lube, and it hurt too much to do it. I knew I wanted both. . . . I could get an erection and orgasm to guys, but I liked vaginas more. I guess I'm still a bit bisexual.

Since then, Casey learned that Joan has been sexually involved with girls and Sloan is in jail.

Casey's first real girlfriend and now fiancée, Jennifer, came into his life six months ago. "She just kicked me in the chest the first time I saw her."

We had been dating for three months and kissed on the second date, and a month later, I felt her breasts. . . . [*Extended rhapsody about her "phenomenal breasts"*] Two months later, I did oral on her in the shower, but she was terrible at it. Why don't they teach them not to use their teeth?

Jennifer was a virgin, and it hurt [her] like hell and bleeding profusely like an artery had broken. . . . I wanted it, and she did as well. I was able to put it in for 45 seconds. . . . Felt like I had become a man! Incredible, felt fantastic, felt like someone who had done a basic biological function on me. Like a human for the first time.

Casey's sexuality has fluctuated from a bisexual child (doing things with boys because it was easier) to a mostly gay early adolescent (more Sloan than Joan) to currently nearly 100 percent straight ("the woman I'll marry") to an ideal fluidity (possibility of swinging with his wife). Although Casey's bisexuality is "in remission," he's attracted to the genitalia of both sexes, though he's "pretty much heterosexual" romantically—he's never dated or been in love with a guy. Casey said he wouldn't change his sexuality even if he could.

José Luis

I established early on that I am exploring both genders. . . .
María was more romantic, and Miguel was more erotic. . . .
I am more comfortable telling people I like men and
women. . . . So what?
—José Luis, age 21, Mexican American, student

José Luis's parents divorced when he was 4, and he grew up with his
mother in an apartment in downtown San Antonino. A fellow 5-year-old
day-care boy produced José Luis's first sexual memory: "harmless bodily
voyaging." The two kissed and touched each other's bodies in a school
closet, but it never "really got into genital contact or anything." After two
months, the two boys were caught by a day-care staffer, who shamed
them and instructed them about "good touch, bad touch." A year later,
José Luis also had a sexual connection with a girl his mother babysat.

> We only met like four or five times when we played doctor. After the first
> incidence, I didn't forget about it, but I kind of let it slide under the mat, I
> guess, if I can use that term. If we were caught, there would be less of the
> guilt and shame. If we were caught, they would be like, "Hey, kids don't
> do that," and we would be sprayed with a water bottle.

José Luis's first adolescent sexual contact was with his best friend,
Miguel. They lived in the same apartment building with single mothers
who worked, so at the end of a middle school day, they had the apart-
ments to themselves. Play wrestling led to sexual experimentation.

> There was a lot of genital grinding, a lot of making out, oral sex even.
> There was a point where I tried anal sex, but it didn't work out. We did
> that for a couple months at a time and never got caught or anything. . . .
> He knew it was something he wasn't supposed to be doing, whereas I
> already had those feelings. I learned about it, but I didn't let it affect me

because I knew it was going to be something secret. . . . At one point when we were doing it, I was about to perform oral sex on him, and he was, "What are we doing?"

When I specifically asked about romantic feelings for Miguel, José Luis backtracked his former denial and admitted it was an *intense* friendship.

At about the same time, José Luis was also sexually and romantically involved with María, beginning when he fingered her in the closet during Seven Minutes in Heaven.

I was very proud of myself at the time and I felt like I hit one of those milestones of becoming a man. We were making out, and I had an erection. I was grinding against her, but she didn't want to do any stuff. . . . I had erotic attractions to María, but they never got fulfilled [intercourse]. . . . I defended her a lot because a bunch of my stupid-ass friends in middle school would say she was fat. María wasn't fat . . . built, not fat, meat on her bones.

Both Miguel and María were sexy figures for José Luis, who "had erotic and sexual wants with men and a romantic side for females." He assumed he was straight with gay tendencies. Middle schoolers, however, spread rumors that José Luis and Jesús, an out gay 13-year-old, were going "into the janitor's closet and make out or whatever, apparently fuck": "One time we made out, but that was about it." In high school, José Luis was called "like totally gay": "Which I denied. I would like, 'No, I'm not!' And I would think, 'only partially' or 'you're half right.'" He officially lost his virginity the summer after high school with a girl who was his first relationship after María. "I really loved, really liked how that felt. So after, in college, that has become easier for me to have sex with both men and women."

José Luis is dually attracted but struggles with a rather large discrepancy between his sexual and romantic orientations. He has been aware of his bi-erotic nature (can "get a boner" to either) since childhood.

María was his most intense relationship, but he also has bromances, mostly with straight boys. Despite his history of casual sex, José Luis described himself as primarily a romantic guy. He reported that his sexual orientation is "bisexual leaning gay" and that his romantic orientation is "mostly straight." That's a large gap between the two. José Luis can easily see himself in a heterosexual marriage but not in a gay marriage. Marrying a woman would be far easier, and he would receive kudos from family and friends. Bromances complicate things, creating uncertainties about whether he is romantically attracted to men or whether his guy emotional feelings are merely best friendships without love yearnings.

In his ideal world, José Luis would be 50-50 sexually and romantically. To achieve that ratio, he would need, in a somewhat convoluted way, to decrease his sexual attraction to men while increasing his sexual attraction to women and, in parallel, to increase his romantic attraction to men without decreasing his romantic attraction to women. Throughout his life, José Luis's major problem has been failing to convert his male hookups to romance and moving too quickly from a crush to sex. José Luis is willing to marry a woman when he is in his 30s if she agrees to "play" with his casual male sex partners. We will see how that works out.

Gene

I do enjoy watching heterosexual porn and seeing naked women and such. It is something that I do want to experience at some point.
—Gene, age 20, white, student

A senior at a rural college, Gene is a dancer who exudes traditional masculinity. Growing up in a small Midwest town, everyone was friends with everyone else, regardless of gender, personality, and life status. He considers himself masculine, largely because boys growing up in the country have to be masculine. Now, he's the one his friends call to help them change their tires and oil.

Gene developed crushes on girls from childhood onward, which serves to reinforce his irrefutable bisexual identification. "Talking to my friends who identify as gay and comparing the crushes they had with girls back then, . . . that's what kind of led me to more solidly think that I am bisexual." With the onset of puberty, the full bi-erotic force was amplified when he dated Kathy and she stuck her hand down his pants.

> I was really taken aback because that was the first time I had ever done anything. . . . I think she had been waiting for me to initiate it up to that point, and I just hadn't felt ready. So then finally it came to a point where she was like, "Okay, I'll do it."

Hand-mouth-genital contact followed, but never to the intercourse she requested—he wasn't ready. Gene has never had intercourse with a woman.

Two months later, Gene texted his friend Greg, a boy he met at a regional high school dance concert, a perfunctory "Happy Birthday." Greg texted back, "I just wanted to say, 'thanks,' and I also want to tell you that I really like you." Gene got his drift, asked for a couple of days to process, and then texted: "All right, I have never really considered dating a guy before but, yeah, you and I are really good friends and I really trust you." Later that summer, they arranged a camping trip, discussed who would bring condoms, and talked about their emotions about having their first gay sex. All went well until they realized that in their inexperience, they forgot to bring lubricant. "I bottomed for him, so the negative part of it was the pain of it."

> Talking to other LGBT guy friends that I have, their first experiences on the whole were nothing like what I have, like having dated for a few months beforehand and having the talking, the impact of it, and how it might happen. . . . If a boyfriend and I decide to have sex, I am very much so about talking about it beforehand. . . . I want to have the emotions as part of it because I had that as my first time.

When Greg left for college, the relationship ended. Greg, not Kathy, was Gene's first love.

When Gene came out, his father said, "I just want you to know I don't want you to give up the idea of having sex with girls because sex with girls is the bee's knees." His father, supportive of Gene's boyfriends, treats them no differently than he treats his daughter and her boyfriends.

Throughout life, Gene has had sexual attractions, fantasies, sex, and crushes with males and females—including two relationships with women and six with men. Recently, he and his boyfriend celebrated their second anniversary and are making plans to marry and have children. One issue they haven't resolved is monogamy. Gene wants at least one sexual experience with a woman before settling down monogamously with his man.

> I think it is something that I do want to experience because I know fantasizing about it, it is something that I would enjoy. . . . He says that he would feel more comfortable with me having sex with another man than another woman because he is afraid that I might discover that I like sex with a woman better.

If in a crowd, Gene would definitely look more at men than women because there is a wider range of guys he is attracted to. His sexual preference is to go down on women (oral sex) with little desire for vaginal intercourse. With men, physical lust and infatuations dominate.

Roberto

If I find a girl that I eventually fall in love with, then great!
Then if not, I would eventually have to come out.
—Roberto, age 21, Puerto Rican, student

Prior to first grade, Roberto and his family moved to the South Bronx to be with "familia extendida Puerto Rican." His earliest sexual memory was sitting "Indian style" in preschool and noticing a girl who wasn't wearing any underwear. "Wow, I don't have that kind of thing." A year later, Roberto and a girl went to the bathroom together, and he taught her how to urinate standing up. He told no one about his boy crushes because, coming from a very Puerto Rican family, "Your masculinity is very important. It's very central. That machismo type of thing." Roberto claims to be both macho and metrosexual. "I like to take care of myself and how I look. Coming from New York, that's every guy there. I shave my legs. People here think that's kind of weird, but back there, that's completely normal." Indeed, Roberto's appearance was stunning, with an Afro hairstyle, tinted glasses, a tight-fitting tee-shirt proclaiming Ricky Martin's concert tour, and pink shorts that contrasted with his brown skin. On personality ratings, Roberto's was exceptionally high on sensation seeking.

Although Roberto's parents are fairly progressive Puerto Ricans, they would not want their son to be bisexual. Yet, they would accept him regardless. He believes both suspect. "Moms always have a way of knowing things." Roberto's father is in denial; he told his precocious adolescent son, "'You're supposed to have girls, bang girls, and have sex. Do what you have to do,' . . . It was never like, 'He's too young to have sex.'" If he told his older brother that his little brother has sex with guys, "he would be destroyed."

During early adolescence, Roberto was obsessed with porn and Yahoo chat rooms.

> We would get on the webcam, and we would strip down. And I remember mostly doing it with kids my age or maybe two years older—boys. Just because I was always curious, I think I did it once or twice with a girl . . . [and] with a lot of straight guys or guys that aren't out.

Roberto has never had genital contact with a girl, "bare nude." While dancing, he'll "grab her ass or rub her vagina, but over clothes": "I've never gone that far with a girl." From his perspective, "Girls never really saw me in a romantic kind of way. I was always friend zoned." They'd talk for hours, and Roberto might secretly have a crush on them. But he knew they wouldn't want to "be" with him. He casually dated girls but didn't want to go further with them because he feared they had done everything and he had done nothing. "What if they tell someone, and they say I sucked?"

By contrast, Diego, Roberto's best friend since sixth grade, always had a girlfriend and thus surprised Roberto one day when Diego demanded, "Show me your penis."

> I was like, "I am not showing you my penis, man!" . . . He just took off my basketball shorts, . . . and then he kind of like saw my penis. But then he ran away with my clothes, and I kind of chased him. We were both laughing, but it was uncomfortable, and we knew it was kind of gay. And I remember he was by the door, and I remember running up to him and kind of like holding my penis and touching him with it. And he was like, "Dude, that's gay." And I was like, "Well, you took off my clothes. That's kind of gay!" . . . I had a hard-on. A lot of the times it feels like because I am his best friend that he needs to know everything about me, including what my penis looks like. . . . That's kind of weird. I just brushed it aside because I don't want to go to that level with my best friend.

However, Roberto remembered "jacking off to him a lot at night."

Roberto's first sex was with a "raunchy" Craigslist recruit. "It was just anal sex. I don't think he even gave me a blowjob. I had an orgasm pretty much straight away. Because it was my first time, I didn't really last long." At least Roberto got it out of the way, and now he can move on to "better things."

Although Roberto has never experienced love, he has been in long-term hookups.

> Someone you have sex with for a long time but there might be feelings or a connection, but it's not something that is going to be followed through

with. You don't call each other "boyfriend" or "girlfriend." There's no commitment. We're hooking up, and it may be or may not be exclusive, but we're hooking up.

When mutual feelings emerge, Roberto ends it because he is not ready to settle down.

True to his stated preferences, Roberto gave himself a 90+ percent on same-sex sexual and romantic attraction, fantasy, genital contact, infatuation, and romance, but these assessments do not preclude him from being every once in a while "really sexually attracted to a girl": "And I will be like, 'Wow! She's so hot.'" In his ideal world, he would be 50-50 on all domains, but he cannot simply "wipe out and erase" his attraction to guys. If he finds a girl he can eventually fall in love with, then everything would be great. If not, he would eventually have to come out—but as what? This was never clear. Ideally, he'd like to have one special person he can confide in and do things with. Until then, he's just looking to hook up.

Roberto believes he's bisexual because girls never really paid any attention to him. So, he went "the other way." Though Roberto reported a nontrivial number of child crushes, adolescent dates, and youthful sexual indiscretions with girls, all have been more recurrent and intense with boys from the same time periods and continuing into the present. He has had considerable genital contact with guys but none with women. Roberto reluctantly accepts his homoerotic nature; the romantic side is somewhat fuzzy. He wants to marry a woman and raise a family, but he believes he will eventually marry a guy and have kids. The real question for him is how strong are his heteroerotic desires—where on the bisexual spectrum is he? This is his unsolved enigma.

3

Women

Stories across the Bisexual Continuum

I began to realize that I had a crush on a female friend—the
only one I'd leave my boyfriend for. I said okay to the threesome, and then he flipped out.
—Elizabeth, age 18, Native American Indian, student

Elizabeth grew up in a small city in Maine with a divorced mother
(teacher) and two younger brothers. Both parents are now engaged to
others. Last year, as a high school senior, Elizabeth's life seemed set: she
was attending her top-ranked college; in the lottery, she received her
first-choice roommate; and she and her boyfriend, Jackson, were "talking marriage." Now that she has been a college freshman for several
months, things seem less certain, especially with Jackson.

Similar to her friends, since early adolescence Elizabeth has admired
the beauty of other girls. She didn't think of it as anything special because she was dating guys; she figured she'd outgrow it—plus, she had
Jackson. Their first sexual interaction was when they were 16, six months
after their first date. It was emotionally but not physically good. "He had
no idea what he was doing!"

It was mutual and unplanned. There was kissing, fondling, then intercourse. He had an orgasm, and I didn't. And I never did with him. We
had a pregnancy scare. . . . Sex was never tremendous with him, but he
got better, especially at oral sex. Intercourse was never anything special. I
liked the holding, but he always went to sleep too soon.

Elizabeth would have preferred less sex and more emotional closeness and cuddling.

At several points in the relationship, Jackson suggested that for variety they ought to change things around. "He kidded that we ought to bring in another female into our sex. I started to think that it was not so bad, and then I began to freak out. This is ridiculous, but there was something appealing about it." For the first time, Elizabeth understood her natural attractions to women, and she shared this with Jackson. He was confused and hurt because she had not told him earlier.

> We're very close and tell each other everything. He's one of those guys who loves to be of help, so he was very supportive. I was worrying that this was wrong, immoral, etc., and he helped me by saying he'd love me no matter what. He's very homophobic, like my oldest brother, but with women he is okay, probably because of the sexual thing.

Elizabeth's first kiss with a woman was her lottery college roommate, who had questioned her sexuality but decided she's straight. One day they talked about sexual issues, and they kissed. "Boy, was she terrible!" Before this encounter, Elizabeth wondered if she could enjoy the physical aspect of being bisexual; oddly enough, the terrible kiss confirmed that kissing another woman would be pleasurable.

After telling Jackson, Elizabeth told her closest friends, but not those she was attracted to. She is also out to her parents and her homophobic brother.

> Mom was very cool about it. She said she didn't understand, and she asked questions about it. She thought being bi meant I'd be promiscuous, having both boys and girls, and so I had to educate her. . . . Since then, she has been fine, though it doesn't come up much.

Elizabeth and her father have a "weird relationship": "He's very non-confrontational, and his way is to throw money at everything. We're not close, and so sometimes I've taken to shocking him to get a reaction." He is okay with it, but if he wasn't, he wouldn't say anything. Then came the 16-year-old homophobic brother. "I told him because his best friend is gay. . . . My brother is the Republican in the family. But he was good about his friend, so I thought I could tell him." He was surprised but fine with it. Her other brother is too young to understand. She thinks he might be gay because "he's so sweet, creative, and artistic."

Elizabeth described herself as masculine because she's ambitious and competitive and has hung out with boys while growing up, but she also described herself as very feminine, loves to dress up, and wants kids of her own. Similar to her male friends, she is attracted to feminine girls: "not butch!"

Rachel

Everyone knew that we were a couple. This was when I was 15. I guess that I am less out now since I've been to college.
—Rachel, age 19, white, student

Rachel, a sophomore at a northeastern university, grew up in an upper-class Boston suburb with three sisters. Her parents separated when she was in the seventh grade and divorced three years later. Rachel lived with her mother, with limited contact with her father. Throughout childhood, Rachel was considered "a real tomboy."

I hung out with both girls and boys. I was into sports. Then it was 99 percent guys, especially during recess when we played kickball. But my friends were really girls. When I was teased for being a tomboy, I always spaced out, listening to my imaginary friends listening to imaginary music with me. Girls teased me for not playing with them, and boys teased me because of my hairy legs. I was teased by the guys a little for being a dyke and basically by the girls for being a tomboy and not being normal.

To stop the teasing, as an adolescent Rachel tried to be more gender conforming—playing softball with the girls and smoking with them, growing her hair long, and wearing "flowering dresses, sun dresses," and cleaning her nails: "I tried to learn how to cross my legs and wear makeup." Rachel admits she has never stopped "thinking masculine."

Rachel traced her first same-sex attraction to fifth grade after "fooling around with other girls with kissing and rolling around, touching each other" during sleepovers. Two years later, she knew her feelings were "homosexual," which did not particularly trouble her, though she knew she had to keep it a secret—which she did until sophomore year, when she declared herself as bisexual to her closest friend. This was after she began a close friendship her freshman year with Rita, an older girl at her school. Rita was beautiful, and Rachel sensed considerable tension between them: "Rita was attracted to me. She was an open lesbian." The relationship lasted eight months off and on, with many teenage fights, some of which centered on Rita's demand that Rachel should be more out to her parents and others.

> It was an awkward situation, and I said to myself at this time that I must be gay. But I avoided it altogether, except from time to time when I thought about it. I just avoided labeling myself, but after the disclosure [to her friend], then I was certain that I was bisexual. This was the beginning of my identity.

Though sex with Rita was "great," sex with Ron, her official dating partner during this time, was "not great but something to get over." On reflection, Rachel recalled, "[It] didn't make me less heterosexual, and it wasn't for pleasure. Ron was 15. So, I had attractions to males and females at the same time."

Now dating both Rita and Ron, Rachel proceeded to race out of the closet.

> I was very out in high school, especially to my close female friends. I was already an outcast, so I didn't really care. I was in a romantic relationship

[with Rita], and we cuddled in the cafeteria and were going to go to the prom together. But a family outing prevented that. . . . Just recently have I got involved in campus groups. I'm open to all who know me, but I've become more closeted because of the campus atmosphere.

Rachel's mother is "very homophobic," so she does not officially know about her daughter's sexuality. It is not that she would disown Rachel, but she would simply not want "to hear about" Rachel's sexual and romantic relationships. Her distant father would be "indifferent toward these kinds of things." Both will only be told once Rachel is in a serious relationship. All sisters know and are hugely supportive.

With regard to Rachel's identity, she has always felt attracted to both sexes, but in different ways. Although she "likes boys a lot," it is more at the sexual than the emotional level. Here is how she splits the distinctions:

I am physical/sexual 60 percent heterosexual and 40 percent gay. I find orgasm with a female harder, but it is a better experience. I find it harder to please a woman, and this is bad for my ego. My fantasies are often with a woman, but I'm intimidated by heterosexual-type women. In the emotional realm I'm 30 percent heterosexual and 70 percent gay. For me, it is an issue of the person and not gender. I am attracted to certain types of males, both feminine and masculine, and females, feminine ones.

Rachel is probably on the pansexual spectrum, though gender matters to her. Overall, Rachel says she is 50-50 if you put everything together.

Jen

I don't look like a stereotypical dyke. I look like a normal
nice girl with long hair and painted nails.
—Jen, age 21, white, student

Despite being a classic suburban, upper-middle-class young woman with parents who own a small family business, Jen always felt as if she did not fit in. "I was awkward, more intellectual than my peers, and read books and thought about things they did not." Another source of her uniqueness was her sexual and romantic attractions. Although the young women I interviewed frequently recalled childhood memories of sexual attractions to females, most specified a particular girl or woman rather than a broad-based spectrum of female recollections. Jen is an exception.

> I've always been fascinated with girls, in class, day camp, everywhere. I wanted to walk and talk with them, to emulate them. In day camp when I was 7, I remember I had a talent for mimicking, and anytime I wanted to be a girl's best friend, I'd mimic her. And I would be her for about a week until she found a new best friend. I realize now that I had strong attractions, not obsessive ones, with females. I wanted to be around them all the time.

Although Jen easily passed as "your typical-looking, mall-trotting, boy-crazy kind of a girl," inside she felt "a whole lot more masculine."

> I do my nails, dress up, wear makeup, wear jewelry, have long hair. . . . I think in a mathematical way, in physical terms. I want to be a lawyer, a masculine thing. I've always wanted to be one of the guys, to joke around. But I just couldn't carry it off. I've a very androgynous inside. . . . I liked boys and the things they do. From junior to senior high school, I sat with boys and played card games and role plays. . . . I feel more comfortable in a room of guys than with girls who may be chitchatting. I like talking direct, like about how things work, like mechanics, and I'm accepted as one of the guys. So, I'm crunchy. I aspire to be butch, but I just don't make it. My girlfriend says I couldn't look butch even if I took hormones.

Jasper, one of the guys Jen hung out with, became her first boyfriend and sex partner. Friends since fifth grade, they began dating during their junior year, "fooled around," then played strip poker at his house (parents gone).

> It was a very intimate moment. It was okay, but it hurt a lot because of our size. I was 5 foot and Jasper was 6 foot 3, and we were proportional to those heights. Even after my hymen broke, it hurt. We continued several times. I knew I desired females, but here I was having sex with a guy, so I had to be heterosexual. . . . After a couple of times, I said to myself, "I've got to be heterosexual because I'm not lesbian."

She thought those were the only two options. Having a boyfriend was easy, but having a girlfriend made her "nervous and petrified." Her first was a summer fling that lasted three months, but she was devastated when they broke up because she was emotionally invested, something absent with Jasper.

Going from her small hometown to a large college changed everything for Jen. In one of her many in-depth conversations with her freshman roommate, the roommate nonchalantly asked, "Aren't we all inherently bisexual?"

> Well, I didn't know, or have the language of bisexuality, but then I began to understand the language and what her question meant for me. This was the tail end of my freshman year, and I began to wonder how would I be able to handle the rigors of marriage. I had all this mythology about bisexuality. It just didn't fit in with my plans.
>
> I wrote this tearful diary entry. Now I think back on my life experiences, and I can remember very clearly why I stared at this one girl all the time in high school. I had a crush on her. I remember having the conversation in my head that I can't be a lesbian because I am interested in boys and I am dating a boy. Because I did not have the word "bisexual," and it was really not until I acquired the word "bisexual" that I acquired the identity. I mean, the feeling was there, but I never had a name for it, and I never knew what to call it until I came to college.

Once Jen had the word and the realization that it applied to her, she had "this huge coming-out-party experience." The first person she told was a gay male friend. "He hugged me and said he knew and was happy I finally came out. . . . 'Welcome to the family! My little girl is growing up!'" Then followed "bunches" of people, and no one was surprised; indeed, several of her friends had taken bets about when she would finally come out. With these outings, Jen acknowledged to herself that she is a member of an "underrepresented and often looked-down-upon group." Her natural instinct compelled her to become an activist, in the footsteps of her feminist mother and tracking her Jewish heritage of activism.

The first family member she told was her 11-year-old brother over Thanksgiving break. He said, "I gotta think about this for a minute." A couple minutes later, he said, "I think it is okay because you're still the same person anyway and I still love you." By contrast, telling her parents provoked a "huge screaming match that lasted all night long." They wanted to put her in psychotherapy to cure her, they read nothing she gave them, and they cared little that she was a student leader. Some progress was recently evident when her parents objected to Jen's Catholic boyfriend. "We rather you dated a Jewish girl than a non-Jewish man." Her mother, however, took the boyfriend as evidence that Jen is no longer bisexual. "She doesn't understand that just because I am dating a man doesn't mean my bisexuality disappears. That I find really frustrating."

Jen takes particular joy in being a role model who doesn't fit a stereotype, because then she can better help others who struggle with their bisexuality. "I don't really fit the stereotype. And I needed to be visible and I needed people to take me seriously, so I could speak up and be out. In my experiences, you need to be out to be taken seriously." Perhaps this is Jen's path to feeling authentic, her compromise between femininity and masculinity.

Madeline

I'm not straight. . . . I would call myself lesbian, but I haven't
struggled long enough to know.
—Madeline, age 21, white, student

Madeline grew up in a family that fought to stay above the poverty line
in rural Colorado. Her parents separated when she was 10, after her
father was transferred to the Grand Junction police force. Her parents
eventually divorced, leaving her mother to enter a number of low-level
health-care jobs before returning to school to become a health techni-
cian. As a child and adolescent, Madeline never had crushes or romantic
infatuations with other girls, but she did have sex with them beginning
in fourth grade, when she played house with her best friend.

> I was the dad. It was very sexually oriented for couple of years. In seventh
> grade, I initiated the same game with another best friend. . . . I was hiding
> things from myself. I never asked. Neither did I have an outlet to know
> what it was about. Finally, in sophomore year of college, I labeled it.

Prior to college, Madeline claimed to be "a real tomboy" and on occasion was called "dyke." She took no offense because she loved her sports.

> I did basketball from fourth through high school, making the boys all-star
> team, and then played on the female team. In seventh, I made the eighth-
> grade team, and in eighth, I made the JV starting varsity. Had Barbie dolls,
> but they were at the bottom of my toy pile. Played with my brother's Tonka
> trucks, so my parents got my own. Hiking, football, Matchbox cars, GI Joe,
> anything outdoors, kickball. Also did track—disc, shot, hammer, javelin. I
> was recruited for Division II basketball and Division I track.

In seventh grade, Madeline was frequently mistaken for a boy after
she cut her hair, which so angered her that she grew it out again, because

she was tired of being referred to as "sir." Madeline views herself as "feminine, sensitive, emotional, sentimental, and nurturing, especially in a relationship," and as masculine, aggressive, and competitive in sports and classes and has recently cut her hair again. "I wore it in a ponytail when long, and it just seemed so stupid to have it long."

Madeline is adamant about her distaste for any label, sexual or otherwise. What she is "is not straight."

> My eyes may be open to date males in the future. One may be the love of my life in the future. I questioned myself a lot last year. I saw this female competing in a track meet and felt overwhelming attractions toward her that I never had before, and I said that this is it. I had experiences before but none so overwhelming.

Then, Madeline met Whitney online, and they arranged to get together, spending the weekend together. A couple of hours after meeting, they kissed, and later that night, they had sex. After two months, Madeline tried to break up because Whitney was ready to "settle down" and Madeline "wanted not to"—plus Madeline doubted she was solely attracted to females.

> I also wasn't all that physically attracted to her, but I couldn't tell her that. She fell head over heels over me. Now some email and we call. She is a friend if I ever needed her. It was a rocky relationship, and I changed my mind every couple of days about it. It affected me in that because it wasn't so satisfying, so perhaps not that attracted to females. . . . Didn't persuade me one way or the other.

Before and after Whitney, Madeline also had sex with Eric, her best male friend. It was, however, quite "unsatisfying," prompting Madeline to seek out the LBQ women's group on campus. "It was great cuddling with Eric, and the emotional attachment was great. But the sex wasn't so wonderful."

Madeline first disclosed her sexuality to an anonymous person on the internet before she told a good friend—who was not surprised. Madeline wants most of her college friends to believe she's straight, so she dresses conservatively, talks about boyfriends, and doesn't mention her lesbian friends.

Equally difficult has been coming out to her mother. In anger over the phone, they had a screaming match.

She had been questioning me about Whitney and why were we spending so much time together. She said that I wasn't being myself lately, like distant and hiding something from her. We were both upset, and I was trembling and said to her, "What do you think is going on?" "Maybe you're experimenting." "Maybe so, or maybe it's more than that." . . . She was most upset because I had hid something from her. She thought I was being influenced by older women. Said I was not sufficiently resisting Whitney, who is a psych major.

She thought she was open-minded, but she is very uninformed. She got so upset because I kept interrupting her. She usually sits me down and lectures to me for hours, but I wouldn't let her. She said couple of times, "This is not my daughter." . . . Time was what she needed. She wanted me to go to counseling, and then she would accept it. Said she loved me no matter what, but it was just that she didn't believe me. She didn't want me to come out to her because she thought I was brainwashed by the LGB community. And I do still question myself, and not sure I'm ready to declare myself.

She is now very good, though she won't fly any banners in the parade. But if I was in a romantic relationship, then she would support me if I was happy. She still hopes I'll find a man, but she would invite my girlfriend home on Christmas. This is monumental shift for her.

Regarding other family members, Madeline's father is not in her life. "He's broke my heart so many times that I don't talk to him, and I never intend to tell him. . . . When I was 8, he said never bring home any 'brownies' home as dates. My boyfriend was Black, so I could never mention him." Her brother is a freshman in college, and although they were once close, they drifted apart once he moved in with their father.

> He's the football player, classic he-man. He once said jokingly that he wanted to beat the faggots on my floor. He said this when he was mad at his computer. . . . He says, "Shut up, faggot," all the time. If told him, he'd be okay with it. He has defended me before when my friends called me a dyke in high school. I know the kind of person he is.

What continues to bother Madeline is the potential effect of being bisexual on her desired veterinary career. "Farms are rural, and the acceptance is low. Not very open communities. Keeps me closeted. I joke with myself that it is all a put-on and that I can pull it off." I have my doubts.

4

Generational Rebellion

If I just had been attracted to boys, that would have been so
much easier than having this sort of duality, and so I didn't
know what label to use or what to call myself.
—Caleb, age 21, white, student

Sexual terms such as "straight," "gay," and "lesbian" have been seriously
questioned or discarded altogether by Zoomers, with some going so far
as to eviscerate the very concept of a heterosexual-homosexual dichotomy.[1] Yet, in popular parlance and research surveys, sexual categories
resolutely remain, despite not fitting with the lived experiences of many
people under 30. They resent such questions as, "Are you straight or
gay?" "What is a pansexual?" "How can you be gender fluid?" "Are you
through experimenting?"

These reservations are occurring even as media outlets have heralded
the sharp increase in the bisexual population. The 2021 Gallup Poll is an
example. Nationwide, 3.1 percent of the population identifies as bisexual,
though this varies immensely by generation. In the Traditionalist and
Boomer generations, it is 0.3 percent; in the X generation, 1.8 percent;
in the Millennial generation, 5.1 percent; and in the Z generation, an
astounding 11.5 percent.[2]

In part, this increase is probably the result of more young people, especially Zoomers, feeling comfortable under a larger and more inclusive
bisexual umbrella. If youths cannot locate their sexual label among those
listed by a researcher, they tend to feel that their lived experiences are
ignored, which is "painful and alienating." Thus, the health-care providers Kathryn Scheffey and colleagues include in their research not only
the traditional three sexual identities but also eleven others (and twelve

gender identities). Importantly, the identity chosen varied depending on whether the individual was talking with parents, friends, health-care providers, or the extended family. The limited options that are traditionally provided lead to oversimplified and inaccurate conclusions about the prevalence and experiences of individuals' lives. The resulting misinformation can have dire consequences for clinical care. Patients might avoid answering questions altogether or give answers that do not reflect their real sense of self. The net effect would be further marginalizing them in health-care settings and causing them to avoid help-seeking services that could potentially perpetuate disparities in health-care access and outcomes. So, too, with a sample of disadvantaged, low-income urban girls, ages 14 to 22, the clinical psychologist Johnny Berona and colleagues warn that if we only use one sexual dimension rather than inclusive multicomponent measures to identify the widest range of youth, intervention efforts to recognize girls who have faced harassment and stigma because of their sexuality will fail. This is particularly relevant for girls and young women who are known to report a variety of terms to describe their sexuality.[3]

Assessing Sexual Orientation

By "sexual orientation," the American Psychological Association means "an enduring pattern of emotional, romantic, and/or sexual attractions to men, women, or both sexes [and] a person's sense of identity based on those attractions, related behaviors, and membership in a community of others who share those attractions."[4] As far as I can tell, no one uses this definition in their research; rather, they define sexual orientation on the basis of whatever numeric data they have available—survey questions assessing one (usually) of three domains: sexual attraction, sexual identity, or sexual behavior.

In most cases, researchers measure sexual orientation using some version of the 7-point Kinsey Scale, which was published nearly a century ago. It includes ill-defined concepts of "psychological sexual reactions" (attractions?) and "overt sexual behavior" (what constitutes sex?). One's Kinsey score could thus range from exclusively attracted to a sex not one's own (heterosexual, or a score of 0) to exclusively attracted to the same sex (homosexual, score of 6), with gradations in between.[5] After initially measuring sexuality along this continuum, however, most experts subsequently and inexplicably collapse the scaled responses into three discrete, mutually exclusive categories such that Kinsey 0s and 1s became straights, 2s to 4s became bisexuals, and 5s and 6s became gays. In this process, two multiattracted points along the continuum, mostly straights and mostly gays, are hijacked and considered straights or gays.

Several additional problems with this method have garnered criticisms. One, despite early attempts by several sexologists to complicate matters by expanding our notion of sexuality by adding new dimensions to measures (are thoughts, attractions, emotions, and affections relevant?), they are now essentially ignored.[6] Two, the focus has nearly always been on sexual behavior, attraction, or identity—though, as we will see, many individuals are discrepant in these domains. Three, sexual orientation is equated with sexual identity, and the two become so intricately and inappropriately synonymous that they are used interchangeably. Four, to add further insult to the notion of a sexual spectrum, more than occasionally all those who are not heterosexuals are combined and named "nonheterosexuals" or "sexual minorities."

To correct these long-standing problems, the clinical social work professor Mark Friedman and colleagues asked focus groups of adolescents and young adults of mixed sexualities the question, "How does someone know if he or she is gay, straight, heterosexual, queer, lesbian or whatever?" The youths surprisingly (to adults) came up with two necessary components. One, *sexual attraction*, consists of both a cognitive sense of being attracted to a person and an intense, internal, physiological reaction to another person. Two, *romantic attraction*, entails "being in love with, forming a long-term commitment to someone, being in a primary relationship with another person, or wanting to have these experiences."

Sexual orientation, according to these teenagers, is not just about sex but also romance, about being in love. Yet, we seldom listen to these spot-on youths in our research protocols—or in our families, for that matter. We overlook complex measures of sexual orientation and, especially, neglect indicators of romantic orientation altogether. We thus sacrifice truth for convenience and in that process construct, according to Friedman, "significant barriers to understanding the nature and complexity of adolescent sexual orientation."[7]

Against the advice of these youths and methodological rigor, in nearly all research to date, investigators use a single question to measure sexual orientation. Usually, it is a variation of "What is your sexual orientation (or identity)?" or "Who do you have sex with?" Three or four response options are inserted into a 200-plus item survey. This method is easy and, perhaps, progressive compared to previous decades, when sexual orientation was neglected altogether in national data sets. But these created data do not adequately capture and may even distort the lives of multiple-attracted individuals.

Also worth noting is that the Friedman youths, in reaching their decision about sexual orientation, explicitly *excluded* two dimensions frequently used to evaluate sexuality: who you have sex with and how you label yourself. If bisexuality is assessed solely by either behavior or identity, as the youths warned us not to do, we run the risk of losing the essential attributes of sexual orientation, resulting in the omission of youths who regard their sexual orientation as directed to both sexes. Margaret Paschen-Wolff and her colleagues in public health conclude that research that focuses only on simple measures to capture sexual identity or behavior and fails to assess sexual attraction misclassifies many individuals. This is especially true for youths who exhibit "branching" among various aspects of their sexuality. One such group would be straight-identified youths who engage in same-sex behavior (see chapter 6). These errors can potentially lead to overlooking health disparities among individuals and, I would add, miscalculating their prevalence.[8]

Since the Friedman study was published in 2004, it is difficult to find research that has implemented the youths' recommendations. Reasons for this exclusion are less theoretical and, perhaps, more practical: researchers only have available preordained sexual orientation questions in the data sets they analyze, or they simplify their research design to cut out the messiness of multiple measures of a construct. They justify these decisions by citing other researchers who do the same thing. Bad follows bad, and bisexuals are the worse for it.

Another option, only rarely taken, is to offer young people the opportunity to describe how they identify or describe their sexuality in an open-ended response box. When given this opportunity, youths are quite creative, listing 39 terms in a study by the psychologist Arielle White and colleagues, including "grayromantic," "confused," "figuring it out," "demisexual," "polysexual," and "polyamorous."[9] In the popular press, a 28-year-old Californian woman answered a Match.com sexual identity question with "all of the above." She has been with men and women—whomever she happens to be into at the moment. "Sometimes I say I'm heteroflexible. Sometimes I spell it out and say I'm attracted to *everyone*. Labels just don't do it." Alok Vaid-Menon, a gender-nonconforming performance artist, poet, and activist does not identify as one gender: "Nonbinary is so oxymoronic. We're defining ourselves by an absence and not our abundance." Others have placed labels on Vaid-Menon, which they (Vaid-Menon's pronoun preference) reject: "I really try to escape having to put myself in these categories. I wanted to be free from boxes—not end up in a new one."[10]

To give Baby Boomers their due, some parents are less naïve about these developments. When Caleb was 19, he came out to his father. "He asked me why I even needed a label. I was super impressed that he was so progressive." When 18-year-old Leila was in junior high school, her liberal parents told her if she were gay, they would love her regardless. She suspects her mother is not totally straight because she was attracted to women in college. "Mom and I talked about most people are on a continuum, and this helped me realize that I was on it by having a relationship with a woman."

To repair our assessment of sexual orientation (attraction) to better reflect the life experiences of young people, I recommend—rather than asking them, "Are you attracted exclusively to males or females or equally to males and females?"—asking them to indicate, "How sexually attracted are you to each sex?" They would be given a scale for each sex they nominated, running from 0 percent to 100 percent, with no obligation that totals must add to 100 percent. This discourages posturing the sexes as opposites and allows individuals to vary their attractions across the full range, including degrees of asexuality (low percentage to each sex). In addition, the same questions asked of sexuality should be posed regarding romance, which would net us individuals who are aromantic or biromantic. These two measures allow for complexity in sexual and romantic attraction to emerge separately for each sex, as they did for Jacob, Emma, and Caleb—who fail to fall into one of our traditional identity boxes.

College freshman Jacob adores women, falls in love with women, is struck by the beauty of women, and becomes physical with women and yet masturbates daily (or more) to gay male porn. Jacob reported that he is 80 percent sexually attracted to men and 100 percent romantically attracted to women. He rated himself "mostly gay" by sexual orientation and "exclusively straight" by romantic orientation. College junior Emma doesn't like the term "bisexual" because to her it means equally attracted to both sexes. "I'm always attracted physically to girls and emotional attractions are toward guys. It differs, but right now I guess 75 percent attractions to women. But then that may be because I'm getting out of a bad relationship with a guy, and I'm seeing my whole life better." Though college senior Caleb is more sexually attracted to men than to women, romantically he is "pansexual" because it is about the person that matters most, not their gender.

The psychologists Anna Salomaa and Jes Matsick warn us, however, that to present such intricacy in our surveys stands little chance of being adopted by those who normally include only a single sexual orientation question in an already long battery of questions. The usual goal is to succinctly collapse information into a line of code—a difficult task given "the complexities of measuring a fluid, multifaceted, and hetero-geneous variable such as sexual orientation." The task is thus "balancing the scientific desire for standardization and the often-fuzzy nature of real-world sexuality."[11] Most scientists assume, whether explicitly or not, that sexuality is not about romance, that attraction to one sex comes at the cost of having attraction to the other sex, and that, regardless, it is not about a fluid continuum but about static categories.[12] My strong preference is to return to basics and listen more openly and intently to the fuzzy life stories of real-world youths and young adults. They might help us understand.

Sexual and Romantic Orientations

Following the Friedman youths' lead, it is necessary to separate orienta-tion into two: a sexual orientation and a romantic orientation. Later, I elaborate on the romantic and how it influences what we know about multiattracted individuals. I define "sexual orientation" as a deeply rooted predisposition toward erotic or sexual arousals, fantasies, thoughts, or affiliations with members of one sex or another, multiple sexes, no sex (asexual), or oscillating among sexes (fluid). Sexual orien-tation is seldom alterable because of its genetic and/or prenatal genesis. Awareness of sexual orientation usually solidifies as individuals are given more information and become more familiar with sexual issues. Few individuals state that they chose their sexual orientation, and it need not be identical to romantic orientation.

On the other hand, I define "romantic orientation" as a deeply rooted predisposition toward romantic arousals, fantasies, thoughts, or af-filiations with members of one sex or another, multiple sexes, no sex (aromantic), or oscillating among sexes (fluid). Romantic orientation is seldom alterable because of its genetic and/or prenatal genesis. Aware-ness of romantic orientation usually solidifies as individuals are given more information and become more familiar with romantic issues. Few individuals state that they chose their romantic orientation, and it need not be identical to sexual orientation.

By contrast, "sexual identity" is a self-label based in part on a consideration of one's sexual and romantic orientations and behaviors. I define it as the term(s) individuals assign to the self, grounded on the most salient sexual and romantic aspects of life—such as attractions, fantasies, desires, behaviors, and relationships. It gives meaning and significance to the configuration of feelings, perceptions, and cognitions that individuals have about the various domains of sex and romance in their life. They may give priority to some domains over others (e.g., sexual over romantic attractions) or may consciously or unconsciously attempt to deceive the self or others about the nature of their proclivities. Individuals can choose and unchoose a sexual identity over time and across situations (fluidity). This identity can be private, known only to the individual, or public, known to a few or everyone. The private and the public need not be congruent. Because sexual identities are historically and contextually specific, terms come and go across various cultures and time periods, frequently without universal meaning or acceptance. For example, over several decades, "sexual inverts" became "homosexuals," who became "gays," who became "queers," and who have become who they are today—an open market of terms and phrases.

I have yet to come across the concept of romantic identity independent of a sexual identity, except among asexuals—individuals who, according to the Asexual Visibility and Education Network, "do not experience sexual attraction—they are not drawn to people sexually and do not desire to act upon attraction to others in a sexual way."[13] Romantic terms that asexuals use include "aromantic" (does not experience romantic attraction); "panromantic" (romantic attraction to all sexes and genders); "heteroromantic," "homoromantic," and "biromantic" (romantic attraction to multiple sexes); and "demiromantic" (only develops romantic attraction after forming a strong, emotional bond). Perhaps we should borrow these terms from asexuals.

With ever-changing meanings and conflations of terms in young people's world, it is difficult to use identity terms to assess sexual and romantic lives and be certain whether they are comprehensive, consensual, or current regarding what participants mean by the expressions they use.

A comparable muddle exists for the meaning and significance of sexual and romantic behavior that participants engage in. What counts as sex is a controversial issue with its own literature: Must it be intercourse, or does oral sex and deep kissing count? When emotional feelings become romantic feelings is also unsettled. Here are several not-unusual, tangible life circumstances from young adults I interviewed that complicate how we understand and measure these constructs:

- A girl is sexually attracted to both sexes and identifies as straight.
- A boy has oral sex with both sexes and identifies as straight.
- Across a girl's life course, she fluctuates among identifying as straight, bisexual, and lesbian but claims no change in her sexual orientation.
- A boy has sexual fantasies and physiological arousals to other boys but has infatuations and crushes only on girls and is a virgin.
- An individual engages in sexual intercourse and has romantic crushes unrelated to their stated sexual orientation, romantic orientation, and sexual identity.

These seeming contradictions across sexual and romantic domains might baffle adults, but they are now common among young people. More so than earlier generations, young people are living nonbinary lives, as the stories in this book illustrate.

Categories versus Spectrums

If we believe in sexual categories created by professionals from various disciplines rather than listening to those who live their lives along sexual and romantic spectrums, then we are missing out on the world that young people are creating. Anna Salomaa and Jes Matsick highlight this basic problem: when defining and measuring humans, most individuals live outside of bounded categories. The rebellion is starkest among those who defy scientific expectations that they fit into—and stay in—one of a few distinct categories with strict boundaries and assumptions that are stable over time. The hitch that flusters researchers is individuals who "continually eschew attempts to be neatly defined by the scientist attempting to carve nature at its joints."[14]

For example, growing up, Dave felt "plundered by hetero messages," which he now rejects, especially after he recognized his romantic feelings for Smith. "Pansexual" is his preferred identity, in large part because it appeals to his self-image as insubordinate and unruly. Ida, a senior at a small college in West Virginia, sometimes identifies as "queer but philosophically bisexual": "I've had relationships with guys but definitely more toward females. Sometimes I say 'dyke,' and when with lesbians, then say 'lesbian' because they're uncomfortable with 'bisexual' as a term." The writer and activist Chirlane McCray echoes these youths, telling the lifestyle magazine *Essence*, "I am more than just a label. Why are people so driven to labeling where we fall on the sexual spectrum? Labels put people in boxes, and those boxes are shaped like coffins."[15]

This is a long-standing, heated debate in sex science: Are sexual and romantic orientations a matter of a few discrete categories, or are they gradations along a spectrum?[16] In a presidential address to the Society for the Scientific Study of Sexuality, Charlene Muehlenhard warns us about the tendency to "reify categories after we create them and our tendency to exaggerate the differences between the categories that we create."[17] Some bisexual and biromantic boys have more sex and romance with girls than straight boys do, and some bisexual and biromantic girls have more sex and romance with girls than lesbians do. Millions of straight- and gay-identified youths have sex with both sexes and yet do not claim to be bisexual or biromantic.[18] Trying to label these youths with a singular, traditional identity would not do them justice and might well distort their reality. Margaret Paschen-Wolff and colleagues express concern with the one-dimensional manner in which sexual orientation is assessed, particularly as applied to bisexual individuals. Their preference is for a "dynamic, continuous conceptualization of sexual orientation." That is, identifying as bisexual does not require engaging in sex with multiple sexes; "rather, a decision to identify as such may involve consideration for and accumulation of the individual's identity (or identities), behaviors, and/or attractions throughout his or her life."[19] When sexuality and romance are evaluated along multifaceted, multidimensional bases, what is readily apparent is that sexual and romantic orientations are frequently fluid over time, which wreaks havoc on those who statistically adore categories. However youths define themselves today might not be forever fixed in time and place.

Overall, youths experience various incarnations of self because their sexual and romantic preferences emerge in response to their changing life histories from childhood to the present and beyond. Perhaps they are born with flexible sexual and romantic orientations that allow them the freedom to change depending on how they live, whom they know, and what they read, watch, and text. Perhaps they seek sexual pleasure whenever possible, do not fear same-sex crushes, and pursue emotional bonding with both sexes. These realities among girls have been acknowledged for decades, and now boys are living them as well. Many youths have coexisting and varying degrees of attractions to females and males, and this ratio might easily change depending on "how things go." In this, the high school dropout and car mechanic Sawyer and Alicia, with a stockbroker mother, are in step with new generations of young people who proclaim sexual and romantic lives that exist as gradations.[20]

Sawyer is primarily attracted to men and more than occasionally attracted to women. To him, "There's everything out there." Sawyer believes most guys are neither totally straight nor totally gay and whatever they have been or are today might not be what they are in the future. Whether he'll always be as sexually and romantically fluid as he is now, he doesn't know, but what he does know is he'll be forever sexually and romantically attracted to men and women, though he might prioritize them in a different order under different circumstances.

Alicia only recently woke up to unimagined possibilities for herself. Even though her father produces television shows that frequently cover sexuality issues, she said,

I never thought of myself as anything other than heterosexual until last week. . . . I observed that I was always very interested in female bodies and that I had close emotional ties. With men, I'm always the caretaker—they cry to me and never vice versa—but with women, it is more mutual in all my relationships with women. I guess I'm heterosexual with lesbian tendencies. If given the right situation and if given a chance, I'd definitely try it, the physical part.

I wasn't quite sure what her options were until she said,

I look at women and see them as beautiful, "fuckable." This is just my new openness. Kissing a girl is soft, different and better than with boys. I'm jealous of women who can kiss each other. Something you can get from a girl you can't from a boy. I can understand bisexuality in a big way. Most of the girls I know complain that they'd like to meet boys like their girl friends.

These issues of defining and measuring sexual and romantic orientations, identities, and behaviors might well confuse us—as they do many young people. Yet, it is critical to increase our awareness of these issues if we want to understand ourselves, our families, and our world. More specifically, we need to ask, "Who is bisexual?"

5

Who Is Bisexual?

I look at girls the way I look at boys—not fair I can't find
boys like her!
—Alicia, age 22, white, student

Many young people struggle to define exactly what bisexuality is. In
Zane's case, his middle school classmates assumed he must be bisexual because he befriended a gay boy, played the piano, sang in the
chorus, and did not date girls who wanted to date him. Early adolescents, with their newly energized sexual and romantic arousals, may
be initially confused about their options given their attractions to
multiple sexes. During early adolescence, Flora didn't believe she was
bisexual; she merely wanted to live in two houses, side by side, with
a husband in one and a wife in the other and kids in both. She need
not feel alone regarding her perplexity because few people know how
best to approach bisexual topics in research, clinics, and interpersonal
situations.

An "equal attraction to all genders" definition of bisexuality seldom
satisfies young people today. Multiattracted youths have questions they
want addressed, as noted by the Bisexual Resource Center:

- Is bisexuality defined by identity, behavior, attractions—or some combi-
  nation of these?
- Where does bisexuality begin and end?
- Human sexuality is sometimes seen as a continuum. . . . Bisexuality, then,
  must fall somewhere in the middle. But where?
- Does bisexuality refer only to the middle point, or 50/50 attraction?
- Does bisexuality encompass all the space between the extremes?

- How much bisexual attraction and/or behavior does it take to make a person bisexual?
- Does bisexuality encompass people whose attractions change over time?
- If you are once bisexual are you always bisexual?
- If you are in a long-term relationship, do you stop being bisexual and "become" gay or straight?
- And for each of these questions, who gets to decide?[1]

Answers central to this book include that one need not be attracted to all sexes and genders to the same degree, at the same moment, or at all times. Fluidity in attractions characterizes many bisexuals; others are not bisexually fluid but stable in their ratio of attractions across time. This capacity for multiple attractions depends on the person's biological makeup, cognitive awareness, personality characteristics, and the allure of other persons—including their gender expression. A young woman might be romantically attracted to shyness and sexually attracted to self-confidence regardless of the person's biological sex; a young man, romantically attracted to femininity and sexually attracted to masculinity regardless of the person's biological sex; and a nonbinary person, romantically and sexually attracted to people as individuals. Clearly, one need not feel equal sexual and romantic passion for each sex and gender.

The quandary for youths is how best to evaluate their status given that they have some, but not necessarily all, components of bisexuality. Is simply having at least some degree of sexual and romantic arousal to multiple sexes sufficient? Decisions made about definitions have profound consequences on the prevalence and characteristics of bisexuals. Unfortunately, few can turn to research for answers because these complexities are essentially ignored.

With regard to social science research, the gold standard is usually a nationally based, representative sample of a country. This is not trivial, because thousands of scientific articles are based on the information such research generates. In turn, the data influence public policies, health decisions, and politics that affect all of us. One of the longest running such data sets is collected by the National Opinion Research Center at the University of Chicago. The creators and sustainers of its ongoing General Social Survey (GSS) provide "politicians, policymakers, and scholars with a clear and unbiased perspective on what Americans think and feel."[2] The intent is to explain US societal trends in attitudes, behaviors, and attributes. Historically, bisexuality was defined by individuals reporting they had engaged both male and female sex partners "in the past 12 months, the past 5 years, or since age 18." What constituted sex or a sex partner was not defined; neither was the number of sex partners specified for what counted, whether 1, 20, or 100. Ignored was how to interpret motives for sexual activity and whether the sex was meaningful, desired, or forced. A decade ago, a sexual identity question was added to the GSS: "Which of the following best describes you?" Options were not expansive but limited to "straight," "gay/lesbian," "bisexual," and "don't know." Why the switch from a behavioral to an identity definition was not explained in published research; whether it made a difference in results and to those who were completing the questionnaire is also unknown.[3]

Similar problems plague other large data sets. The Youth Risk Behavior Surveillance System (YRBSS) is a Centers for Disease Control and Prevention survey, initiated in 1991. It claims to be the "nation's premier system of health-related telephone surveys that collect state data about U.S. residents."[4] Yet, it too severely limits its sexual identity options to the Big Three categories.[5] More helpfully, the Australian Study of Health and Relationships includes these three plus "queer," "questioning," "no label," and "other."[6] Sexual attraction and sexual experience were also assessed; all three variable can be combined to calculate who is bisexual, though no explicit explanation is given about how this should be done.

So, too, the National Epidemiologic Survey on Alcohol and Related Conditions (NESARC), "based on a nationally representative sample of the civilian noninstitutionalized population of the United States," assesses sexuality on the basis of identity, attraction, and behavior.[7] However, all three are presented as categories and not points along a continuum.

Sexual identity: Which category best describes you? heterosexual (straight), gay or lesbian, bisexual, or not sure?

Sexual attraction: Which category best describes your feelings? only attracted to females, mostly attracted to females, equally attracted to females and males, mostly attracted to males, or only attracted to males.

Sexual behavior: In your entire life, have you had sex with? only males, only females, both males and females, or never had sex.[8]

Researchers using the data set must decide, usually without justification, which one or combination of indicators gauges sexuality in their findings.[9]

Do These Research Gaffes Matter?

In a word, the answer to whether these research gaffes matter is a resounding yes. One the most influential data sets is the National Longitudinal Survey of Adolescent to Adult Health (Add Health). It has spawned perhaps more publications than any other nongovernmental national survey and has thus affected millions of lives. It originally defined a bisexual as someone having "romantic attraction" to both sexes, though "romantic attraction" was not defined (some youths apparently thought it implied friendship), and the vast majority of those who reported same-sex romantic attraction at Wave 1 as adolescents did not recount it one year later or ever again in subsequent waves during young adulthood. This is shocking because our general understanding is that the number of youths coming out of the closet *increases* rather than decreases from early adolescence to young adulthood. In part, because of this and other glaring conundrums, in Wave 3, a sexual identity question was added: "Choose the description that best fits how you think about yourself." "Bisexual" is defined as "attracted to men and women equally"—which we know runs counters to almost everyone's understanding of bisexuality. The other two spectrum points ("mostly straight" and "mostly gay") are typically combined by users of the Add Health data with the monosexual "straight" and "gay" categories, usually for unspecified reasons but which nevertheless misidentifies them as not being bisexual—though they have attractions to multiple sexes.[10]

One interpretation of these dubious assessments of same-sex sexuality in Add Health was the failure of data managers to delete from the data set youths intent on pranking researchers by claiming to be gay, lesbian, or bisexual.[11] These "inaccurate responders" were likely to be careless, confused, or jokesters, individuals (mostly boys) who might have intentionally provided false answers to sex questions. Unless they are weeded out, such tricksters are in every survey, especially those given to teenagers, some of whom have a tendency for "immaturity and rebelliousness." The forensic psychologist Dewey Cornell and colleagues note the possible effects of including such youths, who are "tempted to offer inflated reports of their engagement in socially proscribed or illicit behaviors, or they may not take the survey seriously and mark it haphazardly, producing an elevation in otherwise low base rate behaviors."[12]

Supporting these views regarding the possibility of dubious responses from problematic young responders, several years ago the psychometric professor Caihong Li and colleagues asked nearly 7,000 southern college students to complete an online survey on campus climate. Nearly 5 percent of the young adults were determined to be invalid responders; they misreported data, either through carelessness ("intentionally providing random responses," "didn't pay attention to how answered the survey") or zealousness ("choosing highest scores, responding invariantly"). Their bogus responses included claiming to be transgender or gender-nonconforming and victims of sexual assault or intimate-partner physical violence. The authors conclude that by removing these responders from the sample, more accurate prevalence information emerges. In general, the most vulnerable surveys are lengthy, personally sensitive questionnaires—that is, the national surveys reported throughout this book that have formed what we believe we know about bisexuality.[13]

These troll-like response patterns from mischievous respondents are problematic for obtaining accurate estimates for a range of information,

including sexual and gender identity. They are known to increase response rates to supposedly rare occurrences—such as having artificial
limbs, siring multiple children prior to high school graduation, being
seven feet tall, and weighing 300 pounds, aside from claiming to be bisexual. As such, they need to be ferreted out. For example, 253 youths
stated on the Wave 1 Add Health questionnaire that they have an artificial hand, arm, leg, or foot; when interviewed later at home, only two
had an artificial limb.[14]

Although no double check was conducted regarding a bisexual identity, might these jokesters who are supposedly seven feet tall and have
mental illnesses also claim to be bisexual? And, if we extrapolate these
possibilities to larger issues, might it be possible that these "fake bisexuals" are misrepresenting the general population of bisexuals? That is,
should we believe this research that documents the suicidal, depressed,
criminal nature of bisexuals? Is it true that bisexuals are overrepresented
among individuals who have been waylaid by their drug use or cutting
behavior and who are dangerous sexual predators with eating disorders?
Are these the authentic bisexuals or merely the dubious bisexuals who
are having fun with gullible researchers who are misrepresenting bisexuality? Although the consistency with which these self-fashioned, *accidental* bisexual youths are removed in other surveys is uneven, they can
certainly lead to deceptive results in counting and portraying bisexuals,
which in turn distorts survey findings and, subsequently, professional
and policy recommendations. Might they also distort the perceptions
of young people who are just beginning to recognize they might be bisexual? If so, this is tragic beyond words.

Unknown in specific terms is the extent to which the failure to recruit
representative samples of bisexuals affects research findings, such as the
prevalence of bisexuals, their unique characteristics, or their mental
health profile. The social work, education, and community health sciences professors Wendy Bostwick and Sean McCabe, working with the
NESARC data, found that it mattered which domain was selected—a
common failure of most research—whether identity, attraction, or behavior. For example, with regard to the *number* of bisexuals, over three

times more individuals had sex with both sexes than identified as bisexual; with regard to *mental health*, those with a bisexual identity had considerably more anxiety over their lifetime than did those who reported equal attraction to males and females.[15]

Also unstipulated are the "what ifs." Does it matter if the time frame for having sex is "last year," "last five years," or "ever"? Imposing a time frame might also affect responses to questions regarding attractions, identities, and crushes, especially for fluid individuals. A girl might engage in sex with boys in high school because of social pressures but then later pursue sex with multiple sexes because of the opportunities in college to do so; now, however, as a young adult, she only has sex with a woman to remain faithful to her same-sex relationship. A boy might feel he is gay rather than bisexual because his same-sex attractions are stronger; prefers to be straight rather than bisexual because of the advantages accrued by his straight friends; and identifies as bisexual because it is "in" to be on the spectrum in his group of friends. If youths have crushes on multiple sexes during elementary and middle school, which is not unusual, does this imply they are bisexual? Perhaps it is their culture and not themselves that is defining how to interpret similar emotional feelings (girls = she's a crush; boys = he's a buddy).

Terms such as "having sex" are nearly always undefined in surveys— usually because we try not to include explicit sexual behaviors in surveying youths and young adults. For example, the sociologist Laura Carpenter notes that a self-identified lesbian respondent considered herself a virgin because, though she had sex with her girlfriend, she never had intercourse with a man.[16] We are left to wonder, Do anal sex, oral sex, genital touching, mutual masturbation, and deep kissing count as sex and, if so, equally? For a boy to kiss another boy is quite different from having anal intercourse with him—yet both can count as sex. Do girls masturbating together imply something different than vaginally or anally penetrating each other with fingers or sex toys? How deep does deep kissing need to be to count as sexual rather than "how are you?" Do words used in the stems of questions influence responses?

Participants have been asked to "describe," "prefer," "feel," "think," and "identify" their sexuality. Whether these distinctions make a difference is unknown.

One radical alternative taken by the psychiatrist Austin Blum and colleagues is to omit sexual categories altogether and assess sexual orientation on a scale from attraction only to one sex to only the other sex. Their rationale is spot-on: "Our use of a continuum to describe sexual orientation reflects considerable evidence that many people show non-exclusivity in their sexual attractions, behavior, or both." This innovation resulted in findings pitched not in terms of categories but as "students reporting a greater degree of same-sex attraction were significantly more likely to . . ." The problem, of course, is that little can be inferred about the middle of the range given the overwhelming number of exclusively other-sex-attracted individuals. However, it might be a useful technique for characteristics in which the degree of same-sex attraction matters, such as the greater the score, the more likely is an individual to engage in same-sex behavior or romantic attachments.[17]

How Did I Become Bisexual?

These surveys do not address the concern of some young people: How did I become bisexual? Research seldom instructs us because, as noted earlier, we are not sure who actually is bisexual. Real-life dilemmas, such as contrasting sexual and romantic entanglements, are essentially disregarded, and thus the disconnect between actual bisexual lives and what we understand bisexuality to be is a source of bewilderment for many youths. If they were to turn to science for answers, they would be, once again, disappointed because, as best as I can determine, few if any scientists actually care what causes bisexuality. Listening to public health officials, clinical practitioners, and educators also might not help because these professionals have read, cited, or created a wealth of potential misinformation that severely limits knowledge and outreach to those who have questions about their multiple attractions or genders.

At the most fundamental level, by design or by neglect (it is difficult to discern which), we seldom agree on how to assess whether a person is bisexual and thus have little idea how an individual *becomes* bisexual. Maybe Freud was right that everyone is bisexual.

Possible explanations include family genetics, which might cause a young person to consider whether a parent, sibling, or aunt or uncle is also not exclusively straight. Another is both biological and environmental: the mother was stressed during her pregnancy due to marital problems, cigarette smoking, drinking, using drugs, or the like, which altered her unborn child's levels of prenatal hormones, causing sexuality to shift away from exclusive heterosexuality. A popular theory among evangelicals posits that sexual or physical abuse by relatives or pedophiles while growing up changes sexual orientation from straight to not straight. Another theory, somewhat similar, is based on family dynamics: having a dominant mother or submissive father (or the reverse has also been proposed) causes sexual orientations to switch.

Of all theories, the most frequently heard by the youths I interviewed was one articulated by Billie Joe Armstrong, the lead singer of the band Green Day: "Everyone is born bisexual and your parents or society pushes you to be straight. I think I've always been bisexual. . . . I think people are born bisexual, and it's just that our parents and society kind of veer us off into this feeling of 'Oh, I can't.'"[18] This idea appears to be derived from the psychoanalyst Sigmund Freud's *Three Essays on the Theory of Sexuality*. In brief, according to Freud, everyone innately incorporates attributes of both sexes anatomically and psychologically, with sexual attraction to both sexes being one part of psychological bisexuality. Usually, the masculine becomes most dominant in men and the feminine in women, resulting in heterosexually; if it is reversed, then homosexuality. In neither case, however, is either the masculinity or the femininity totally erased, with the result that, at some basic level, all of us are bisexual.[19]

Although the everyone-is-bisexual line is usually applied to girls and not boys, several of the young men I interviewed believed it applied to them as well. Toby believed that everyone, to varying degrees, has sub-conscious bisexual fantasies. Donovan was less certain about everyone, but the term "bisexual," according to him, "should be applied far more to people, . . . so many more than usually think." Roberto concurred: "A good majority of people are bisexual." He later added, "I would say most people are." Dave was more scientific, pointing out that sexuality is a "bell curve and people toward either end [straight, gay] with most in the middle [bisexual] and afraid to admit it." As for himself, he was not sure why he was attracted to whom he was: "I am a free person about every-thing. I never like to hear that I can't be attracted to guys and that I really [have to] like girls." Most of the young men believed in the power of bi-ology, though Casey believed it was complicated: "Society doesn't mold you. . . . I was born straight and happened to have homosexual urges."

The young-adult women I interviewed, for their part, were generally less concerned about how they became bisexual—largely because, simi-lar to Casey, "it's complicated."

KRISTIN: I'm a biology major, and I never thought about the evolution-ary significance of attractions to both. I think homosexuality because tied to other genes, and that keeps it in the population. Could be a biological component of getting stuck in the middle, but I never thought about it.

VALERIE: I abandoned my quest to figure out why God gave me this plate, and I have to deal with it. I thought it could be genetic (not a gay gene, which I find disgusting), but there is something in my mind, my chemistry, my brain, my mentality, something. Not that I chose this somewhere out of my ass without it coming from some-thing inside me.

EMMA: Oh shit! I don't believe in the nature part. I grew up with guys, and my peer group was guys and who I interacted with and I learned how to be. My family didn't raise me to be girly, allowed me to play sports, and didn't have to wear dresses. All of that maybe, but I don't know.

EDEN: I took [this] course freshman year of college, and I discovered
that females can be attracted to females. . . . Not a biological issue
but rearing can orient one toward females, like a social/psychological
developmental issue.

Ultimately, the bottom line was Valerie's conclusion: "This kind of
conversation doesn't matter to me anymore. It's sad that society can't
deal with just this. I don't care where it came from, but it's the same
as heterosexuality." In part, Valerie's assessment might be based on the
paradoxical reality that the majority of those who engage in sex with
others of their own sex identify as straight.

6

Straights Having Sex with Each Other

It's not like two straight guys get drunk and start making out.
—Roberto, age 21, Puerto Rican, student

The Savage Love columnist Dan Savage received a letter from a 29-year-old single straight man who wondered if it would be possible to have a "one-time thing" (sex) with his close gay friend because, he wrote, "I am now experiencing a sexual attraction to him." Although Savage said no out of respect for the gay friend, I wonder if the straight man's real concern was not for his friend but for his own status as a straight man if it were to happen.[1]

What puzzles many of us, and perhaps this young man, are the research findings of the sociologists Aaron Hoy and Andrew London: self-proclaimed heterosexual women and men account for approximately half (more so for women) of all same-sex sexuality. Hoy and London note, "Same-sex desires, attractions, and behaviors are a part of life for large numbers of heterosexually identified people. . . . These individuals make sense of their experiences with same-sex sexuality in many complex ways and even integrate these experiences into their sexual and gender identities."[2]

Over the past decade, about 4 percent of straight-identified high school girls and 2 percent of boys reported having sex with another girl or boy, respectively. Given that these acknowledgments are *reports* of behavior, they are unquestionably a substantial undercount of the total. Because straight-identified youths make up the overwhelming majority of the population, this 2 percent to 4 percent translates to a large percentage of the total number of youths having same-sex encounters.[3] Should we consider these straight-identified individuals to be bisexual?

If there is sex, is there not sexual desire? Why are they not identifying as bisexual? These individuals challenge the very meaning of bisexuality.

Women

Given the greater cultural unease with gender nonconformity among boys than girls—especially boys having sex with each other—it should not surprise us that twice as many straight-identified high school girls than boys report having same-sex relations. Combined with the common finding that straight-identified women are more likely than straight-identified men to report inconsistencies between their sexual behavior and sexual identity, the question becomes, What is the meaning and context behind what is sometimes labeled as "gal-pal sex"?[4] One common explanation is that women are having sex with each other for the showpiece of men—their sexual encounter titillates men (at least straight men) and causes women to be perceived as more desirable, which enhances their prestige. The writer and professional dominatrix Natalie West has a problem with this explanation because "[women's] sexuality is often not only invalidated, but also made into a performance."[5] The greater latitude given to women than men to dabble in same-sex behavior was corroborated by my interviewee Roberto. "Coming from a place where the party scene is huge, it's so normal to walk into a party and see two girls making out. No one would assume anything of it. You would just think they were having fun or partying."

This "performative" aspect was explored by the sociologist Janelle Pham among nearly 5,000 college women who had at least one sexual experience with another woman. The predominant pattern (over three-quarters) was among women who engaged in nongenital sex—making out with a woman, touching a woman's breasts or bottom, or having their breasts or bottom touched by a woman. The straight women were usually in sororities, with the sex occurring in a public place, frequently at a fraternity party or a bar in the presence of alcohol (thus lowering inhibitions). Pham notes that in "male-dominated, heterosexually predominant party scenes . . . sexual acts between women are eroticized [to] facilitate sexual encounters among women." This public performative bisexuality was deployed by women, Pham hypothesizes, to garner the desired male attention ("for fun or male benefit"). The women were invested in "hegemonic femininity" and hence distanced themselves from known lesbians and from identifying as lesbian. They also tended to be sexually experienced with men and to be white. Pham reminds us that white straight women enjoy greater flexibility than do women of color, who may feel their sexual behavior is "open to greater scrutiny and more likely to be taken as representative of their entire communities," especially on predominantly white college campuses.[6]

Rebelling against this female performative bisexuality are contra "Skirt Clubs," not a place for the benefit of men but a setting reserved for women. Several years ago, when founder Genevieve LeJeune went to sex parties with her boyfriend, it was her "boyfriend edging her on to do something for him to watch or indulge in." LeJeune wondered how she could explore her own bisexuality if she were constantly performing for someone else (her boyfriend), which began her process of envisioning a different kind of environment: "A safe, judgment-free space where women could act out their desires on their own terms, away from the male gaze, . . . away from the demands of boyfriends and husbands, even if just for a night." As a result, LeJeune created "straight-but-curious all-female sex soirées" with a strict no-boys policy, thus negating the possibility that women are performing for men. The women told her they "wanted a girlfriend in addition to their boyfriends or husbands: someone just for them." Lejeune wondered if the women were "so eager to find intimacy with another woman that they would fuck anywhere." Or, perhaps, similar to Laura Carpenter's interviewee, they felt comfortable because what they were doing did not really count as sex. "It was adventurous, but not too adventurous. It was lesbian, but not too lesbian." Although women are usually less concerned than men are in maintaining the charade of heterosexuality and a straight identity, these hideaways ensure safety and anonymity.[7]

Given the cover charge for Skirt Clubs (upward of $200 per visit), few women from lower socioeconomic means would be able to attend. Yet, many might want to. Counter to the belief that women who hook up with other women are primarily from selective, progressive universities, national data reported by the sociologist Jamie Budnick indicate that we have the social location backward: women with the lowest levels of educational attainment report the highest lifetime prevalence of same-gender sex. These are the women Budnick interviewed who engage in sex with women—defined both sexually and romantically with the question, "Have you ever had physical or emotional contact, such as kissing, dating, spending time together, sex, or other activities with a woman?" Many have never attended college, are from low socioeconomic classes, are married or cohabitating, and have a child. Why do these, for the most part, straight-identified women sexually and romantically engage women? Budnick proposes two interlocking reasons: One, early motherhood forecloses the possibilities of claiming or developing a bisexual or queer identity. Motherhood and self-sacrifice take priority over personal identity (but not, necessarily, same-sex behavior or romance). Two, within their friendship networks, they find opportunities to explore same-gender sex and desire in safe circumstances devoid of sexual assault. If they were to adopt a not-straight identity, most would embrace bisexuality and not the more incendiary terms "queer" or "lesbian." For Budnick's interviewees, "'bisexual' is a relatively untainted and utterly intelligible term, and 'queer' is an alienating slur rather than an anti-label panacea."[8]

Many questions remain, in large part because of the limited literature on women who have sex with women. Are women less invested than men in maintaining the myth of a straight identity? Is it about power? Are there down-low women within particular ethnic/racial groups? Are cultural mandates to be gender appropriate in sexual behavior less restrictive and punitive for women? Is there something totally unique to straight women having sex with women, perhaps mirroring reasons why lesbians have sex with men? Or, as some people would have it, are all women bisexual? The evidence certainly does not support this last question, though more women than men identify and act as if they are bisexual.

The young women I interviewed were initially motivated to have heterosexual sex because of their curiosity, social expectations, and desire to feel normal. Then why explore something other than heterosexual sex? One frequent answer was that sex with men, especially the first, was not so great and largely disappointing, and thus they were motivated to try something else. None indicated that bad sex with boys or good sex with girls changed their sexuality—but they did open new opportunities to explore.

The woman who was most animated about her first sex with a boy was a young woman I interviewed who vividly (with volume) recalled her first heterosexual experience at age 15. "It hurt a lot, so I yelled, 'Take it out! Take it out!'" A girl might blame herself or her boy partner for the bad sex, but she usually faulted their inexperience. For example, Alicia and her boyfriend had a seventh-grade crush on each other when they decided to go a step further.

> I gave him a hand job at his request and looked the other way. I was not very good, and he did not come. I didn't know what I was doing, and it was his first experience, too. I did it for acceptance, what we were supposed to do, the sex norm. I did not enjoy it—awkward experience. After this, I always tried to be a pleaser, what supposed to do with a boyfriend. I don't think I have ever been sexually awakened. It was a degrading experience—like a chicken with its head cut off.

Another young woman was several years older and had been dating her boyfriend for two months when he asked, "Is it okay if I touch you? You don't have to touch me."

> What to do with it? He didn't know how. I then attempted a hand job on him, but it was disastrous. He touched me in an adolescent sort of way,

but he had no idea how to make it work. Complete disaster! I liked it, but embarrassed that I had done it. This was the only time. I was afraid that he would tell others that I was that kind of girl. He fingered me.

Other than women who have sex with other women for male-oriented performative purposes, Pham identified another group of straight women who have sex with women—those on team-based sports. By contrast to their sorority sisters, these women were more likely to engage in *genital sex* with a female partner, including genital stimulation, oral sex, or vaginal/anal intercourse. In general, Pham notes that sex-segregated team sports tend to be female affirming and accepting of sexual minorities, bringing together young women into intense physical and romantic bonds with each other that builds team cohesion. "This may have a facilitative partnering effect, with women engaging in sexual relationships with other teammates, or may signal a subcultural dynamic that is supportive of women's same-sex eroticism." These women might currently or eventually identify as bisexual.[9]

Men

A widely debated and highly provocative literature has evolved around an incongruous class of straight-identified men who have, on their own volition, sex with men—labeled "bud-sex" or "dude-sex." The gender and sexuality studies professor Jane Ward views these men as super-straight, hetero-masculine men who engage in sex with other men as "often necessary, patriotic, character-building, masculinity-enhancing, and paradoxically, a means of inoculating oneself against authentic gayness." For these men, heterosexuality is "natural, normal, and right"; dude-sex does not challenge their heterosexuality but is rather an affirmation of it and secures the dividing line between gay and straight. It is sex with a bro, who must be of the same race, straight, and masculine. Nobody here is *really* bisexual because genital contact with other men is not about sex but about playing a "central role in the institutions and rituals that produce heterosexual subjectivity, as well as in the broader culture's imagination of what it means for 'boys to be boys.'" According to Ward, the straight men have to "avoid being mistaken as sincere homosexuals" by signifying that the sexual encounter is not about sex. Rather, "it was compelled by others (such as older fraternity brothers) or by circumstances that left them little choice (such as the apparently quite dire need to obtain access to a particular fraternity)." It is as if these fragile men with toxic masculinity are saying, "I'm so straight that I can do this without it actually having any consequence whatsoever for my daily sexual orientation, which is straight." They continue to date and have sex with women; they would never grace the steps of queer subculture or associate with gays.[10]

In the book *Still Straight: Sexual Flexibility among White Men in Rural America*, the sociologist Tony Silva makes similar claims about rural men and their sexuality, which serves as an example of the *performance* of heterosexuality. For the straight-identified men he interviewed, sex was not merely a matter of math, counting one's relative degree of same-sex behavior was not relevant. Context and interpretation are the critical factors in sorting through the identification process. Silva applies this approach to bud-sex, which is similar to dude-sex in that it is sex with men but differs primarily by location: dude-sex is within an urban, collegiate, or military context, while bud-sex is between rural men. Both should, in the scheme of the math problem, disqualify a man from identifying as straight, but it does not. It is one of the many complex ways in which the additive power of sex between men is discounted; rather than subtract from heterosexuality, it, once again, reinforces normative masculinity and straightness. To be clear, bud-sex participants are not, at least in their own eyes, closeted bisexuals but straight-identified men who have sex with men—preferably masculine men with no promises of romantic connections or meaning other than sex. They normalize and authenticate these sexual encounters as expressions of masculinity; besides, they are doing a favor for their wives: "The married men framed sex with men as less threatening to marriage than extramarital sex with women, helping to preserve a part of their lives that they described as central to their straightness." It is "secretive sex"; the men are "helpin' a buddy out" by relieving him of his sexual urges. Quite strikingly, they do this without being inconsistent in their own minds with hegemonic masculinity.[11]

In another social context, the sociologists Héctor Carrillo and Amanda Hoffman remind us that it is not just about the gender of one's sex partner but also about the sex act itself. For a Mexican man who engages in male-male sex, if he is the top in anal sex, then he is masculine and straight, both publicly and to himself; his partner, of course, is feminine and hence gay. From the point of view of the top man, he maintains his straight identity because he is exclusively or primarily sexually and romantically attracted to women. Besides, there is "no real personal or social advantages that would stem from publicly adopting an identity as bisexual or gay." However, his "pinch of bi" is bisexual nevertheless, at least in his attractions and behavior. On the sexual orientation continuum, he believes he is on or close (bisexual) to the heterosexual end. Carrillo and Hoffman argue that these men are "not drawn toward male bodies in the same way as they are drawn to female bodies, and some observe that the only physical part of a man that interests them is his penis"; and penises "are disembodied objects of desire that provide a source of sexual pleasure." His interest in men is purely sexual, not romantic.[12]

Men might privately admit that they not totally straight while maintaining their visible heterosexuality. Are their traditional protocols of finding ways to have sex with other men without giving up a straight veneer decreasing among younger generations? I believe so, because young people now have the freedom to break free from cultural gender demands. Plus, they have a new identity that blends their various degrees of romantic, sexual, and gender behavior and attractions without endorsing a bisexual label that many of them feel is "too gay" or not applicable to them—"mostly straight."[13] Left out, however, are some ethnic, racial, and socioeconomic populations, such as rural and low-income Latino young men who believe in the *activo/pasivo* phenomenon.[14]

Complexities of Straightness

Are straight-identified women and men who engage in same-sex activities closeted bisexuals? Is the sex motivated by mere pleasure or an assertion of power? By having sex with both sexes, are they by definition not straight but bisexual? Does the sex they have make a meaningful statement about their sexual orientation? Is the ultimate sexual identity they assume even important?

Sociologists and gender studies professors differ in their answers to these questions and the inferences they make about both the motivations and the meanings of the same-sex behavior. To address these issues, the sociologists Arielle Kuperberg and Alicia Walker surveyed over 24,000 college students, in part to focus on straight-identified individuals whose last hookup was with a same-sex partner. Within the sample, Kuperberg and Walker describe four types of men and five types of women. From most to least frequent are the following:

Wanting More: enjoys the encounter, wants a relationship with the partner, has had previous same-sex experiences, involves genital contact

Drunk and Curious. is binge drinking at the time, supports premarital sex, does not want to repeat the act, is politically liberal

Little Enjoyment: drinks heavily, knows the partner, has little actual genital contact (more making out)

Just Not Who I Can Be: is heterosexist, believes same-sex relations and premarital sex are usually wrong, is politically conservative

The first three types also apply to women, and there are two more types that apply to women but not to men:

Maybe for Show: takes place at a public location (bar), is binge drinking, has little genital contact, is politically liberal, has no previous same-sex encounters

Loved It, but Religious: enjoys the hookup, wants a relationship, has no prior same-sex experiences, is highly religious

Across all six types, the majority of the straight-identified young adults are sexual experimenters or partying types with public drinking and private same-sex encounters: among men, to have sex once women leave a fraternity party; and among women, to attract men at Greek parties or bars. These men and women tend to be politically liberal, have positive views about premarital sex and homosexuality, and seldom regret their same-sex engagement. The authors suggest that the Wanting More youths were probably in the early stages of transitioning from a straight to a mostly straight or bisexual identity. Other young adults did not particularly enjoy the sex, but it served to reaffirm their heterosexuality.[15]

The foregoing research is particularly valuable because it illustrates that straight-identified men and women have sex with both sexes for a variety of reasons and consequences for their sense of sexual and gender selves. They may feel straighter and more gender appropriate because the sex is in the service of power, pleasure, daring, or curiosity. The sex might be experimental, a means to assess how strong their same-sex attractions are and, possibly, to move them toward a less exclusive straight identity. To understand, we need to know more about how their arousal is played out and its meaning. What is the strength of their same-sex sexual and romantic attractions? What motivates them to act on them? They may seldom identify as bisexual (though they have dual attractions) because they believe bisexual is too far along the continuum toward gayness. Others are more fluid in temperament and lifestyle and are not unwaveringly oriented in their sexuality. Or they are more interested in same-sex others in a romantic than in a sexual sense, or they prefer other identity terms such as "pansexual," "genderqueer," or "queer." I found among mostly straight men that the motive is seldom to maintain normative straight privilege or reputation; rather, it best reflects their true sexual/romantic self. Their orientation has not changed, but what has is their awareness of what it is and how they can live it out in their daily lives.[16]

Are They Straight or Bisexual?

Given that few scientists consider in their research design whether the specific wording, time frame, motivation, meaning, and component of sexuality matter, it is not surprising that the necessary corollary is difficulty determining who is bisexual, how representative those who so identify are, and whether the found results characterize the much larger bisexual/pansexual population. Many would-be bisexuals struggle with or object to the "bisexual" word, and their reservations permeate and hence muddle what is known about bisexuality. My sense from the interviews is that few multiattracted or multibehaving individuals characterize themselves as having equal attractions to all sexes; it might depend on the person's gender presentation, personality, or availability. Others decry the "sexual" in "bisexual" as reinforcing a stereotype of promiscuity—double the opportunities, double the fun. And, among younger cohorts, the "bisexual" label itself has vague meanings and has been usurped by other preferred identities, including "pansexual," "queer," "fluid," and "unlabeled."

What defines a bisexual was debated at a recent roundtable discussion at Indiana University. I asked the gathered crowd of faculty and graduate students whether they like the word "bisexual." There were mixed reactions. The graduate student Elizabeth Bartelt noted, "There is by no means a consensus among the [queer] community with what term is most in use" for individuals who have traditionally labeled themselves bisexual. Ideally, one should avoid terms that are applied in the negative (what it is not), such as "nonexclusive" and "nonmonosexual," or that include only a portion of their essence in the name— the "sexual" in "bisexual" omits the romantic and the gender. Some people adopt a placeholder term, "bi+," with the caveat that this language conundrum will be resolved and more satisfactory linguistic names will emerge. Even though "bisexual" is an imperfect word at best, it is difficult to circumvent the term because of its widespread usage.

The social psychologist Corey Flanders emphasizes that the diversity within bisexuality should be a top priority if we intend to sort through the morass of what bisexuality is. We should start by finding out "how young bisexual people themselves define bisexuality, whether those definitions change with social context, or whether bisexual people define bisexuality differently from pansexual people." For youths, "a single identity encompasses so many different meanings and attractions and behaviors for people who explicitly identify as bisexual" that it "leaves room for the multitudinous expressions of that identity." We must flush out some of those countless meanings—we need to ask about their lives.[17]

Comparable, perhaps parallel, discussions regarding the significance of romantic attractions and behaviors—crushes, dates, love, attachment—further complicate these definitional dilemmas. Passionate friendships and bromances are taken up next as examples.

7

Why Romance Matters

I find things in women I don't find in men. No offense, but
women are more compassionate, they pay more attention,
and their bodies are more attractive—none of this hairy stuff.
—Harper, age 20, white, student

Largely missing from our appreciation of bisexual youths are the
romantic aspects of their lives. Sexual proclivities capture our cultural
imagination and thus gain prominence; romantic attractions, less so. But
are romantic attractions subservient to sexual attractions? The social
psychologist Michael Bailey believes so: "Sexual interest is necessary for
the development of romantic feelings. It sometimes seems that some are
trying to emphasize the romantic at the expense of the sexual, but I don't
think that's how men work."[1] Do women work this way?

In either case, I see no evidence, either from previous research or
from the young people I interviewed, that sexual and romantic attractions are necessarily identical or that one is necessary for the other. The
two are clearly highly correlated for most youths, and one may provoke
or encourage the other. Admittedly, sometimes the two are only periph-
erally connected, as in hooking up with one sex and crushing on the
other. That said, for most youths, the sync between sexual and romantic
intimacy is consistent, if not for the same person, then for the same
gender—but not always. For the young women and men I interviewed,
regardless of their sexual or romantic orientation, the discrepancy between the two ranged from nonexistence to raging divergence; the latter
was particularly irritating for those who believed they should be constant. Yet, it is rare for scientists, parents, and health-care providers to
consider the potential misalignment of sexual and romantic feelings.

When they are misaligned, the incongruity is usually renamed. Love between two boys becomes a bromance, not a romantic pairing. Two girls in love becomes a passionate friendship, not an overwhelming crush.

Romantic orientation is routinely disregarded because researchers seldom ask questions about the nature of romantic attraction, passionate love, or attachment. Although most multiattracted youths date, we rarely inquire about the contrast between their straight and gay dating. We believe their focus is solely on Grindr or BeNaughty (sex apps), not on Tinder or Her (romance apps). Listening to their life histories tells another story. The conversation might begin with sexuality, but it *inevitably* progresses to their romantic crushes and love interests. They might provide few details about their first sexual encounter but wax long and emotionally about the first date. Why are we not following their lead? If we did, what would be revealed, according to the psychologist Michael Walton and colleagues, is "a rich and diverse tapestry of human sexual *and* romantic expression that is beyond current typical recognition and understanding."[2]

At least from a scientific perspective, the romantic and the sexual should be at least loosely linked because, according to the neuroscientist Stephanie Cacioppo and colleagues, "Sexual desire and love, as two highly rewarding experiences, share similar biochemical, neuroendocrine pathways," especially in brain areas that are rich in dopamine and in parts of the ancient brain. Or, as a more popular account has it, "Our brain and heart are known to be in close communication," and in this, there are "no differences between brain systems regulating romantic love in homosexuals and heterosexuals"—and, I might add, bisexuals. According to relationship science, both the sexual and the romantic enhance and reinforce pleasure and emotions. Becoming infatuated can create sexual desire for that person, and perhaps more than young hearts recognize, having sex might ultimately lead to having romantic feelings for that person, especially with repeat performances.[3]

Passionate and Companionate Love

Two primary distinctions are usually made when considering romantic orientation. One is *passionate love*: having an intense craving for uniting with another. In common jargon, passionate love is a crush, infatuation, puppy love, and being in love. When reciprocated, we feel ecstatic; when unrequited, we feel anxious, empty, and despondent. Children are as likely as adolescents and boys are as likely as girls to experience passionate love. In the mid-1980s, the social psychologists Elaine Hatfield and Susan Sprecher developed a Passionate Love Scale with three components:

Cognitive components: intrusive thinking; preoccupation with the partner; idealization of the other or of the relationship; desire to know the other and be known by him/her

Emotional components: attraction to the partner; longing for reciprocity, to love and be loved in return; desire for complete and permanent union; physiological (sexual) arousal

Behavioral components: actions aimed to determine other's feelings; studying the other person, service to the other; maintaining physical closeness[4]

A second aspect of romantic orientation, *companionate love*, is a cluster of emotions, romantic intimacies, attachments, and commitments. We must be in close proximity with the object of our desires, and in that person's presence is calm, comfort, and security; if the person is absent, loss and bewilderment. Although adolescents might experience companionate love, it is more commonly a feature of late adolescence and young adulthood—for both sexes.

The psychologist Sandra Langeslag and colleagues developed a 20-item questionnaire to assess both love components: the Infatuation and Attachment Scales (IAS). They point out that infatuation and attachment are not inexorably linked but are two distinct constructs that are moderately related in an inverse manner. That is, once passionate love fades, there is now room for companionate love to take hold. In the question-naire, an individual mentally thinks of a beloved person and then agrees or disagrees on items related to their feelings toward the person.

Passionate IAS questions include the following:

- I get shaky knees when I am near _____.
- I have a hard time sleeping because I am thinking of _____.
- I search for alternative meanings to _____'s words.
- I am afraid that I will say something wrong when I talk to_____.

Attachment IAS items include the following:

- _____ is the person who can make me feel the happiest.
- _____ is part of my plans for the future.
- I would feel lonely without _____.
- _____ knows everything about me.

Langeslag and colleagues conclude, "Given the ubiquity of romantic love and its enormous impact on people's lives, these are extremely impor-tant topics for scientific research." Yet, the romantic lives of bisexual, pansexual, fluid, and nonbinary individuals are habitually ignored, and, thus, little is known about those who report both types of love, at the same time or not. The review here is drawn generically, with specula-tions about how the known information might relate to multiattracted individuals.[5]

Evolution of Love

Although many of the young people I interviewed were vaguely familiar with theories about their sexual orientation, when I asked about their romantic lives, most had little idea about how they developed their romantic orientation. Some felt it was as hardwired as their sexuality; others attributed it to socialization pressures. Most, however, simply accepted their romantic orientation regardless of origin. Except for a relatively small number of evolutionary biologists and anthropologists, scientists have generally ignored the issue. Without denying the impact Western society has on its members regarding who they are supposed to fall in love with, evolutionary biologists have noted that having a romantic orientation is probably built into the basic DNA of all sexes and hence universal across historical times and societies. Our romantic orientation is rooted in our species's physiology, which fosters bonding, procreation, and survival.

Consistent with this perspective, prehistoric humans improved their chances of passing along their genes to future generations if they were inclined to bond with others of their own sex. By becoming emotionally attached with same-sex others, they enhanced cooperation, voyaging and hunting skills, and, ultimately, success (more protein)—plus the pleasure of having (possible) sexual intimacy in the absence of other sexes. We know that heterosexual bonds directly heighten mating opportunities; so, too, same-sex bonds create procreative advantages by improving personal survival as well as the survival of one's mate.

These possibilities, which do not challenge the effects of socialization processes per se, are too seldom acknowledged by social scientists, especially those from sociology, gender studies, and developmental psychology. Though an evolutionary argument has been made for females to focus on their relationships, data on male affiliative and bonding behavior are sparse because interpersonal relationships among males—even among our primate kin—are usually cast in relation to dominance and aggression. One exception is a review of the nonhuman-primate literature by the comparative psychologist David Hill and the primatologist Jan Van Hooff. They found romantic-like (passionate) and bonding (companionate) behavior among males. They summarize their evidence in the following way:

1. Affiliative behavior between adult nonhuman-primate males is both more widespread and varied than has previously been sup-

posed. Bonding behavior varies by species, manifested in groom-
ing, spatial proximity, hugging, cuddling, spending time together,
and alliances.

2. While kinship remains an important explanatory factor regarding
   male relationships, it is not the only one, nor is it a prerequisite of
   affiliative relationships among males.

3. The propensity for males to show affiliative behavior to each other
   in their group increases when competition between them and non-
   group males occurs (greater need for bonding—think of athletic
   teams, fraternities, and gangs).

4. Whereas relationships between females adjust according to ecological and social conditions, the development of male bonding
   is more dependent on how females adjust to their environment
   (perhaps among humans as well).[6]

Building on Darwinian sexual selection theory, the psychologists Barry Kuhle and Sarah Radtke propose an evolutionary case for
human females forming romantic bonds with each other and possessing sexually and romantically fluid orientations. Ancestral women
routinely faced problems related to securing resources for themselves
and their offspring because of "a dearth of paternal resources due to
their mates' death, an absence of paternal investment due to rape, or a
divestment of paternal resources due to their mates' extra-pair mating
efforts." Given these occurrences, a fluid sexuality would have given
ancestral women the ability to "secure resources and care for their
offspring by promoting the acquisition of allomothering [nonmater-
nal infant care] investment from unrelated women. Under this view,
most heterosexual women are born with the capacity to form romantic bonds with both sexes."[7]

In email exchanges with the evolutionary psychologist Menelaos
Apostolou, I discovered that similar theoretical work regarding sexual
and romantic fluidity in men is nonexistent. Apostolou believes that few
evolutionary benefits would accrue to fluid men.

Men can develop strong bonds with other non-genetically related men through other mechanisms such as friendship and reciprocity. They do not have to sleep with other men to develop such bonds. Also, if we assume that same-sex attraction has been beneficial for men to enable them to build strong bonds with other men, then most men should experience same-sex attractions, but 90% of the men do not.[8]

There are several problems with his argument. First, the conclusion that men are not fluid is incompatible with recent empirical evidence (see chapter 10). Second, it is noteworthy that Apostolou grants that "in terms of prevalence rates, male heterosexual orientation with same-sex attraction appears to be relatively common (about 8%) and more common than male homosexuality," which implies some degree of sexual fluidity. Third, defining fluidity as sexual omits romantic fluidity, which might be more common, especially given a functional perspective. That is, if women *and* men wanted to improve their chances of passing along their genes to future generations, it would have been advantageous to form sexual and emotional bonds with both sexes. That is, while heterosexual behavior encourages the production of offspring and homosexual behavior enhances same-sex bonds that result in cooperation among group members in social situations and during hunting excursions, bisexuality combines the best of both. The species benefits, thus encoding bisexuality in the DNA of our successful progenitors.

Consistent with the view that we are built to bond with both sexes, the clinical psychologist Michael Kauth argues in *The Evolution of Human Pair-Bonding, Friendship, and Sexual Attraction: Love Bonds* that from a biological and evolutionary position, intimate same-sex friendships served as an adaptive trait because they "harnessed love, affection, and sexual pleasure to navigate same-sex environments for both men and women, ultimately benefiting their reproductive success and promoting the inheritance of traits for friendship."[9] That is, we are born with the capacity for loving, meaningful, and sexual relationships with both sexes. The neuroethologist Andrew Barron adds that same-sex social bonds are critical aspects for individuals living within a social group. They confer a selective advantage by "facilitating engagement in sociosexual behavior with the associated benefits of social reinforcement, affiliation, play, appeasement, and conflict resolution."[10]

It is not, however, a necessary or inevitable outcome that boys and girls will bond with their own sex. The greatest doubt usually centers on boys. They face cultural mandates—such as being aggressive, independent, and powerful—which neglect the basic bonding DNA of males. The human evolutionary biologist Joyce Benenson summarizes the problem confronting males: "Men engage in conspicuous public contests for status and directly interfere with others' success. Despite frequent and intense contests which occasionally turn lethal, men typically employ ritualized tactics and accept status differentials within a group."[11] I believe we can do better by emphasizing that females and males of all ages and sexualities are also created to bond with each other—not just with regard to sex or the pursuit of physical activities but also with regard to emotional and intimate relationships. It is in our nature to do so, as demonstrated across nonhuman primate species and across human history and cultures. The impediment is rooted in cultural messages to act, look, and behave in a *gender-appropriate manner*. Otherwise, we face mental health disturbances, especially loneliness, depression, anxiety, and emptiness. Sounds like a bum deal to me.

Assessing Romantic Orientation

Relational aspects connected with sexuality across the spectrum were present in early theoretical models of sexual orientation—sometimes referred to as "affectional disposition." These romantic features were subsequently dropped in both theory and research practice.[12] Yet, to fully understand the complexities of bisexuality, we need to incorporate the full meaning of bisexuality in individual lives. I have noted this omission in the literature and propose a romantic orientation alongside but not identical with sexual orientation.[13] We know how to measure romantic dimensions—we just seldom do it. Here are several exceptions in new research designs that address this shortcoming:

- Girls indicate whether they had a boyfriend and/or girlfriend—referred to as "same-sex romantic partnering."
- If individuals are in a romantic relationship, a domestic cohabitation, or marriage, record partner's sex. If not romantically involved, name the preferred sex of a dating partner and how important it is for that person to be male/female.
- Participants indicate whether they have ever been romantically attracted or in love with a male, female, both, or never.
- Individuals answer, "I am romantically attracted to individuals of the same sex / other sex," on a 7-point scale from "almost never true" to "almost always true."
- Individuals respond on a 9-point scale from "exclusively men" to "exclusively women" to 13 questions assessing passionate love, including "in love," "felt euphoria," "infatuated," "desired by," "possessive," "flirted with," "wanted to cuddle with," and "despair if rejection."
- Participants provide their romantic orientation on a 7-point Kinsey-like continuum from exclusively female to exclusively male and the percentage from 0 percent to 100 percent of their child, adolescent, young adult, and ideal infatuations and romantic relationships that is devoted to each sex.

Incorporating these measures into our research designs will provide a greater opportunity to appreciate the diversity of the bisexual population.[14]

Bromances and Passionate Friendships

One question raised by several youths I interviewed was whether "bromances" and "passionate friendships" count as signs of romantic orientation. Both exist within an extensive literature developed around sex differences in basic friendship styles. One early researcher portrayed the distinction as women have "face-to-face" and men have "side-by-side" relationships with same-sex others.[15] Women self-disclose and give emotional support; men share interests and activities. Women embrace; men fleetingly touch each other. Women are personal; men, impersonal. Although these disparities are overblown, they nevertheless have some truth to them, perhaps because of the way masculinity and femininity are constructed in modern Western cultures. On the male side, Eric Anderson's Masculinities, Sexualities and Sport lab named it "homohysteria": the "fear of male homosexualization and its associated femininity."[16] Bromances among men are unmasculine (too much intimate physical contact) and thus culturally problematic because "highly intimate and affectionate same-gender friendships are more likely to engender suspicion of homosexuality when they occur between men than when they occur between women."[17]

Whereas women can be passionate with each other and stay straight in the eyes of others, if men are passionate with each other, they are tagged gay—as was the 8-year-old Ricardo Jaramillo when he was caught holding hands with his best friend, Pedro. They never held hands again. In a "Modern Love" essay, Jaramillo, a college senior with a multiracial heritage, wrote about his struggle to say "I love you" to his current best friend, Kichi. When he uses these words, Kichi says, "Yeah, bro, I'll catch you soon," rather than what Ricardo wants to hear: "I can't help but wish that one day Kichi will forgo all the masculine clatter, look me in the eyes and simply say 'I love you, too.'" His essay addresses the question, "What keeps nearly all young men from being able to tell their male friends that they love them?" He believes it is adhering to the traditional bounds of manhood and mastering "the linguistic gymnastics [of] masculinity." Ricardo first learned this lesson with Pedro. "Men in America have learned repeatedly that tenderness must be tamed in accordance with a set of codes we must become fluent in, as if our survival depends on it. This lesson is learned over many years, passed between generations." Otherwise, a boy/man feels uncomfortable, a weirdness inside of him. "The lesson is burrowed in that deep. I hesitate, flinch." It's unmanly, it's gay, and it's breaking the code of masculinity.[18]

Bromance as a concept became trendy among Millennials at the beginning of the 21st century—think Matt Damon and Ben Affleck, Adam Levine and Blake Shelton, and Justin Timberlake and Jimmy Fallon.[19] A bromance is generally understood to be a *nonsexual* male-male friendship that is exceptionally affectionate, emotional, and intimate—again, the hallmarks of a romantic orientation. Homosocial bromance bonding exceeds normative male friendships and, in some circumstances, matches or surpasses heterosexual romance, as noted by Anderson and colleagues: "Our participants mostly determined that a bromance offered them elevated emotional stability, enhanced emotional disclosure, social fulfilment, and better conflict resolution, compared to the emotional lives they shared with girlfriends."[20]

Although it does not lessen the prohibition against expressing love if a young man says it is not about sexuality but romance, having more romantic encounters between men might be a good thing. Two men can love each other and say so without having sexual relations, marrying each other, or identifying as anything other than straight. Certainly, there is no romantic identity or label they are expected to adopt. Research notably demonstrates that intimate same-sex bonding is not the sole province of women or Western cultures; these relationships exist among men with appropriate celebrations in Africa, India, New Zealand, and elsewhere. As the anthropologist Robert Brain notes, the characteristics of these bonds are not universally similar, though male-male relations across a number of countries include displays of emotions and affections that resemble more the passion of heterosexual lovers than the calm friendship of equals. They fall in love, share beds, bond for life, and ritualize their relationship.[21] Without doubt, some of these displays of affection contain sexual desire, but the men are usually reticent to engage in sexual relations because of cultural prohibitions; others might well have been passionate friendships—dare I say, bromances. Clearly, bromances resemble "traditional expectations of romantic companionship, namely, the declarations of love, kissing, cuddling, and exclusive emotional confidence."[22]

Among women, passionate friendships have a long history in the lesbian lexicon, as noted by Lisa Diamond. Across many cultures, anthropologists have documented these intense, emotional friendships among adolescent girls. They would appear to be romantic relationships but lack explicit sexuality: "These bonds inspired their own unique terms in different cultures and historical periods, such as romantic friendships, smashes, Tom-Dee relationships [a masculine woman sexually involved with a feminine partner], or mummy-baby friendships." They are characterized by proximity seeking, self-haven, cuddling, hand-holding, mutual gazing, possessiveness, separation distress, and security.[23] Again, these are the trademarks of both passionate and companionate love and hence romantic orientation.

Although nearly all of the young women I interviewed had passionate friendships with other girls during childhood and adolescence, it seldom occurred to them that this might imply they are bisexual. With other girls, there "is a lot more touching, closeness, kissing but not sexual as in penetration with men." Another, with excitement, said, "I definitely need my quality girl time. I'd love to spend the rest of my life with my best friend." The friendships were often so intense that one young woman wondered if this was a sign of codependency.

Amy differed from the rest by naming her passionate friendship as a sign of her bisexuality. Growing up as an only child in a Long Island suburb, Amy and her best friend "experimented, playing doctor and exploring," when she was 6-years old. As a 13-year old, she developed a passionate friendship with another best friend. "It was not 'homosexual.' She came over every day and slept in my arms. So emotional, soul sisters, but not sexual. She said she was bisexual, so I figured I must be as well because so close to her. It felt okay to say it to myself."

Given this review, we return to the question raised by youths: Do bromances and passionate friendships count as a sign of romantic orientation? Is developing same-sex crushes and infatuations making a meaningful statement about romantic orientation? Perhaps in such situations individuals are fully sexually and romantically straight or are straight in one but not the other or are bisexual in one or both. Similar to bud-, dude-, and gal-pal sex, bromances and passionate friendships might have been "invented" as a cover, an acceptable cultural script manufactured to let men and women be emotionally vulnerable with each other while being protected from the stigma (or cultural dishonor) of gayness. They satisfy romantic arousals and desires to be attached to same-sex others without blowing their gender appropriateness—he keeps his masculinity and she keeps her femininity intact.

One of the more controversial features of the distinction between a romance and a bromance or passionate friendship is the absence of sex—at least theoretically. An enlightened, mostly straight young man, Dillon, a collegiate hockey goalie, was ambiguous about whether he would have sex with one of his man crushes: "If the guy is attractive enough . . . You just never know."[24]

Caleb had several best friends in his high school all-male a cappella group, but he couldn't tolerate the thought of "crushing on anyone" of his gender. He was in love with a girl, though he said, "I found guys in my classes attractive, but it was more of a window-shopping-type deal. Never trying to purchase the merchandise." Things changed in college when Caleb met Deke in the a cappella group; eventually they became a bromance. Deke was cute, a bit sassy, and they understood each other. Neither at first realized that his bromantic feelings ran deep; they tiptoed around each other for months but eventually dated and became sex partners. In retrospect, Caleb recognized that several of his intense high school male friends were not always about just friendship.

Stacey, age 22, had always assumed while growing up in a small Georgia town that everyone was straight. But in fifth grade, while she and her friend were looking at a nude photo book of women, she felt a weirdness and "wondered what this was all about." To this day, she has not had sex or a romantic relationship with a woman, but she would be open to the idea.

In high school, I never thought I was gay, or could be, but thought it was okay. . . . I feel comfortable with my attractions to women, but boys is where my preference is. It feels natural. . . . I have just wondered what it would be like. I've not had any experiences but because not in the right situation or the right person, and if so today, I would go for it. It would not bother me if I was.

Stacey identifies as straight and dates only boys, but she has begun the process of questioning her emotional relationships with girls as several of her close friends have begun dating other girls.

With or without sex, the young people I interviewed frequently felt that their intense same-sex relationships were healthy and desirable. The pansexual-identified Dave was particularly poignant on his opinion at several levels, including societal values.

There is no problem with young men having close friendships emotionally, and closer friendships of that sort should be encouraged in order to create healthier and more easily adaptable adult men. . . . This would also help create a more peaceful society by deemphasizing the necessity for competition and machismo just a bit. . . . Let people do what they want, what makes them happy, as long as it does not directly and intentionally hurt other people.

Given these varied experiences, how does one differentiate among the emotional responses a youth has with members of the same sex versus other sexes? Is the distinction easily made between a best buddy and a passionate friend? At what point do the feelings become infatuations rather than merely intimate friendliness? I raised these questions with several of the young adults I interviewed. One young woman spoke for many: "With females, it would start as friends and then move to passionate." A young man acknowledged that most guys "want to have camaraderie or those really good friends that you turn to when you have trouble." To the question of what happens when the friendship turns romantic, he shrugged. Toby muddled the difference, without the intent to do so: "With a [female] relationship, there is physical attraction—touching, kissing, sex, dinner, movies—and you can do with a male friend lots of the same things." The difference for Toby is that you wouldn't pay for a male friend's dinner or movie.

Social media, of course, has entered the conversation, offering modern interpretations of bromance. Bryan Hawn's parody, viewed by millions on YouTube, portrays two singing hunks with obvious but repudiated sexual interest in each other. It is a bromance to escape "with dignity" from any indication of gayness—though they carefully remind us, "Bromance. There's nothing really gay about it. . . . Not that there's anything wrong with being gay. I love you in a heterosexual way."[25] As one might expect, there is an app—BROapp.com—to help men who are "looking for friends, bromance, or more!" What exactly is "more" is not defined.

The question of whether a passionate friendship or a bromance is a platform for an infatuation in disguise or whether either partner can be totally straight rather than fall under the bisexual umbrella remains ambiguous. Certainly, one can have a crush on or fall in love with a member of the same sex without having sex—just as having sex with a same-sex individual does not mean one is romantically in love. I have a lingering suspicion that defining an emotional relationship between two men as a bromance and two women as a passionate friendship might serve to conceal or deny their romantic attraction for each other.

I am left with three concerns. One, by overlooking the romantic in determining who is bisexual, we limit our knowledge about bisexuality—and what we think we know might well be distorted. Two, as to the fundamental question, my perspective is yes, we should consider bromances and passionate friendships as potential indicators of romantic orientation, which may or may not be linked with sexual orientation. Three, why not just call it what it is? What is so wrong with two straight-identified boys or girls being infatuated with or attached to each other? To lose the connection because of toxic masculinity or femininity is tragic. Straight girls and young-adult women have these relationships all the time with impunity and male envy. Perhaps we should just celebrate these relationships for both young women and men.

8

How Many Bisexuals Are There?

I'm not gay, straight, or lying. Possible to be bisexual and was
against the study that says bisexuality does not exist.
—Donovan, age 21, white, student

The question of how many bisexuals there are turns out to be extremely
difficult to answer. Given the complications of whom to count and
what domains to count as bisexual and cultural factors such as bisexual erasure and biphobia that inhibit individuals from declaring their
bisexuality, it is perilous to estimate how many individuals are not exclusively straight or gay. Among young adults in the United States, it could
be 300,000 or 3,000,000 (or more). Yet, the vast majority of what is
known about bisexuals is based on the 300,000, the 1 percent to 4 percent reported on national surveys.

The public health professors Brian Dodge and Theo Sandfort, in their
review, uncovered several other major stumbling blocks in calculating
how many bisexuals exist: "The prevalence of bisexuality has varied
widely depending on the recruitment venue and the demographics of
the participants, particularly in terms of ethnicity."[1] It turns out that this
was only an opening salvo when reckoning with the number of bisexual
individuals: First, we must consider what elements in one's life are critical to be bisexual. Then, we can estimate the prevalence of bisexuals,
their characteristics, and their mental health status.

Answers Vary by the Sex of the Person

The question of whether bisexuals exist has been passionately debated,
with opposing answers that range from the idea that everyone is born

bisexual (see Freud) to one must choose to be bisexual, to no one is bisexual, and to females can be bisexual but males cannot. With regard to the last of these, cultural stereotypes of girls and young women complicate matters. Do they identify as bisexual or act as if they are bisexual merely because they want to match the fashionable moment in their friendship group? Is it superficiality that causes them to identify as bisexual because they long to have the contemporary cachet that everyone else is embracing the bisexual mantra? Is it that girls want to attract boys, and having sex with other girls helps them to recruit boys? Or do they aspire to identify as anything other than the straitjacket of heterosexuality, which is so boring? Not being boxed into the straight or lesbian category gives young women a bisexual option, which can be reworked and magnified into other related identities such as pansexual, fluid, and queer. It is difficult to answer yes to these questions, in large part because we seldom ask young women *why* they adopt the labels they do.

The sexologist Meredith Chivers's extensive review of women's sexual responses found that they were not distinguishable based on self-reported sexual identity. That is, we cannot easily assess women's sexual orientation by measuring how aroused they become while watching pornographic videos featuring explicit depictions of sexual behavior.[2] This does not, however, imply that women have no sexual or romantic orientation. That women tend to respond similarly among erotic cues, whether male or female, and are also slightly aroused by videos of bonobos (pygmy chimpanzees) engaging in penile-vaginal intercourse suggests to Chivers "that women have a nonspecific pattern of arousal to sexual stimuli," and not that "women's sexual orientation is inherently bisexual."[3] Thus, at the very least, we can tally the number of women who identify as bisexual, those who have sex with multiple sexes, and, the largest number, those who report sexual and romantic attraction to multiple sexes, but we cannot do so by biological measures, which fail us in counting bisexual women.

What about men? Less than half as many men as women identify as bisexual on national surveys, and some of these are not truly bisexual but jokesters, delusional, or merely hanging out as bisexual until they have the muscle to accept who they really are or will be in several years: gay. They thus avoid gay stigma (homophobia) and what they perceive to be the consequences of being gay in the United States. If true, then contemporary same-sex-attracted boys should be moving more swiftly to gayness because the shame and disgrace have softened across the United States. Hence, there are fewer reasons to conceal their true gay nature. One problem with this proposal is that the number of young men who identify as bisexual is growing, not shrinking.

The stereotype that there are no (or few) bisexual men is as widespread as the stereotype that all women are bisexual. The male typecast was underscored in a rare example of social science reaching a mass audience, largely because of a *New York Times* article titled "Straight, Gay or Lying? Bisexuality Revisited." Researchers, led by the personality psychologist Gerulf Rieger, reached the controversial conclusion, "With respect to sexual arousal and attraction, it remains to be shown that male bisexuality exists."[4] Are we to conclude that no men are bisexual? Before declaring yes, a closer look beyond the headline is essential.

What was not publicized in the newspaper article was the fact that the researchers did not actually deny the existence of male bisexual behavior or identity in their genital-arousal study. And, in addition, they freely admitted that modest bisexual arousal was commonplace because *most* men who watched explicit erotic videos depicting male porn actors pleasuring themselves were more genitally aroused—that is, their penis was slightly enlarged—than when viewing a landscape video taken from a nature documentary. This suggests that men are potentially bisexual in their genital arousal, and as previously documented in these pages, quite a few are, regardless of their sexual identity, bisexual in their behavior (e.g., dude- and bud-sex).

Five years later, the controversy regarding the existence of bisexual men was laid to rest. From the same Northwestern University lab, using the same definition of bisexuality and the same assessment tools, the clinical psychologist Allen Rosenthal and colleagues established that bisexual men exist, with distinctive bisexual patterns of both genital (penis engorgement) and subjective arousal.[5] The difference between the two studies was in the recruitment of samples. Whereas Rieger advertised in gay-oriented magazines and an alternative newspaper, Rosenthal recruited from bisexual sources. To be eligible, men were required to have had sex with at least two partners of each sex and a romantic relationship with at least one person of each sex. Later, psychologist Jordan Rullo and colleagues supported these findings using a different methodology: length of time viewing sexually provocative pictures on a computer screen. Bisexual men and women "viewed other-sex pictures significantly longer than gay men/lesbian women viewed other-sex pictures and rated other-sex pictures significantly more sexually appealing than gay men/lesbians rated other-sex pictures."[6]

Less than a decade after the Rosenthal study, the psychologist Erlend Slettevold and colleagues discovered correspondence among young men in their assessment of sexual identity and penile enlargement. Consistent with the perspective presented here, bisexual young men showed considerably more variability in their arousal patterns compared with other men; few were equally aroused to all sexes. "Based on their physiological sexual arousal, bisexual men appear to be a more diverse group than men who identified as heterosexual or homosexual." Men who identified as "mostly straight" or "bisexual leaning straight" were most likely to show bisexual arousal. Social pressures might explain this pattern: "These men might experience strong attractions towards both sexes; however, because they can be aroused to females, they lean in their identity in the heterosexual direction, acting more in line with social expectations." Bisexual men who indicated strong attractions to men identified as "bisexual leaning gay" or "mostly gay." They were in contrast to other bisexuals in that they showed stronger genital arousal to males over females, and some even failed to exhibit bisexual arousal at all (perhaps those in transition to being exclusively gay).[7]

How can we explain these discrepant findings from the original Rieger paper, which appeared to deny the existence of bisexual arousal?

Rieger, who coauthored the Slettevold study, and colleagues suggested that during these progressive times, gay men can more easily skip bisexuality as a transitional stage. Thus, bisexual young men are likely to be those whose sexual-arousal pattern matches their identity. That is, current generations of young men have less need to disguise their sexual selves, which results in a greater congruency among their sexual identity, sexual attraction, arousal, and behavior.[8]

I am convinced by the scientific evidence that both bisexual women and men exist. Few researchers have doubted over the years that bisexual women are a real phenomenon, and now we can add to the mix *real* bisexual men. Aggregating nearly all of the available data produced by the major players in the debate regarding the existence of bisexual men, I agree that the robust evidence shows that bisexual-identified men's physiological and subjective arousal patterns are more dual oriented than are those of men who identify as straight or gay—that is, there is a sexual continuum rather than categories for women and men. A final confirmation comes from an unlikely source: the lab of Brendan Zietsch studying the "underlying genetic architecture" of sexual orientation. The researchers describe the biology of orientation as highly complex because there is "certainly no single genetic determinant (sometimes referred to as the "gay gene" in the media). Rather, many loci with individually small effects, spread across the whole genome and partly overlapping in females and males, additively contribute to individual differences in predisposition to same-sex sexual behavior."[9]

We now have final answers to two major questions:

1. Not all women are bisexual.
2. Bisexual men exist.

The next big question, which has plagued us throughout this book, is why the official count of bisexuals is so low. This turns out to be a far more difficult and unsettled question to answer—in large part because so many bisexuals are concealed from our view because we do not know how to find them.

Concealing Bisexuality

Given that contemporary youths are talking, texting, and singing about their sexuality and embracing a wide range of sexualities, with bisexuality writ large having particular cred, it is sometimes difficult to imagine an alternate universe that is silent about bisexuality. Even now, however, some young people decide for personal or political reasons to avoid the perceived hassles of not being straight and conceal their sexual and romantic status. They can also inadvertently hide because of the way we attempt to find them, define them, and sign them up. One example is a study conducted by the sociologist Jaime Budnick. She observed that "queer," "genderqueer," "fluid," and "pansexual" constitute a particular lexicon among college populations—and, I might add, among social-media-savvy teenagers in general—not shared by people in lower socioeconomic positions and mixed ethnic young women in her sample. Some of the women were young mothers, and most had sexual friendships with other women but felt little pressure to label their experiences or themselves as bisexual. With appropriate probing, many of the straight-identified women complicated identity definitions by describing themselves with considerable flexibility. They were comfortable discussing their adolescent sexual and romantic experiences, their intimate friendships with women, their ambiguous boundaries, and hooking up with women but were unsure if those experiences mattered with regard to their identity. It is highly unlikely that these concealed women are included as bisexuals in our sex surveys.[10]

Then how can we count the prevalence of multiattracted individuals? Should we tally straight-identified men and women who have periodic dude-sex or gal-pal sex? Because three-quarters of adults in the United States who report any incidence of same-sex attraction or behavior identify as straight, should we count them as falling under a bisexual umbrella?[11] Are bromances and passionate friendships relevant? If one accepts the premise of this book, then those should be included in the total bisexual population regardless of their degrees of sexual and romantic attractions. As such, nearly all pansexual- and fluid-identified individuals should be counted, as well as many of those who report they are queer, nonbinary, kink, trans*, questioning, unsure, unlabeled, and scores of other identities created by today's youths.[12] There are few agreements as to what counts, as will be apparent when considering the official numbers provided by national studies—which nearly always include only those individuals willing to report a bisexual identity, attraction, or behavior.

On nearly every national and international study across various Western countries, relatively few individuals report that they are bisexually attracted (4 percent), engage in bisexual behavior (2 percent), or identify as bisexual (2 percent).[13] Although they are few in number, it matters which domain is assessed and the year information is collected. The largest variance is with regard to domain, as the sociologist Edward Laumann and colleagues documented 25 years ago. Both women and men were more likely to report same-sex sexual desires than to engage in same-sex behavior or identify as not straight. Of those who had at least one of these three, only about 20 percent had all three.[14]

What has remained constant across all domains is that women report higher levels of bisexual indicators than men do. Most illustrative is the 25-to-34 age cohort in the National Survey of Family Growth (NSFG). Identity, attraction, and behavior were less aligned among women than men, and more women than men engaged in bisexual sex and romance, had bisexual sexual and romantic attraction, and identified as bisexual.[15] Similar findings were reported in Add Health's 24-to-32 age cohort and in other Western countries, including the United Kingdom, Australia, Sweden, the Netherlands, and New Zealand.[16] The overall numbers are so low that one could say that bisexuality hardly merits consideration as a sustainable sexual category, or it appears to be a measurement error, an accidental choice, or a farcical performance by jokesters punking researchers.[17] If true, perhaps the *New York Times* headline questioning the vitality of bisexuality was not so far off.

One basic problem with these national surveys is that although prevalence depends on which domain is assessed, there is little consensus about which is the best or most appropriate one to count. As Tsung-chieh Fu and associates concluded from NSFG data, in future research we should not merely interchange measures of sexual identity, attraction, and behavior but consider using multiple measures in order to capture the complexity and variability of sexualities.[18] Another perspective, not counter to Fu and colleagues' recommendation but an extension, is to use the domain most relevant to the topic of interest. For example, if exploring the spread of sexual infections, it is most relevant to ask about sexual behavior, while realizing that many but not all bisexuals have sex with both sexes.

If we adopt an inclusive, multidimensional definition of bisexuality, the number of bisexuals significantly increases for women and men. The size of the increase depends not only on the dimension assessed but also on the time period designated (currently, past year, lifetime); the recruitment venue (bisexual organizations, online surveys, national samples); and, inherent in the last, characteristics of the population, such as ethnicity, social class, age group, and geographic region. Unfortunately, because scientific data are seldom available on sociodemographic aspects, their influence on prevalence rates is largely guesswork. Given that we know little about people in non-Western countries who are erotically or romantically attracted to multiple sexes, whether information summarized here applies to them is questionable.

I believe the exceptionally low frequency of bisexuals in national samples is less about the domain, time period, recruitment venue, and sample characteristics and more about the *omission* of individuals who should be counted. That is, potential bisexual candidates have been unthinkingly or systematically excluded. For example, in Add Health, probably the best ongoing study in the United States, although less than 2 percent in the 24-to-32 age group specifically identified as bisexual, if mostly straight and mostly gay identities are included (they are, after all, attracted to more than one sex), prevalence increases to 19 percent for women and 6 percent for men.[19] In a recent study involving middle and high school students from 66 schools in the southeastern U.S., 4 percent identified as bisexual; if counting the adolescents who identified as mostly straight and mostly gay, the proportion increases fivefold to 21 percent.[20] Perhaps mostly straights are pooled with straights because researchers assume that they are merely progressive straights or straights who have experimented with friends when drunk and thus that their behavior does not really mean they are bisexual. Mostly gays, for their part, are routinely sorted with gays because researchers assume that they are transitioning from bisexual to gay and thus will be gay shortly—on the cusp of gayness. However, neither mostly straights nor mostly gays identify as straight or gay when given the opportunity to do so, and neither has exclusive sexual or romantic attractions or interactions with only one sex. They should be considered legit multiattracted individuals and should be counted as such.[21]

The same trends hold if the dimension assessed is not sexual identity but sexual attraction or behavior. In the NSFG, 5 percent of women and 1 percent of men reported dual attractions; if those who are mostly attracted to one sex or another (but not exclusively attracted) are counted, prevalence increases to 19 percent of women and 8 percent of men (almost identical to Add Health). Reports of bisexual behavior in Add Health move from 2 percent to 14 percent among women and 5 percent among men when the tally includes those who report that they have had sex with males and females. Technically, these individuals have dual sexual behavior. Why do we exclude them?[22]

Actually, I cannot fathom why we do not count this supermajority of multiattracted and multibehaving individuals under a large bisexual umbrella. It is tempting to imagine a sinister motive or incompetence, but perhaps the kindest explanation is to believe that researchers, clinicians, educators, and parents do not believe that these individuals are *really* bisexual. The fault may also be due, in part, to culture's biphobia, pressuring young people to conceal their sexuality—to be normal.[23] The psychologist Jonathan Mohr and colleagues report that bisexual college students are less likely to be out than lesbian/gay students are and more likely to use a variety of identities, including straight. This lack of disclosure creates problems for researchers, as the sociologists Tristan Bridges and Mignon Moore note: How do you "extract information from respondents that some may not want to share?"[24]

Even if we could include the *concealed*, I believe the result would probably remain an undercount, for several reasons. One, if we expand the definition of attractions—as youths tell us we should—to include romantic aspects such as crushes, passionate love, attachment, and romantic relationships, I believe the number of bisexuals would increase dramatically. How many youths would be added under the bisexual umbrella? Little is known because those who count seldom include romantic domains as indicative of dual attractions. In interviews with presumably straight and gay male youths, I have discovered that many are not "totally" straight or gay because of their romantic arousals.[25] By embracing the notion that bromances and passionate friendships are common, my guess is that the prevalence of bisexuality skyrockets far beyond previous estimates. Suffice it to say, many multiattracted youths diverge from the sexual = romantic equation because of discrepancies in the degree to which they are sexually and romantically attracted to each sex.

Two, when youths are given a three-category option to calculate their sexuality, characteristic of most large surveys, some are forced to choose something they are not. When mostly straight young men were limited to the tripartite option, over 60 percent chose "straight" because that was closest to what they understood themselves to be; in their eyes, bisexual was too gay. Yet, they are not really straight and are thus misidentified as straights rather than the bisexuals that they are. In addition, nearly 20 percent of mostly straight young men rejected all three responses and checked "unsure" or "questioning"—and thus faced the likelihood of being dropped from the data set. This is consistent with most studies: if a participant rejects the identity boxes and checks "none of the above" or inserts an alternate identity that does not fit a predetermined category, their data are removed from statistical calculations. Thus, not only do mostly straight men and women not identify (self-reports) as straight, but physiologically—as shown by my research with young men regarding pupil dilation and, more recently, genital arousal by Jeremy Jabbour and colleagues—they are not straight. Furthermore, mostly straight men report "more childhood gender nonconformity, greater male sex partners, and less self-reported disgust or aversion to sex acts with men. Mostly heterosexual appears to be a gradation of male sexual orientation." That is, they are bisexual, not straight.[26] Misplacement of these men as straight results in inaccurate counts; deletion means that some number of nonconforming young men and women are uncounted. Although we know little about these men and women, we *do know* that many are attracted to multiple sexes.

Three, some individuals do not *identify* as bisexual but are sexually or romantically attracted to multiple sexes because they prefer another identity, such as one of the several dozen that White and colleagues extracted from student-generated terms.[27] In addition, one-third of those who are kink-oriented or trans* (born one sex, transitions to another gender) are multiattracted. How do they respond to the three-option choice? We do not know.

A final suppressing factor in counts of multiattracted individuals is the one we know the least about: those who do not answer our sex questions. As the psychologist and evolutionary biologist Qazi Rahman pointed out to me, these nonresponders might not have been at school that day, refused to participate, withdrew consent during the survey, left early before sex questions were asked, skipped the sex questions or, as I argued with regard to Add Health, made a joke of the sex questions.[28] These possibilities complicate our task to tally sexual groups. In one study, the number of youths who were "not sure" or did not answer the sexual orientation question was four times the number who identified as gay or lesbian; in another, over one-half of young adults who selected "unsure" had bisexual emotional or sexual attractions; in another, of the young women who marked "unsure" at one point in data collection and then chose to identify at a later wave, 29 percent wrote "bisexual," and 46 percent wrote "mostly straight"; and, in another, nearly as many men marked "something else" or "don't know" as indicated they were bisexual/gay and, for women, as indicated they were lesbian.[29] In the psychiatrist Austin Blum and colleagues' study of nearly 10,000 students at a public university, 39 percent completed an anonymous survey. Of these respondents (60 percent female), 25 percent did not complete the Klein Sexual Orientation Grid; this compares with the considerably lower number of the total participants who failed to answer the gender and race questions (3 percent) or the grade point average question (1 percent). That is, more students were hesitant to answer the sex questions than the gender, race, or academic questions. Why did one-quarter of the young adults omit the sex questions? How many are attracted to more than one sex? If the number is substantial, how typical are they of bisexuals in general? Also recall that the majority of those who were eligible to take the survey but did not were young men. They might have been even more likely to omit or distort the sex questions.[30]

In other nationally representative studies, the portion of nonresponders reached 10 percent or more. The psychologist Lara Greaves and colleagues investigated two issues with the New Zealand Attitudes and Values Study: those who answered the sexual orientation question outside the scope of the question (uncodable = 9 percent) and those who did not answer the question (nonresponders = 11 percent). Greaves and colleagues were able to decipher characteristics of individuals who were willing to answer the sexual orientation question from those who did not, and the negatives were more likely to include women, ethnic minorities, lower-socioeconomic-status individuals, and the religious. Greaves and colleagues concluded that participants "need clear *refused* or *unsure what this question is asking* options to maximize the potential for them to respond accurately." One possibility would be to include in surveys a short definition of "sexual orientation" or "identity."[31] The sociologist Emma Mishel emphasizes that a considerable fraction of those who do not identify as straight mark unusable responses; hence, "the proportion of men and women who would be dropped from analysis is quite substantial." Excluding individuals who do not choose an offered sexual identity category probably skews what we know about sexual minorities.[32]

Despite these concerns, the usual procedure in calculating the percentage of the population in each sexual orientation group is to omit those who leave sex questions blank, write a response that cannot be coded because it is inappropriate ("comfortable," "happy," "hopeful"), or write a response that represents a small fraction of the total ("pansexual," "queer," "heteroflexible"). In addition, some participants do not have the requisite knowledge to respond to questions about their sexual identity, behavior, orientation, or attractions, or they do not understand the question—and this is especially true if it is a child or adolescent population. For example, in one study of over 4,500 children ages 9 to 10, only 43 (0.9 percent) said they are or might be gay or bisexual, but over 1,000 (24 percent) said they did not understand the question. Only one parent reported that their child is gay or bisexual.[33] With a slightly older sample of Puerto Rican adolescents (ages 11 to 13 at Wave 1) in the South Bronx and the San Juan / Caguas area of Puerto Rico, the clinical psychologist Katherine Elkington and colleagues found that about 20 percent of youths reported during the three years that they were not sure which sex they are attracted to or they refused to answer the question. Higher than found in other studies, 14 percent of girls and 12 percent of boys reported same-sex attractions prior to age 16.[34] As Mishel points out, among children and adolescents, "it is imperative to clarify whether the respondent does not understand the question, or just does not know how to label their sexual identity yet."[35] I would add the question of whether some youths in the bisexual range are unwilling to disclose their sexuality on surveys because of privacy concerns or because of fear of ramifications or retaliation ("threat of discovery").[36] They might well forestall questions about their sexuality so as to evade potential rejection from family, friends, and communities. In a Canadian sample, 60 percent of bisexual men (versus 14 percent of gay men) concealed their sexuality to an interviewer.[37] We can only guess why they were not as forthcoming as gay men about their same-sex attractions, but this gap in our knowledge base adds to a long list of items that handicaps our ability to know how many bisexuals exist. From any reasonable perspective, it is clear that the hidden population under the bisexual umbrella is huge and seldom sampled or represented in what we believe we know about bisexuality and multiattracted individuals.

Bisexual Erasure

One of the primary impediments handicapping our understanding of young people with multiple attractions is *bisexual erasure*. As defined in the *Urban Dictionary*, "Bisexual erasure is the tendency to ignore, remove, falsify, or reexplain evidence of bisexuality in history, academia, the news media, and other primary sources. In its most extreme form, bisexual erasure can include denying that bisexuality exists."[38]

Bisexual erasure affects all sexes but is especially insidious for young men, which was well illustrated several years ago when the world champion British diver Tom Daley disclosed that he was dating a guy. Did this mean that Daley is gay, given his attraction to males? Daley did not initially label himself as either gay or bisexual. He is married to the director Dustin Lance Black, and they have a son—but on a YouTube video, Daley admitted that he still "fancies girls," which thus implies that he has dual attractions. After waffling slightly, Daley clarified his identity in a 2018 interview by stating that he is neither gay nor bisexual but "queer": "It doesn't define you, it's questioning. . . . I am not 100 percent straight, I'm not 100 percent gay, I'm just queer. My generation, I think, are more fluid." Daley thus reflects his generation's perchance to use nontraditional terms or to refuse labels to describe their sexual and romantic lives. What cannot be ignored are the words of Daley's husband, who has an insider's perspective: "I don't know if I'll be in trouble for this; his head still turns for girls."[39]

As publicity escalated around Daley's sexual orientation, gay elders such as the journalist Andrew Sullivan (who is gay identified) were not buying Daley's "nongayness." Sullivan, a conservative political commentator and author, exemplified this approach: "Daley will never have a sexual relationship with a woman again, because his assertion that he still fancies girls is a classic bridging mechanism to ease the transition to his real sexual identity. I know this because I did it too." According to Sullivan, "male sexuality is much cruder, simpler and more binary than female."[40] Thus, to Sullivan, Daley was simply avoiding the gay label to circumvent the inevitable cultural stigma of gayness. Daley's dual sexual desires were judged by Sullivan to be a ruse, a bisexual phase or cover, until he found the courage to declare his *real* gay identity. Thus, a bisexual identity as a transitional phase was reinforced, as a stepping-stone to the "real gay truth."

Although many lesbian and gay young adults during their development identify as bisexual for a day, a year, or a lifetime, it is fabricated logic to assume that all multiattracted youths will ultimately transition to gay or lesbian. If Daley were merely attempting to dodge gay stigma or to avoid the wrath that some lesbians and gays experience in our culture, what evidence is there that homophobia is better or worse than biphobia for one's mental health? None that I can find. One could say that because bisexuals can pretend to be straight, by dating or having sex with another sex, they avoid the perturbations of not being straight. But are deception and concealment more detrimental for their sense of self and place in the world than just being open about their same-sex attractions is? Daley's decision to select "queer" was the best resolution— because it is the most truthful for him.

So, too, my interviewee Sawyer did not lose his attractions to women when he became engaged to a man. Bored with high school, Sawyer dropped out at 16 and enrolled in car repair and mechanics classes at a local community college. Coming to the interview directly from his job, Sawyer was dressed in black except for the car dealership's logo on his V-neck shirt. As if to prove his credentials, a grease streak on his arm's underside was rubbed away during the first few minutes of the interview. His self-assessment concluded with, "I can see myself getting married to my current partner [male], but I also wonder about the possibility of having some sexual relationships with other people—men and women." His homoeroticism increased rather dramatically over his brief lifetime, such that a large percentage of his crushes, sexual attractions, and sexual fantasies are now male oriented. Marrying a man would not make him gay or even mostly gay. Similar to Daley, Sawyer doesn't want to forsake his deeply felt sexual desire for women.

Biphobia

Being gracious, I could argue that the mismatch between the lives of ordinary, contemporary young adults and scientific research is due to the exceptionally broad and diverse range of bisexual developmental pathways across their life course. Or, less diplomatically, I could place the blame on the incredulity of older generations that two sexual categories are insufficient to encapsulate all possible identities for young people. Complexity is rarely seized on in research designs that typically forgo inclusiveness and depth for simplicity and universality.

Biphobia is one culprit, apparent not only in stereotypes, overt harassment, and discrimination but also in the cultural denial (erasure) of queerness and in our general suspicion or silence as to the reality of having attractions to multiple sexes. This cultural script also applies to young women who identify as something other than straight or lesbian. We may believe more easily that they are bisexual because the straight-male gaze can effortlessly fantasize and encourage two women having sex or holding hands in public. At a small Pennsylvania college, the psychologists Megan Yost and Genéa Thomas found that bisexual women were perceived as "sexy" and as "really heterosexual," which was "reinforced by the belief that bisexual women were performing for the purposes of attention."[41] However, the young women I interviewed noted negative consequences from their families, culture at large, and even lesbian community members. Mothers fear that if their daughter says "bisexual" now, she will eventually say "lesbian," which to them implies social ostracism and no grandchildren. Queer community members might demand complete allegiance to *womyn feminism* and politics. My interviewee Laura felt intense hostility from lesbians after she came out as bisexual because they suspected she was still grasping onto heterosexual privilege.

It is as if we can understand Laura and Sawyer better if they were lesbian or gay because then we would have a recognizable and understood box in which to place them. Although lesbian and gay athletes such as Brittney Griner and Jason Collins in basketball, Megan Rapinoe and Robbie Rogers in soccer, Laura Ramsey and Orlando Cruz in boxing, Kate and Helen Richardson-Walsh in field hockey, Michael Sam in football, Brittany Bowe and Gus Kenworthy in skiing, Tillie Walden and Adam Ripon in figure skating, Greg Louganis in diving, and, recently, the high schooler Jake Bain in football have been widely accepted, it is far more difficult to name bisexual athletes. Is this because bisexuals can hide through heterosexual dating or because we simply erase bisexual athletes from public view?[42]

Less debatable is the vast literature documenting the compromised life that bisexuals purportedly have, not because they are by nature psychologically perverse but because of the assumed biphobia that causes them to experience sexual and gender stress and invisibility. Without personal and social support from family, friends, and sexual communities to buffer them from ensuing stigma, bisexuals as defined in these studies report high levels of most major mental health indicators, and this is more severe among bisexual women than men. Indeed, a fair amount of research—which I will later contest—says that bisexuals have more mental health problems than even gays and lesbians. It is noteworthy that absent from this literature is any indication that bisexual, pansexual, fluid, or queer individuals bring unique contributions to the table—that is, because of their fluidity or multiple attractions, they have particular gifts and resiliencies that surpass those of other sexualities.

Prevalence: Final Answer

The importance of these issues is readily apparent in many areas. For example, the public-health-care researchers Travis Salway Hottes and colleagues emphasize the importance of being more inclusive in our research of individuals who have attractions to multiple sexes. The underrepresentation and invisibility of bisexual individuals in population health surveys suggest a need to understand obstacles to (and remedies for) the inclusion and identification of bisexual people specifically. In addition, the diversity of intersecting identities and social positions of bisexual individuals reminds us that bisexuality is not a monolith and that some subgroups are less likely to be included and identified in health surveys.[43]

There is, of course, a problem with the counting. The clinical psychologist John Pachankis estimates that globally, "83% of sexual minorities around the world conceal their sexual orientation from all or most people" and are thus lost to research.[44] This calculation appears reasonable to me and should be applied when counting people under a broad bisexual umbrella—if we grant that it is a matter not only of bisexuals' deception but also of our failure to be inclusive of multiattracted individuals. Given the cultural context of heightened disbelief or negativity toward bisexuality, suppressing effects might be greater for men than for women. In one survey, only one in ten bisexual men but seven in ten gay men reported that most of the important people in their life know their sexual orientation. Bisexual individuals of both sexes can easily dodge prying questions about their sexuality because they are likely—over 80 percent of men in one survey—to be dating an other-sex person and thus do not need to be out as anything other than the assumed straight.[45] They have the proof needed to pass. Besides, some fear that dating partners would leave them if they knew about their same-sex sexual or romantic attractions. Because visible bisexual community groups are usually small and difficult to find, if a "lost" bisexual youth were to attend a LGBTQ community event, it might not be life affirming, given reactions from adults, such as Andrew Sullivan, who believe that because they went through a bisexual phase to hold onto heterosexual privileges, bisexuals will also ultimately ditch their façade of dual attractions and acknowledge their authentic lesbian or gay nature. It bears noting that such assumed privileges do not enhance mental health.[46] Under such conditions, it is understandable that bisexuals choose not to disclose to others, avoid LGBTQ organizations, and conceal their identity on sex surveys. The omission of these individuals from our research or outreach is seldom if ever acknowledged.[47]

A critical but nearly impossible question to answer is, Are individuals who volunteer their bisexual identity, orientation, or behavior on the basis of various recruitment strategies representative of bisexuals in general? More specifically, do these *out* individuals give us accurate information about the prevalence of the bisexual population? I have my doubts, but I cannot prove it. Rather, by my calculation, which includes the legitimate individuals under a large bisexual umbrella who are seldom embraced—pansexuals, fluids, mostly straights, mostly gays, romantics, nonbinaries, kinksters, trans*, unsures, and questionings—my best guess is a prevalence ranging upward to 25 percent of the general population for both sexes. If one were to argue that this is an undercount, I would not disagree.

PART II

The Sexual and Gender Spectrum

9

Pansexuality

I like my boys in skirts and my girls in pants.
—Sierra, age 20, white, technical student

A pansexual individual is someone who is sexually and/or romantically attracted to a person regardless of the person's gender or biological
sex. It is not necessarily about being attracted to a person's vagina or
penis, displaying feminine or masculine behavior, or identifying as a
woman, man, or intersex. Rather, of paramount importance is an individual's internal compass of their attractions. Pansexuality as an identity
has readily been adopted by people in the Zoomer and Millennial generations. The essential characteristics of pansexuality raise four not
completely resolved issues.

One, although the term "pansexuality" is sometimes used interchangeably with "bisexuality," the two are not equivalent. Pansexuality is
broader in scope because, unlike bisexuality, it does not rule out someone solely because of their biological sex or gender qualities. According
to the American Institute of Bisexuality,

> By replacing the prefix bi—(two, both) with pan- (all) . . . people who
> adopt these self-identities seek to clearly express the fact that gender does
> not factor into their own sexuality, or that they are specifically attracted
> to trans, genderqueer, and other people who may or may not fit into the
> mainstream gender categories of male and female.[1]

One might also include attraction to androgynous, genderfluid, trans*,
and intersex individuals. Thus, pansexuality is about the total package
of the person.

Two, it is unclear if pansexual individuals are born without sexual and gender preferences or, alternatively, born with a bisexual orientation and their unique pattern of gender-neutral attractions is socially constructed. According to the Bisexual Resource Center, pansexuality and other identities such as fluid and queer are identities that belong under the larger bisexual umbrella. By contrast, other websites propose that pansexuality is "a much broader form of sexual orientation, in which the pansexual individual experiences sexual attraction towards members of ALL genders (not to be confused with sexes, which is purely physical)."[2] These positions have various levels of merit, but we have little evidence for or against them. Regardless, when participants write in "pansexual" as their sexual identity or orientation, if researchers count them at all, they are usually grouped with the omnipresent category bisexual.

Three, pansexuality has become for some youths and young adults a self-chosen recalcitrant and insubordinate identity, largely because it is sufficiently vague and all-inclusive so as to deliver no information to those who ask inappropriate, invasive gender or sex questions. As such, "pansexual" is transgressive, a placeholder for those who are unlabeled, questioning, not sure, and none of the above and those who defiantly resist being boxed in by convention. These attitudes probably play a role for some significant proportion of those who identify as pansexual.

Four, earlier I noted that a large bisexual umbrella encompasses those who are attracted to, identify with, and engage in sexual and romantic behaviors with multiple sexes. Not everyone would agree, however, that the proper name for the umbrella is "bisexual." In the *Journal of Bisexuality*, the controversy was postured with the question, Which is the larger umbrella, bisexuality or pansexuality? The therapists Christopher Belous and Melissa Bauman proposed that pansexuality as an identity is much larger and more encompassing than bisexuality. Thus, there is "a need for the restructuring of the sexual orientation continuum to include pansexuality as a larger categorical identity under which bisexuality exists—as a specific subset of pansexual orientations." Countering, the applied social psychologist Corey Flanders argued that bisexual is the rightful umbrella to describe a range of dual behaviors and attractions, saying that pansexuals are bisexual in orientation if not in identity. Thus, a bisexual umbrella "covers people who explicitly do not identify as bisexual but elect to be considered under the umbrella; and the umbrella is held over other individuals whose behaviors or attractions may align with the umbrella, but they do not consider themselves as a part of this group." Both would agree that individuals under both umbrellas usually identify with multiple sexual labels.[3]

The psychologist Paz Galupo and colleagues presented a third solution to this controversy: use neither term but instead include both under a "plurisexual" umbrella. "Plurisexual" does not linguistically assume monosexuality as the ideal conceptualization of sexuality but refers to "identities that are not explicitly based on attraction to one sex and leave open the potential for attraction to more than one sex/gender (e.g., bisexual, pansexual, queer, and fluid)."[4] Regardless, the most critical issue is to acknowledge the diversity of multiple sexual and romantic attractions. Because the preeminent concept is a bisexual umbrella, it is my choice—for the moment.

In sum, from a scientific perspective, the limited number of researchers who explore pansexuality follow the clinical psychologist James Morandini's succinct definition: "pansexual" is "a label that denotes sexual or romantic attraction to people regardless of their gender expression (masculinity or femininity), gender identity, or biological sex." Pansexuality per se "explicitly rejects attractions based on binary notions of sex (male versus female) and gender (man versus woman)."[5] From a sociological perspective, Emily Lenning adds, "Bisexuality implies a dichotomy, pansexuality suggests the possibility of attraction to a spectrum of gender identities." She thus centrally locates pansexuality in cultural notions of gender roles, gender expressions, and how gender impacts identity.[6]

Freud to Spider-Man

Pansexuality as a concept dates to the time of Freud but has only recently achieved currency as a nascent option for self-identification—especially on social media, where many who identify as pansexual have attracted considerable attention.[7] This visibility and acceptance have even given pansexual identity a certain cachet. Belous and Bauman acknowledge that this new openness to unorthodox identities is because the "standard, well-known, three sexual identity models" do not apply to some young people. These emerging identities are especially okay for young people because they can relate to them. "One of the ways in which this message is being spread is through the ever-increasing prevalence of social media, blog, and news posts that positively discuss a pansexual identity from a normalizing perspective."[8]

Celebrities who have publicly declared their pansexuality are usually individuals who were assigned female at birth, including US Representative Mary Gonzalez, the rapper Angel Haze, the singer/model Rina Sawayama, the singer/actor/model Janelle Monáe, and the singer/actress Miley Cyrus. In a 2016 interview, Cyrus tracked her adoption of a pansexual identity to fifth grade. Her first relationship was with a "chick." "I don't ever think about someone being a boy or someone being a girl. . . . I saw one human in particular who didn't identify as male or female. Looking at them, they were both: beautiful and sexy and tough but vulnerable and feminine but masculine." Pansexual is the alternative identity that best fits her developmental history: "Yo, I'm down with any adult— anyone over the age of 18 who is down to love me. I don't relate to being boy or girl, and I don't have to have my partner relate to boy or girl."[9]

Few prominent biological men have come out as pansexual, although the singer (Panic! At The Disco) and actor (*Kinky Boots*) Brendon Urie has recently done so. He is married to a woman and is in love with her: "But I'm not opposed to a man because to me, I like a person. . . . I just like good people, if your heart's in the right place. I'm definitely attracted to men. It's just people that I am attracted to. . . . I guess this is me coming out as pansexual."[10]

Consistent with the intensified cultural sensitivity of youths, the actor Andrew Garfield hopes the next Spider-Man will not be the traditionally white, straight, male superstar but pansexual. He would prefer that as a culture we move beyond the conversation "where we can have a pansexual Spider-Man. . . . Why are we so, 'No, it has to be this way, a man and a woman?' . . . Love is love. Skin is skin. Flesh is flesh. We're all wrapped in the same thing. I have no preference." He questions why we are "scared of things that aren't us." Pansexuality fits Spider-Man because it provides an identity for those who want a universal embodiment of gender, sexuality, and supremacy.[11]

What We Know about Pansexuals

Because researchers seldom include pansexuality as an identity or orientation option in their surveys or in other ways incorporate or recognize pansexuals, little is known about how many pansexuals exist or their unique characteristics. Nevertheless, Lara Greaves and colleagues conclude, "People who identify as pansexual are, on average, quantifiably different from those who identify as bisexual."[12] This uniqueness was the focus of the psychologist Liadh Timmins and colleagues in their online research of 160 cisgender pansexuals. In one of the largest surveys of pansexuals conducted, the participants were overwhelming female (86 percent) and significantly younger than were straights, bisexuals, and gays/lesbians. They were very similar to bisexuals in their female-to-male ratio in sexual attractions, romantic infatuations and attachments, and sexual partners. The younger age and female sex of pansexuals confirms an earlier large-scale survey that Arielle White and colleagues gave to high school students. The youths had the option to respond with a sexual identity label if it differed from the questionnaire's predefined labels "straight," "lesbian/gay," and "bisexual." Consistent with other research, "pansexual" placed fourth. Pansexuals were slightly younger than those who adopted a "lesbian/gay" or "bisexual" label, and three times as many pansexuals reported being female as reported being male.[13]

Consistent across all research, the vast majority of pansexuals identify as female—sometimes by a factor of 10. Not unexpectedly, pansexuals are more likely than bisexuals to be gender diverse (genderfluid, nonbinary, or trans*) and thus not cisgender—that is, they report a gender identity, gender expression, and/or gender role inconsistent with their biological sex. As noted in the Timmins study, the majority of pansexuals' sexual and romantic attraction, behavior, and partners' sexual orientation are within the bisexual range. They do not differ from other nonheterosexuals in their ethnicity but are lower in educational attainment and income level—perhaps reflecting their younger age. Pansexuals also report higher psychological distress and are more politically liberal than bisexuals are.[14]

Somewhat more confusing, individuals who are exclusively straight, gay, or lesbian have been known to identify as pansexual, though for inexplicable reasons, given that pansexuality contradicts these monosexual identities. Perhaps their pansexual identity is motivated more by cultural and political than sexual and romantic issues. Regardless, in an online sample of nearly 400 nonheterosexual individuals, Paz Galupo and colleagues found that those who identified as pansexual did not believe that traditional sexual orientation measures (e.g., the Kinsey or Klein instruments) accurately captured their full range of experiences because the scales failed to adequately encapsulate gender issues. Pansexuals were also less likely than bisexuals to state a preferred gender or degree of attraction but described themselves as transcending gender and sex, using multiple labels, and forgoing explicit binary presentations of sex, gender, and body.[15]

Despite the paltry number of research studies that could settle the connection between pansexuality and bisexuality, it is safe to conclude that nearly all pansexuals are in essence bisexual because they are multiattracted, but not all bisexuals are pansexuals because many bisexuals state a strong sex or gender preference. I agree with Belous's conclusion that the two are not identical; pansexuals in the true form are an exceptional sexual identity and (perhaps) orientation with distinct characteristics.[16]

The research leaves many unanswered questions. Why are some individuals pansexual and not merely bisexual? Is pansexuality a social creation born of cultural sensitivities (youthful rebellion)? What are the essential pansexual developmental milestones, sexual and romantic histories, and personality characteristics? How do the limited number of male pansexuals compare to female pansexuals? Does pansexuality vary among sociodemographic variables such as race, ethnicity, and social class? What are our attitudes and beliefs about pansexuals? Until these questions are answered, the future of pansexuality is unsettled and unspecified.

Yet, it is clear from individual life histories that pansexuality is a *real thing* with prominence and repercussion, especially among members of younger generations who search for identities that adequately reflect where they are with their internal sexual and romantic development.[17] Thus, I take exception to both popular media and research which assume that pansexuality is binary—either you are or are not pansexual. Rather, to me, pansexuality is a spectrum on which individuals vary in the degree to which they have sex and gender preferences. Because pansexuality *requires* no sex or gender preference, my guess is that few individuals are truly pansexual in this *purest* form, but it could anchor one end of a spectrum. At the other end are those who are attracted to individuals *because* of their sex/gender, resulting in at least four pansexual subspectrums:

1. Sexual: from *never* to *always* a preference for the biological sex of the person
2. Sexual: from *never* to *always* a preference for the gender of the person
3. Romantic: from *never* to *always* a preference for the biological sex of the person
4. Romantic: from *never* to *always* a preference for the gender of the person

This is not to neglect the most essential characteristic of all pansexuals: the overriding emphasis on "the person as a person." How this idea is manifested and along what axes are critical have yet to be fully understood. We should ask.

To that end, I interviewed several young adults who identify as pansexual. They provide a sense of what pansexuality means to today's youths, especially given the intricacy of their sexual and romantic life histories and their struggle to bypass a simplistic, singular identity. Because the vast majority of pansexuals are born female and have shared their stories with the media and in qualitative studies, relatively little has been heard from pansexual young men. Listening to them begins the process of understanding their unique life trajectories and perspectives about what it means to be outside the three traditional sex categories. First, however, is the story of Sierra, born female.

Sierra

Sierra grew up in a small city in central Florida in a traditional Christian home, though she is now a "pagan, polytheist." Her father worked "somewhere in a big building downtown." Once she completes her associate's degree at a local community college, her future is uncertain. She has always been a southern-styled "super femme."

> I was a ballerina with bows in my hair, long dresses, a know-it-all, had fluffy, curly hair. I identify as a femme! I'm a classic femme. I am 90 percent feminine and 10 percent masculine. I guess I'm masculine in I can be very strong, forceful, aggressive like Dad. I'll yell when I'm angry, and I have my wallet in my back pocket. I don't dress up a lot and wear a lot of tee-shirts and jeans. I'm everyone's mom. I love dressing up full hog and wear makeup. Don't like team sports. Does horseback riding count?

Sierra assumed liking boys meant what it was supposed to mean, until she was 14. While reading a novel, she found herself more than a little intrigued by a description of a naked lady.

> But because I knew I liked boys, I just put it all out of my mind. I forgot because I couldn't deal with it. By 16, the summer before my junior year,

my best friend [Allie] and I fell in love. So, then I figured that I must be bisexual. So, by 17, I said I was bi and queer and very involved in the gay community. Weird and odd, that was me.

The relationship with Allie lasted three years, and sexualizing their relationship happened gradually, a natural aspect of their friendship.

Allie initiated the sex because I was uncertain. I had been taught to be careful about sex, that it is very special, and one should be sure. She pushed it. It is fuzzy and can't remember, but was mutual masturbation at first. Don't think it was with orgasm. Scary and exciting. I was hesitant because didn't know what I was doing. . . . I had poor body image, like many girls. I was told I was fat. Now I had someone to tell me I was gorgeous. We're still friends.

About a year later, Sierra had her first heterosexual experience: "not the best sex I ever had." With the consent of Allie, she dated Billy, also 17 and a friend of both. Sierra initiated sex.

He was startled. We were both nervous. It was the old in-the-back-of-the-car thing. He had oral sex on me, and I had an orgasm and then me oral sex on him and then actually intercourse. But he didn't have an orgasm because we realized we were past our curfews. It confirmed for me that I was bi, which was comforting because I wondered if I was lesbian. The sex was pleasant. Glad that the first time was with him because he was a good friend.

They had no future sex, broke up, and went back to being friends again. Sierra came out to her mother (as pansexual) at age 17 and to her father one day later.

This was a scary moment. She reacted calmly at first. She went through all the classic P-FLAG stages that they tell you about. She was absolutely okay with it but hiding her confusion. Couple of days later, she was freaking out, visibly uncomfortable. . . . She was most upset because I was having sex, so asked me not to. But, hey, we were teenagers! They sent me to a shrink, not to convert me but to help me out. I went to three sessions and then said I wasn't going unless they were going to P-FLAG.

Sierra expected her father to be more difficult because he's conservative and doesn't want to know such things. She promised not to tell anyone at his workplace or his relatives. Somewhat later, she told her younger brother. "After all, his bedroom was next to mine, and how could he not hear and know?!" He believes it is a sin, but it is his sister. "He would not berate me or try to convert me." He stops his friends from saying, "Oh that's so gay" or telling "faggot jokes."

Sierra sometimes gets flack from her lesbian friends for not being lesbian. Although it is unclear where she wants to end up, Sierra loathes being thought of as a "lesbian-identified bisexual" because it's not the person's biological sex that matters but the person. "I like femmy boys and butch women." Sierra is on the pansexual spectrum, though she does have slight sexual and gender preferences.

Charles

Charles is multiracial and identifies as Black. The 18-year-old freshman unmistakably stated the pansexual line in his interview.

> Attracted to the person and not the gender. Nothing to do with them being male or female. . . . I'm not more or less attracted to them because they are male or female but as an individual person. Don't think of myself as gay or bisexual but just attracted to all people the same.

Because Charles has not experienced genital sex or romantic love—though he's looking forward to breaking the dry spell now that he's in college—I remain somewhat skeptical about his neutral sexual and gender preferences. A year later in the follow-up survey, he was still a sexual and romantic virgin. He reported liking girls but said, "if there was a guy who I thought was really, really attractive then I might be interested."

Given this self-assessment, Charles is not an ideal poster child for pansexuality. Although he fits easily on the *gender* pansexual spectrum toward the pure end, *sexually* his preference leans female. I question how strong his pansexual identity will remain once he solicits sexual and romantic entanglements. I have little doubt that he is bisexual; where he is on the pansexual spectrums awaits further determination.

Zach

Zach is multiracial and identifies as Hispanic. The sophomore claimed, "Gender is not an issue. It is the person, the personality." Although he has had more sexual and romantic experiences than Charles has had, it's not by much. He recalled child and adolescent crushes on girls but has never had genital contact with them. Zach and a male friend made out, fondled, "and moved to oral sex." The sex lasted two years but never evolved into a romantic relationship because of "the kind of person he is." His first "real" sex was four months ago, with a male college friend; recently he met a guy who might be "romantic material."

Since high school, Zach has sexually leaned more toward males than females, especially in his masturbatory fantasies, and romantically toward men and women. He identifies as pansexual, though, once again, I do not believe that Zach is on the pure end of pansexuality, especially on the sexual domain, given his stronger attraction to males.

Kenworthy

Kenworthy was 30 minutes late to the interview, eating an apple with a bagel saved for later, barefoot, and wearing Drake PJs. Although it was nearly noon, I had the sense that Kenworthy had just gotten up. He apologized for his tardiness—it had been a drug-induced late night. Tall, lanky, and athletic looking in a skateboarding, Ultimate Frisbee sort of way, Kenworthy talked for nearly two hours. By his own assessment, he is a laidback, free-spirited guy who has reflected deeply about life, including world peace. After wiping his hands with a recyclable brown napkin to remove traces of the apple, he smiled, firmly shook my hand, and asked, "What's up?"

Kenworthy is hanging out, enjoying life before he begins his new job as an assistant research scientist. He is a squatter in his girlfriend's environmentally sustainable co-op, and his rep among friends is the guy who participated in the Genesis 2 Super Smash Bros. tournament, a regular drug user, a rock singer, and a drama coach. Willing to experience whatever life has to offer, Kenworthy has broken the mold his parents set for him. A pansexual identity is the one that best encompasses his sense of self; in the future, he wants to be more, not less, pansexual.

Kenworthy was raised as a suburban, "privileged white American male," a "free thinker," and a "creative person," and his albatross was growing up in a cult-like evangelical religious family keen on zealously sheltering him from the world around him, especially social media. He viewed everyone around him as preppy, materialistic, racist, and sexist. Kenworthy's first sexual memory was at age 5 while "skimming up a pole": "I had this odd feeling in my penis," which was both "outstandingly pleasurable and morally toxic." Sixth-grade hormones caused him to notice he was getting erections: "I'm saying this had a profound influence on me." Guys entered his erotic fantasies when he began masturbating; it was through internet porn that he realized girls also have sexual desire, including his first girlfriend. Hanging out in her room, he "sketched out."

> She asks me what I was thinking, and I was overwhelmed with the desire to touch her breasts. And she said it was okay, and I did. And it blew my mind! At first, very exciting but guilty because still under the influence of my parents. . . . I wanted this, and it did not degrade me but did make me rethink my morals.

A year later, Kenworthy hooked up with another girl, resulting in his first intercourse.

> Twice we did it but not full penetration. I felt some bad because it was sex before marriage, pregnancy worry. I was dry humping her, and occasionally my penis would make a brief penetration. . . . Then on her birthday, we had sex deliberately, and by then I had convinced myself there was no reason to hold back. It was nerve-wracking because I didn't know what to expect or what to do. It lasted a very short time.

In college, James entered Kenworthy's life like a bolt: "a dreamy, a model, good looking, Colombian, slender, straight As, charming, most charismatic male I had ever met." Sexually, Kenworthy's same-sex desires first played out at his dorm's "Rub 'n the Tub" party: several kiddy pools filled with warm, sudsy water in the courtyard, with everyone hanging out naked.

> [Two guys were] hitting on me incessantly and having fun with it. . . . This was premeditated, and the two guys and I fooled around—mainly, one stimulating me orally and manually kissing. Felt weird, uncomfortable, not terribly great. I was disappointed because had been so nervous and not really into it and not enjoyed it as much as I thought I would. . . . Definitely a landmark in my sexual experiences. It did not increase nor decrease my desire for homosexual contact. It increased my desire for experimentation further.

A second threesome occurred a year later with a woman who had a bisexual male friend.

> I was lying on my back and her straddling my face and doing her and him giving me a blowjob. Very exciting and successful. Reached orgasm and lot more enjoyable. Weird because there was a miscommunication in the middle of this, and he wasn't expecting me to come in his mouth.

Kenworthy has had crushes on guys, such as James, but he's never dated a guy, been in love with a guy, or had intercourse with a guy because these go "too far" into homosexuality even for his progressive, free-spirited lifestyle. Kenworthy is convinced he is clearly on the heterosexual side of the ledger, and yet, guys are vital for his sexual and romantic future. He rated himself masculine because he's athletic, intellectual, arrogant, and confident; he's not sentimental and timid (feminine). He rated himself as exceptionally high on life satisfaction and well-being. His life goal is to be a pothead computer-science guy— whatever that means.

On the follow-up survey, Kenworthy reported that he is enjoying his emerging career in California. In his ideal world, he would be in a long-term, sexually open polyamorous arrangement, though he fears that it's impractical in our culture. Sex without love is fine, and society should "learn the difference between infidelity and polyamory and drop the stigma from the latter." Women might be receptive to his proposal but not straight guys because, according to Kenworthy, they're not comfortable sharing their female sex partners and are disgusted seeing an erect penis.

Though Kenworthy is happy with his sexuality, he "might wish more attractions to males simply because group sex is comfortable, easy, curiosity about that experience." Homoeroticism is not threatening because it appropriates "socially imposed psychological taboos." It's the person's spirit that matters most. A pansexual identity would not tie him down or commit him to anything. Kenworthy is also on the pansexual spectrum, perhaps more so regarding the romantic.

Dave

A white 23-year old, Dave is technically a virgin but with more sexual and romantic experiences than either Charles or Zach. As a child, others thought he was gay; as an adolescent, bisexual; as an undergraduate, he "might have said bisexual, maybe not"; and now, "pansexual because depends on the person." In part, this identity emanates from his objection to the mandate to pick a side, and he readily escapes these expectations by refusing to close doors regarding sexual and romantic relationships. Whereas Dave has robust emotional male crushes, his sexual activities (mutual masturbation, oral sex) are overwhelmingly heterosexually oriented—though he would like to meet a guy who inspires him or is receptive to his sexual advances. Dave uses OkCupid to meet women, but I see little evidence that he searches Grindr for men—though he says he's sexually and romantically attracted to men. Last year, Dave edged to the brink of having sex with a guy, making out "under the influence of intoxication. Lots of tongue [with] a free kind of guy"—which is what Dave wants for himself. At this point, he has made out with ten people (nine girls, one boy). Dave favors women because they have more qualities he likes; with men, it is a narrower range, physically and personality-wise. Is he gender neutral? No, because Dave prefers a feminine gender presentation for both sexes.

Dave is currently engaged to a woman but he wants an open marriage with multiple sex opportunities for both of them. His minimal attraction to guys has not abated: "possibly because I consider myself pansexual, and I have just not met any guys I like that way." Intrigued by a world in which traditional gender roles are upended, Dave wants to be free to develop emotional, romantic alliances with men, and besides, pansexuality appeals to his self-image as the rebellious sort, his insurgent persona. He idealizes gay people because they have stronger bonds with other guys, have closer friendships with women, and experience different ways of living. Straight guys are boring, are not into women as people but just want to have sex with them, are poor kissers, and just "stab" the vagina to get off. Dave is not a pure pansexual, but he does label himself as pansexual and connects with the political pansexual domain. If pansexuality is a spectrum, Dave is clearly on it.

Malachi

Malachi, an only child, was born in Haiti, where his father worked in Port-au-Prince before the family moved to a conservative Georgia suburb to be with extended family. Malachi's first sexual memory was a girl crush when he was 4 years old. "We considered each other our first boyfriend/girlfriend"—and everyone thought it was cute. Growing up aware of his dual attractions, he never considered labeling himself as anything.

Once in high school, Malachi joined the school band and met Jade, his first girlfriend. A year into their relationship, they discussed possible sexual interactions. "We both come from very conservative families and with the abstinence-only sex education and all of that." Eventually they had intercourse, but the evolution was slow because of "feeling guilty" because they "weren't married." The first time was "fantastic," and both had orgasms. They've remained good friends. "We're both in this place where we need to do our own things, and if we end up crossing paths again, then that's great. If not, it's fine." According to Malachi, they shared a "true love."

After Jade, Malachi acknowledged to himself pervasive same-sex attractions and boy crushes. What he didn't know was that Jade's best friend, Ajay, had a crush on him. Once Malachi and Ajay became best friends, Malachi interpreted his feelings for Ajay as a bromance, perhaps even a crush.

> I was aware of homosexuality and bisexuality, but I never considered it in terms of myself or anyone that I knew. It was sort of this far-reaching concept. We were very close, and it was the first time I gave thought to the idea of being with a man. And him explaining everything to me and how he felt and whatever, I gained a lot of respect for him. Because we were really good friends, so I felt like it was something that could work if we were somewhere else. But being in that region of Georgia, homosexuality—not to be overly generalizing—but that is something that doesn't happen in my [Black] community, at least that is known about.

Today, Malachi's biggest regret is not turning his Ajay bromance into a romantic relationship. "Based on our personalities and based on our friendship, it would have worked."

In the time between Jade and Ajay, Malachi dated women, had sex with several, but never thought that such behavior implied anything about his desires for men. His bisexuality was not "theoretical"; he simply had not found "the right man to go off in that direction"—that is, until he met Jayden in college. Away from family and community, Malachi decided it was time to pursue.

> And in my head, there was no reason for me to not get involved with a guy. . . . And then I met Jayden in band, who is gay. And we were really good friends, and then I learned that he had a crush on me. And I was like, why not? We dated, and it was fun. We both got along and enjoyed each other's company, and eventually we had sex.

Continuing the equality theme, the two most significant sexual events in Malachi's life were his first sex with Jade and with Jayden. Malachi is attracted to the same kind of woman and man, an independent personality.

> There is this song by Ne-Yo called "Miss Independent," and I think a lot of things he talks about in that song exemplify my ideal. . . . An ideal relationship is one where you have two people who are very independent and have their own lives that sort of come together and are there to enjoy each other mutually but are not dependent on one another. I don't think like the old-school traditional, the woman is dependent on the man to take care of her or any of that. I think you should have two people who are self-sustaining and are with each other because they want to be, not because they need to be.

Malachi is uncertain whether he will end up with a woman or a man, but, regardless, it will be a monogamous relationship. "I don't like to share."

Looking back on his developmental history, Malachi recognizes that his transition has been from a "straight" childhood to a "bisexual leaning straight" adolescence to a "more or less equal attraction" young adult-hood. Now, everything is essentially 50-50 with regard to his sexual and romantic orientations, except that he leans slightly to women for sex and men for romance.

The Pansexual Spectrum

Although these young adults are not theoretically *pure* pansexuals in that none is absolutely free of sex or gender preferences, does this call into question their pansexuality? No, because based on my modified version of pansexuality that considers the nuance inherent in sexual, romantic, and gender desires, they are all on a pansexual spectrum. The one individual who is closest to the pure version of pansexuality, Mala-chi, prefers no label, including pansexual, to identify himself. Malachi has had sex and romance with both sexes, though he leans slightly to women for sex (his pupil dilation in response to pornographic images confirms this) and to men for romance (currently in a long-term male relationship). Regarding gender, Malachi has no preference: "As cliché as it sounds, the personality draws me more. Very driven and indepen-dent. . . . We can make the physical parts work out." With this, Malachi hits most pansexual buttons, especially because it is the person that mat-ters most to him.

The other five young adults are also pansexual because they are sexu-ally and romantically attracted to multiple sexes and genders (to varying degrees). They believe in a spectrum of romance and sex, oppose cat-egorical labels that limit their opportunities, and pronounce that their attraction depends on the person. It is the latter point that is most excit-ing in the continued evolution of gender, sexuality, and romance among current generations of youths.

10

Fluidity

The reason I can't choose is because one day I feel it's completely girls, and another day I could be thinking about guys. I don't know if it's a gay time of the month, haha. But it changes day to day. It's very fluid. Love is love. You can be who you want and love who you want.
—Woody Cook, age 19, white, model

The youths I interviewed frequently spoke about changes in their sexual and romantic attractions from first memories in early childhood to the present. Because personal and cultural demands easily intervene to influence these feelings and the decisions made as a result, neither the homoerotic nor the heteroerotic absolutely rules; both are critical as they weave in and out of the youths' lives. After reassessing existing research, Lisa Diamond was convinced that "sexual attractions, behaviors, and identities among representative samples of adolescents and adults [show] that sexual orientation is not a static and categorical trait."[1] If not, what is the alternative? One answer is sexual fluidity, which has received extensive and, at times, sensationalized coverage from popular media. Although researchers are inconsistent in defining fluidity, in the popular mind it simply means changes over time—but in what? Is it sexual orientation, sexual behavior, or sexual identity that is fluid? Does one choose to be fluid, or does it come instinctively and effortlessly? If sexual orientation changes, then fluidity seemingly upends orientation as an enduring, deeply rooted predisposition of erotic or sexual arousal. Is it possible that fluidity itself is a sexual or romantic orientation?

Sexual fluidity, first defined a decade ago by Diamond, is the capacity for change over time in attractions that results from an individual's heightened erotic sensitivity to situational and contextual influences.[2] Since Diamond's definition, researchers have elaborated the temporal and essentially ignored contextual influences. For example, the psychologist Sabra Katz-Wise defined fluidity with the following questions:

- Have you ever experienced a change in attractions to others over time?
- Did the change in attractions result in a change in the labels you use to describe your sexual orientation?
- Have you experienced more than one change in attractions to others over time?
- How likely is it that your attractions or sexual identity will change in the future?[3]

Diamond later expanded her definition in a more inclusive and somewhat radical manner. "A capacity for situation-dependent flexibility in sexual responsiveness, which allows individuals to experience changes in same-sex or other-sex desire across both short-term and long-term time periods." This definition includes three critical phenomena:

1. nonexclusive (bisexual) patterns of attraction
2. longitudinal change in sexual attractions
3. inconsistencies among sexual attraction, behavior, and identity

Diamond reported these occurred "across a large body of independent, representative studies conducted in numerous countries, supporting an emerging understanding of sexuality as fluid rather than rigid and categorical."[4] This revised definition appears to include the capacity to experience sexual attraction or behavior that runs counter to an overall orientation. A woman might identify as lesbian, be attracted to both sexes, and have sex with men. She is sexually fluid even though there is no documented change over time.

My addition to Diamond's definition is to add two other kinds of related but independent fluidities. One is *romantic fluidity*, which includes romantic arousal, attraction, infatuation, and falling in love. The other is *gender fluidity*, which includes those whose gender changes over time (whether slowly or quickly), resulting in identities such as gender non-binary, genderfluid, agender, bigender, pangender, androgynous, and demigender. Gender fluidity is experienced internally, with or without outward expressions. Romantic and gender fluidities might be congruent with, to varying degrees, or be altogether independent of sexual fluidity.

The Politics of Fluidity

According to the Trevor Project, a nonprofit organization focused on suicide prevention among sexual-minority youth, conversion (reparative) therapy is a pseudoscientific practice of attempting to change an individual's sexual orientation from, for example, bisexual to heterosexual using a variety of psychological, physical, and spiritual interventions. Conversion therapists use shaming, emotionally traumatic, and physically painful techniques to change sexual orientation. Although there is no reliable evidence that they succeed, there is a considerable number of stories from young people who attest to its harmful effects—including suicide attempts, depression, and anxiety. The validity, efficacy, and ethics of conversion therapy have been questioned by many international jurisdictions and medical and scientific agencies.[5]

If sexuality is fluid and hence not inexorably locked in, then reparative and conversion therapists might feel emboldened to give hope to those who are troubled by their sexual attractions and want to change—nearly always from less gay to more straight.[6] On the other hand, conversion therapy and its practitioners are themselves in remission, as an increasing number have come out as gay or bisexual. When the Church of Jesus Christ of Latter-Day Saints "learned" that sexual orientation is probably biological and unchangeable per se, it softened its mandatory excommunication stance to simply banning same-sex behavior, similar to its stance on premarital chastity.[7] More recently, the dean of Brigham University, the flagship educational institution of the church, wrote, "Go for it," in response to Matthew Easton's valedictorian speech in which he said, "I am proud to be a gay son of God." Classmates did not jeer but cheered him—another example of generational change.[8]

The columnist Eric Sasson laid out the opposing political sides to fluidity. On one side are those who do not embrace sexual fluidity because they believe the demand for equal rights is tethered to the fundamental idea that gays are "born this way." To them, sexual fluidity gives license to conversion therapists, parents, and youths to believe that sexual orientation is a matter of choice and can thus be *unchosen*.[9] The polemics were illustrated several years ago after Macklemore and Ryan Lewis sang "Same Love" at the Grammy Awards show. The lyrics include the words, "And I can't change even if I tried, even if I wanted to."

The other side of the dispute was presented by the *New Republic's* Brandon Ambrosino, who takes exception to the aversion that some sexual-minority individuals have to the concept of sexual fluidity. He does not believe we need to prove that gayness is biologically determined to demand equality: "I see no reason to believe that the only sexualities worth protecting are the ones over which one has no control." To deny fluidity is to dismiss fluid individuals in our community, especially bisexuals.[10]

Two days later in the same publication, Gabriel Arana countered by citing an innate, bioessentialist view, calling Ambrosino's view "eye-rollingly naïve" and "hip, post-gay," one that "you might expect from a college student who's just taken their first queer-theory class." Arana argued, "From a political standpoint, it matters a great deal whether sexual orientation is inborn or a choice. Rightly or wrongly, social conservatives object to homosexuality on the grounds that it is a lifestyle choice."[11]

The born-this-way advocates tend to downplay the extent of fluidity among sexual-minority individuals, almost echoing the straight/gay binary conception of sexuality. Yet, personal lives and limited research, especially with women, reveal that fluidity varies from slight to extensive and from rarely to frequently. For example, using the nationally based

GSS longitudinal study, the sociologists Christopher Scheitle and Julia Kay Wolf reported that more than 2 percent of the US adult population changed their sexual identity over four years, with one-third of these individuals changing multiple times. My colleagues and I reported that in the Add Health data, nearly 40 percent of multiattracted young adults changed their sexual identity over seven years. The social scientist Alice Campbell and colleagues reported that across four years, 31 percent of Australian emerging-adult women (ages 18 to 27) changed their sexual identity at least once. Consistent in nearly all studies, the three plurisexual identity labels were the most unstable.[12] How frequent such fluidity is among Zoomers has yet to be documented.

The ultimate question for Lisa Diamond and the law professor Clifford Rosky is which position is stronger when confronting social conservatives and conversion therapists. Regardless of the degree to which fluidity exists, they dispute that the born-this-way or immutability case should be the foundation for advocating for the equality of minorities because such arguments are unscientific and legally unnecessary. It is time "to put it to rest. . . . It doesn't matter how we got to be this way." Basic human rights should be guaranteed to all sexual and gender minorities regardless of the origin of their sexual and gender selves.[13]

Fluid Orientation

When we consider both arguments, an additional concern presents itself. If we grant fluidity significant status, maybe fluidity is not a "let me see what attractions will I have today" lifestyle choice but is an immutable sexual and romantic base that comes from deep within a person that gains visibility and significance with environmental assistance. Because we do not know from a scientific perspective how prevalent fluidity is across various domains or what causes fluidity, we are left with conjecture. One that I entertain is that just as we can be born with a monosexual or bisexual orientation, so, too, perhaps we are be born with a fluid orientation. Lisa Diamond partially entertains this possibility when she suggests that people are born with a sexual orientation and also "a degree of sexual flexibility, and they appear to work together. So there are gay people who are very fixedly gay and there are gay people who are more fluid, meaning they can experience attractions that run outside of their orientation."[14] This degree of sexual fluidity would also apply to straight people, which means that technically some of them are bisexual.

An alternative perspective, not necessarily contradictory, is possible. What if we preserve fluidity not as an "add-on" but as a vital quality of individuals who are probably differentially susceptible to having a fluid orientation, which, as noted earlier, might serve an evolutionary purpose. A fluid orientation would thus be of the same enduring quality as erotic or romantic arousal. As such, fluidity is not a matter of choice either in totality or in degree; rather, the decision is whether and how to act on sexual, romantic, and gender proclivities over time and situations. I see no reason to believe that any one sex or sexuality is more or less inclined to have a fluid orientation.

Another central issue that is generally ignored is whether fluidity applies equally in all sexual and romantic domains. Certainly, factors other than biology come into play regarding sexual identity and behavior, including evolving personal development over the life course about the meaning of attractions, attitudes such as biphobia and social stigma, and other salient factors such as the availability of sex partners. It is easy to imagine that sexual identity and behavior are far more fluid than are internally recognized sexual and romantic orientations as manifested in erotic and romantic arousal and attraction. Because of these differences, the significance of fluidity varies widely depending on whether the focus is sexual, romantic, or gender orientation, behavior, or identity. In a recent longitudinal study of nearly 2,500 urban girls, ages 14 to 22, Johnny Berona and colleagues found widespread (63 percent) change over time across sexual and romantic indicators. Counter to expectations, the most common was in sexual attraction (39 percent), followed by sexual identity (27 percent), sexual behavior (12 percent), and romantic partnering (8 percent). The young age of the girls might have been the critical factor, because cognitive and affective aspects of sex and romance usually occur developmentally before social and behavioral aspects. That is, the girls probably contemplated these matters before acting on their sexual and romantic desires. Consistent, however, with other reports, same- and multiattracted girls were most likely to experience fluidity, which increased with age.[15] Perhaps this is because by definition fluidity implies multiple romantic, sexual, and gender expressions.

I am not arguing that all individuals are born with fluid orientations, only some. How many, I cannot hazard a guess, but it is not trivial, especially among sexual-minority individuals, who as a population are more likely than heterosexuals to report being fluid.[16] Certainly, many bisexuals, pansexuals, and nonbinaries are born with the capacity to freely make choices, perhaps attuned to inner desires even as their culture around them encourages or discourages such decisions.

Female Fluidity

Lisa Diamond argues in her book *Sexual Fluidity: Understanding Women's Love and Desire* that sexual fluidity is primarily a feature of women, not men—almost by definition: "Sexual fluidity, quite simply, means situation-dependent flexibility in women's sexual responsiveness." This fluidity is available to women of all orientations to "experience variation in their erotic and affectional feelings as they encounter different situations, relationships, and life stages."[17] This possibility is, according to Diamond, principally the result of the way the sexes are socialized in Western cultures. More so than men, women are considered to be particularly sensitive to situational, interpersonal, and contextual factors and thus shaped by sociocultural factors such as women's studies classes, passionate friendships, and the media's portrayal of women. They understand themselves through their relationships and alter their identity in response to this variability—that is, they grasp the meaning of their sexual and romantic desires not as discrete categories but as existing along a spectrum over time and across environmental situations.[18] Clearly, mainstream identities are not sufficiently comprehensive to account for the diversity women experience in their daily lives.

Women's tendency to have ambiguous, fluid sexual-arousal patterns led the psychologist Michael Bailey to question if women even have a sexual orientation. He notes that sexual orientation usually implies sexual desire, arousal, fantasy, and attraction and that only one of these, arousal, can be measured directly (usually by genital arousal, pupil dilation, or brain responses). Because women's self-reported sexual identities do not consistently map onto their arousal patterns, either they are all bisexual or they have no stable orientation. "Let me be clear that I am not asserting that most women have no sexual orientation; I am merely raising the possibility. . . . Women are less constrained than men by a focused sexual arousal pattern. Before asking what sexual orientation orients, we should first ask whether anything sexually orients women."[19]

The primary problem, as the health and sex educator Emily Nagoski notes in her book *Come as You Are*, is that we err by attempting to understand women's sexuality by applying male concepts to them, including the equation of sexual orientation, sexual identity, and arousal patterns. Not only do women vary more than men do in their sexual-response patterns, but context matters in eliciting sexual arousal, desire, and orgasm.[20] The overlap between a woman's genital arousal and how turned on she feels can be minimal, a point made by Meredith Chivers. She has found a lack of consistency across a broad range of sexual assessments, which would tentatively appear to support Bailey's speculation that the majority of women do not distinguish between male and female pornographic targets. Chivers raises the question why some women who "report little to no sexual interest in other women, nor few previous sex experiences with women, and few sexual fantasies involving women (relative to frequency of fantasizing about males) exhibit sexual responses to stimuli depicting women that are, in many cases, relatively equal to what they exhibit to male sexual stimuli."[21] For over a decade, this has been on her research agenda. Rather than unilaterally conclude that women do not have a sexual orientation, she suggests several hypotheses in her seminal review for explaining the research findings, including these five:

1. Women demonstrate greater erotic plasticity than men do; that is, women have a sexuality that is more malleable by external influences such as social, cultural, and other contextual factors.

2. Any sexual stimulus, preferred or not, provokes an automatic genital response that produces vaginal vasocongestion and genital lubrication as a protective mechanism, reducing pain and/or injury during wanted or unwanted vaginal penetration (e.g., rape).

3. Women's bodies are ubiquitously eroticized and sexualized in popular media, and therefore women may be doing the same when viewing sexual stimuli depicting women.

4. Women are socialized to be sexually aroused in accordance with how others are aroused by them.

5. Because female babies generally lack the prenatal androgen exposure that male babies experience, which is associated with sexual and romantic responses to females, the lack of these androgens results in no sexual or romantic preference among women.

More directly, Rachel Farr and colleagues have challenged Bailey's view, finding that women have a fundamental sexual orientation even as many are also fluid in their attractions. Farr and colleagues do not support a "universal bisexuality," even among sexual-minority women. "Non-heterosexual women demonstrate a 'core' sexual orientation, regardless of whether they identify as lesbian, bisexual or fluid. The results specifically support the notion that self-identified bisexual women appear to have a 'core' bisexual orientation, with respect to day-to-day variability in their attractions." Women's sexual orientation "depend[s] on a whole host of factors ranging from biology, genetics, and physiology, to environmental factors and social circumstances."[22]

Indisputable is that when fluidity is noted, the reference is nearly always to women. The ultimate answer of why so many women are fluid in their sexual and romantic selves remains unknown and thus a matter of speculation. Diamond's answer is about a basic characteristic of women: the higher prevalence of nonexclusive attractions. "This gender difference drives many of the other gender differences in indices of sexual fluidity (such as the likelihood of change in attractions over time, which appears to be greater among both men and women with nonexclusive versus exclusive attractions)."[23] What if, however, men were just as likely as women to be bisexual? Then, would they be as likely to be fluid?

Male Fluidity

So strong is the belief that men are *not* sexually or romantically fluid that few researchers even make an effort to confirm this conviction. Yet, the 23-year-old actor Lucas Hedges describes his sexuality as a "fluid experience."[24] The researchers Lisa Diamond and Sabra Katz-Wise agree, presenting evidence that men can also be fluid, though the extent of the sex difference is unclear. Katz-Wise recruited an admittedly biased online sample of highly educated sexual-minority young adults and found no significant sex differences in fluidity, with about 60 percent of women and 50 percent of men reporting fluidity in attractions and sexual identity. Fluid women, however, were more likely to believe that sexual fluidity is a real thing and that sexuality can be changed by environmental events. With an adult sample, Christopher Scheitle and Julia Kay Wolf found that women reported more identity changes than men did, and, yet, over 40 percent of fluid individuals were men.[25]

Diamond reanalyzed previously reported data and found that between 25 percent and 75 percent of sexual-minority individuals across national studies reported substantial temporal changes in their attractions. Consistent with Katz-Wise's research, women were not uniformly more changeable than men, "contrary to the notion of a global gender difference in sexual fluidity." Similar results were reported among nearly 2,000 16-year-old Croatian adolescents. As to why research usually shows greater rates of change in women, this finding may be driven, according to Diamond, by women's greater propensity to have bisexual attractions, which in both sexes increases the potential for fluidity (by contrast to those who start from a monosexual position).[26]

What is nearly universal is the finding that fewer straight-identified men than women report sexual fluidity—but why? A biological explanation is that male sexuality is more categorical because it is shaped by genetics and prenatal hormones, whereas women's sexuality is more likely to be on a spectrum. Others argue for a stronger determining role for the socialization of men. They are not to engage other men in sex-like activities except in a limited number of circumstances: during innocent, meaningless boyhood play; when inebriated or high and thus not responsible for their actions; while incarcerated in prison as an exertion of power; when women are not available in all-male spaces such as fraternities, boarding schools, gangs, and monasteries; or for dude- or bud-sex. Straight-identified men are supposedly not watching gay porn or viewing the male body as a potential "sexy" experiment. Society views a man's body less than a woman's as an acceptable target of lust. By contrast, women's bodies are objectified, and if they are making out or having sex with another woman, then it is a matter of straight male titillation and, hence, "hot."

Fluidity Reconsidered

In research conducted about a decade ago using Add Health data, women were more likely than men to initially identify their sexuality not in absolute terms (100 percent heterosexual, 100 percent homosexual) but as nonexclusive (attracted to both sexes) and to experience more shifts over time. Although the prevalence of men's fluidity was considerably lower than among women, it was not zero. Over 5 percent of young men (not just sexual-minority men) shifted their self-reported sexual orientation identity over the six-year period, especially straight and mostly straight men switching in and out of the mostly straight category.[27] In an important refinement, the Bryn Austin research group found the expected sex difference in sexual orientation mobility in their sample, but it was eliminated in the sexual-minority group comparison (similar to Katz-Wise's and Diamond's research), despite the much larger number of female bisexuals.[28]

This research is noteworthy because it reveals that men can be sexually fluid, perhaps in the same way and at the same rate (which is unknown, for either sex) as women. This may be especially true among younger generations and among sexual-minority individuals. This raises the question, If women are fluid because of their feminine socialization—as several of Chivers's hypotheses postulate—and if men have their masculine socialization that discourages fluidity, then how and why are men fluid? That is, if men are socialized in a considerably different fashion than women are, then their route to fluidity might have a different origin. One option is that women are fluid because of their socialization, while men are fluid because of their biology. Or, perhaps, fluidity for both is the result of personality or temperament (openness to experience, curiosity, libido). A third option is that men and women start with the same biological fluidity potential, but feminine socialization encourages it and masculine socialization discourages it. If so, as toxic masculinity decreases and inclusive masculinity increases among youths and young adults, fluid women will be joined by many fluid men.

I lean heavily toward the third option, but before we settle the issue, we should listen to the developmental histories of fluid young people. The stories of mostly straight individuals assist us in several ways. First, in-depth interviews with mostly straight and mostly lesbian women reveal, according to the psychologists Liam Wignall and Helen Driscoll, that by using these terms, women are making an important distinction between bisexual identities and their own fluid identity: "Mostly [it is] indicative of sexuality as a fluid construct, serving to deemphasize sexual identity labels."[29] Second, stories of young men challenge the assumption that fluidity is restricted to sexual domains. Many men and women have the capacity to erotically or romantically respond to their nonpreferred sex. Jacob and Kristin exemplify this fluidity.

Jacob

As soon as Jacob entered the room, you knew the college freshman was an athlete, which he advertised by sporting a tee-shirt proclaiming, "Let's kick some [picture of two soccer balls side by side]." With short brown hair highlighted blond, Jacob was pledging a "relaxed fraternity" with openly gay brothers because it fits his progressive spirit. He's fluent in Spanish, Portuguese, and English (his joke) and wants to work in international relations. With the first question, "Looking back, what is your earliest sexual or romantic memory?" Jacob blushed, mumbling, "I can't remember." Realizing I wasn't moving to the next question, the smile disappeared, replaced by nervous laughter. As he leaned back in his chair, his life unfolded as he relaxed and generously told me his complicated sexual and romantic life story.

Jacob is the youngest of three children, and if he were gay, his white, progressive family would unequivocally accept him. To them, he's straight because he's always had girlfriends and displays none of "the gay stereotypes." After several early girl crushes during early adolescence, Jacob watched porn; gay porn motivated his best orgasms. "I knew I wanted to be with girls, but I knew I was only sexually attracted to guys. . . . I remember it was a pretty bummed-out situation for me when I realized I liked clicking guys [gay porn]." Jacob doesn't believe watching porn made him sexually attracted to guys, because the attraction has always been there.

Jacob's first genital contact was in his junior year of high school when he and his girlfriend were "hooking up" and she gave him a hand job. Intercourse waited until college orientation week. Jacob wants to have more sex with girls, but it's a tricky situation—he can't finish unless he fantasizes gay porn.

When I see a girl, I want to be with her, and I want to talk to her, and I am initially attracted to a girl. And then for as far back as I can remember, I have kind of been only sexually attracted to guys. I've never had an experience with a guy where I see a guy and I'm like, "Oh, I want to go out or I want to be involved with that person." . . . Sometimes it [erection] is hard, and sometimes I get one and it goes away halfway through. Sometimes I am able to finish, but it's not like enjoyable, . . . [which is] horribly embarrassing. It just sucks.

Jacob has hooked up with lots of girls, "like kiss and stuff," but, he said, "it falls apart because I am not sexually able to be with girls. But I only want to be with girls!" Although it's not unusual for adolescent boys to initially experience erection and finishing problems, few straight boys follow Jacob's "click on dick" porn solution. Jacob has never had sex with or been infatuated with a guy.

But never, not one guy. No one has ever touched me. But I know I would. I know myself. I've spent the past four years entirely in my head. I don't know how to talk to guys in a romantic way or flirt with guys. It's not that I would be embarrassed about it. I just don't get those feelings with guys. I don't see a guy and think, "Oh, he's attractive. I'm going to go talk to him." That never happens. There was a [fraternity] brother in the house who I am friends with, and one night after a party he was pretty drunk, and we were in a room together, and if it had been a girl, I would have hooked up in a second. . . . He was kind of leaning in, and I just didn't want to hook up with him. It's such a divide.

Does having sex with a guy interest Jacob?

I don't know how I would act. I guess I could, but I have never really thought about it. I wouldn't really want to do that. . . . Yeah, it will happen. It's going to happen. I just don't know how to play it out if it happens. . . . I don't know if you've gotten this from the interview, but in my mind, I am a bottom. I just don't know how that would play into it. It would have to be a good-looking guy. . . . Someone who is muscular. It's hard to say. I am very turned off by very effeminate guys. . . . It is more of what they have [genitalia].

Because Jacob is a student-athlete in a fraternity, dates women, and acts masculine, his best friends disbelieve him when he tells them he daily gets off on gay porn.

> Aside from a few people who have really taken the time, is that people simply don't understand what I am telling them. . . . It's such a divide, and people just can't break up their own mind to see it how I see it. . . . They say, "Oh, it sounds like you're bisexual." The way I describe it to people is—I just can't! No one else I have ever talked to or seen online or anything has anything remotely like me. . . . It's so annoying.

Once or twice a day, Jacob watches gay porn to "get off," and yet he's fervently, romantically, and physically attracted to women. He adamantly refuses to identify as bisexual, and several times during the interview, he volunteered, with passion, that his unique blend of sexual and romantic feelings and behaviors means he's *not* bisexual. Yet, one could argue that averaging his romantic and sexual selves justifies cataloguing him as bisexual. Gay friends tell Jacob he just hasn't met the *right boy* to fall in love with, and straight friends tell him he just hasn't met the *right girl* to turn him on sexually. If he had, the dream boy would bring Jacob's sexual and romantic orientations into harmony (he'd be gay), and if the hot girl with the great body and personality were located, he'd be straight.

About the possibility of being gay, Jacob said, "Honestly, I would be so fine being gay. . . . It wouldn't be an issue. I am not for any reason of religion or anything—that's not what's holding me back. I just have this mental conflict, this mental divide." Jacob should not, however, turn to research for clarity because it would lead him to dead ends, arguing that he's either gay or straight, or bisexual if splitting the difference. Given his strong sexual attraction to males, is his adulation of women merely the gay eye admiring feminine beauty? Perhaps he'd like to be a fashion designer on *Project Runway*? Other research, however, might lead Jacob to conclude that he's straight given his real-life genital contact with girls and his love of the female body, except for loving the male penis, which is unremarkable among some straight male youths.[30] Most critical, he

believes, are the romantic butterflies for girls (never boys) as proof he's
not gay.

On the survey given before the interview, Jacob marked sexually
"mostly gay" and romantically "exclusively straight." His pupil-dilation
scores from the physiological part of the study indicate that Jacob is
aroused (his eyes enlarge) by both men and women, slightly higher by
women. How does Jacob square these seeming contradictions?

> I wish I could take an MRI and a PET scan and see anything I can do to
> help. . . . I have to silently struggle with it. Even the gay kids who I talk
> to about this all don't understand either. Because they are dealing with
> issues that I wish I was dealing with. . . . And the whole, "It Gets Better"
> campaign—it doesn't seem like it's going to get better for my thing.

With that, I turned off the tape-recorder and provided Jacob the
student-health phone number, a medical consultation, reading recommendations, and my availability whenever he wanted to talk.

Jacob voluntarily returned sophomore year to tell me that over the
summer he hooked up with a guy on Grindr for his first gay sex. He easily
got off, but it wasn't great sex because of the guy's personality. His summer experiences with women were more numerous, but with a common
outcome: getting to penetration but unable to finish without fantasizing about gay porn. The persistence of homoeroticism didn't, however,
dampen his desire to spend the rest of his life with a woman, but would
she understand his need to go to gay porn to finish? Would he tell her?

Senior year, Jacob texted, "Sorry I have been MIA since we last spoke
two years ago." With the addition of a scruffy beard and a "Brasil" shirt,
Jacob brought me up-to-date.

> Eight months ago, I was dating a girl, and three or four months in, I told
> her 95 percent of my issues. It was a fulfilling relationship, and I finished
> quickly, and she did as well, always before me. I was romantically very at-
> tracted to her. I could get it up kissing her and get hard. Never a problem.
> Just fantasized being a bottom with a guy I'm attracted to.

They had sex multiple times a week, usually initiated by Jacob. On off days, he masturbated to gay porn: "makes stronger images I can use with her." While in Brasil, Jacob was anally penetrated by a Grindr male and had oral sex at a gay bathhouse. Since then, he has blocked his Grindr account.

Two years later, we had a FaceTime appointment. Jacob met a woman who, he said, "really turns me on romantically and sexually."

Able to come within a minute without any male images. Was just there in the moment, and that was the turn-on. Actually, I've not watched gay porn for three weeks because of involvement with women sexually. Haven't needed it. . . . With a girl, I can get aroused just by touching, going down on her—so arousing and don't need anything else. So amazing to totally go there 100 percent and finish without thinking of guys.

Now while watching gay porn, Jacob sometimes imagines himself in the active role, penetrating a guy. "Never about the characteristics of the guy, just their sex organ. I'm the one pleasing him. This works best when going in and out . . . to get me off, finish, climax with a girl." He never craves sex with guys, but if watching gay porn, he comes in two minutes. In his ideal future, he doesn't want to go to porn, and he'd be married to a woman, without "multiple guys or other arrangements."

At the end of our conversation, Jacob assessed his sexual and romantic self:

- *Sexual orientation*: bisexual leaning gay, situationally not bisexual
- *Romantic orientation*: exclusively straight, extremely heteroromantic
- *Sexual identity*: not confused but fluid

Though these three do not seamlessly mesh, Jacob can live with the ambiguities. He's fluid because he's on a spectrum, consistent with his generation's tendency to invent labels of choice. Jacob's dilemma was resolved once he realized he didn't have to define himself as straight, bisexual, or gay. It wasn't a matter of homohysteria or bisexual erasure; he simply resisted the mandate to pick a side. Jacob hasn't reached his final resolution, but that's okay with him.

Kristin

Kristin's family began at the low end of the socioeconomic order on a rural military base in South Dakota. The family frequently moved to other military bases commensurate with her father's promotions. Now he's on Wall Street. During this time, her mother has been a stay-at-home mom raising Kristin and her two younger brothers. All family members are devout Scandinavian Catholics, though Kristin only smiled when I asked if she was as well.

When Kristin and her same-age cousin budded breasts, they were curious about them, talked about them, and looked at them, causing Kristin to "ponder what being physical with another girl would be like." These feelings ran parallel to her growing outspoken and confident persona in middle school. She questioned her Catholic understanding of what a girl should be. "I was reluctant to be pretty. I wanted a career and to do things not normal for girls to do." Then and now, Kristin did not characterize herself as being overly feminine.

> I don't fuss over nails or makeup. All of these things are overrated and a waste of time. They're beyond just being presentable and attractive. [I'm] on the masculine side of feminine: features more masculine, and I prefer to wear pants or overalls. Little-girl games frustrated me, hated dolls, content being with guys and going fishing and climbing trees and playing outdoors.

Kristin was occasionally teased by other girls for her unfeminine ways, but she didn't care.

Kristin's best male friend became her first sex partner, nine months after they switched their friendship to officially dating.

It was the first time I was in love. And we were on this double date, and it was a big deal, with dressing up, ballet, champagne, etc. . . . [We] then began fooling around, and we had before—only this time went further. It was romantic and comfortable. I had wondered about what it would feel like not being a virgin. It was a positive experience until we broke up, and then I wished I had it back. Very intimate, but I wasn't mature enough, but I was happy I had the experience. . . . It was intercourse, with him having orgasm but not me. It neither pushed nor pulled me or made me pick one [sex] over the other.

It was not until freshman year of college that Kristin's same-sex attractions became intensely explicit. What was the meaning of her attractions to women? Here is a sampling of her equivocal process:

I noticed that I was noticing female bodies, and I felt a crush on a sorority sister for a couple of months who I knew to be lesbian. I was never scared of being a lesbian because I had heterosexual attractions. This was confusing, and I had no one to talk with if I acted on it. It's like a mood with me, not there all the time. I was conscious of feeling different from my friends, but that did not mean a label.

My sexuality seems more fluid than most, but I just don't talk about it. . . . I have sincere attractions to both. With females, it is more of a mood when I notice women. . . . On one scale, I'd evaluate how attractive everyone is and where I fit in. The other part is, Who am I attracted to? When it is intense, I don't know what to do about it. Should I try to do something or ignore it? There are weeks when I don't think about it. I'm looking at women more, but I'm not more attracted to them. With most guys, I dismiss them, but some I can get intense about. I can get intense with women. I can't act on it because I'm in a relationship [with Trey]. With guys, it's not physical as much as intellectual and their personality.

Kristin concluded that her sexual/romantic orientations are bisexual, but her identity is fluid.

Kristin and her boyfriend, Trey, have been on and off for three years. He once asked why she was hanging out with her gay friends so much. "Are you gay?" Trey, a music major, was once a supportive friend for someone who came out as gay. So shouldn't he be for her as well?

> He would provide a cushioning environment for me to say it, and yet I couldn't. I screamed at him, "Are you trying to get me to say I'm gay?!" It is hard to keep a secret from Trey, but he'll wonder if I'm content with him or will want to experiment with women. His insecurities could spring up, yet I hate keeping secrets. Don't want to tell him, and this frustrates me.
>
> Should I pursue to see if this is more that an attraction, or do I go down that path? At this point, I'd act on it. You know, for women being physical is only a small baby step from what we have with our girlfriends: lots of sharing, talking, hugging, emotions, admiring, looking, comparing. I have been hit on by women, especially after I cut my hair.

At the time of the interview, Kristin had not had sex or a relationship with a woman.

Kristin is only out as having same-sex attractions to one person, a sorority friend who has also wondered about herself. "Most of her friends have come out to her, so she says that she attracts them. She was very supportive and helped me clarify." Kristin has no plans to tell her "very traditional Catholic" mother.

> She probably only slept with my dad. She hasn't seen the world, but she is a strong person who clings to her faith to get by. She's from a small town [in Scandinavia] and did not finish schooling so she could marry dad. She had no real young adulthood and not exposed to things. She'd say it was wrong, sick, confused. She'd say ridiculous things, and we'd argue.

Kristin is very close to her father. They talk without embarrassment about her body, puberty, and sex. When she was listening to a lesbian band, he asked her, "Is there something you want to tell me?" It would take him a while to adjust, but he'd be supportive. The same is true with her oldest brother, a senior in high school. "He looks up to me and appreciates me."

Although fluidity confuses Kristin, it has been a private, positive experience. But, of course, she has not had to cope with the ramifications of disclosing to her family and friends. She wants to experiment, but she's not sure how to get there.

Life Happens If You're Fluid

As each young person narrated their developmental history, the inconsistencies in erotic and romantic attractions became quite evident. Sexual arousals and romantic crushes might include femme but not masculine individuals (or the opposite), and to complicate matters, they might be fluid in their sexual or romantic life but not in both. With regard to variability over time, nearly all attested to fulfilling the conditions of fluidity during adolescence and young adulthood. They swapped out portions of their sexual and romantic inclinations devoted to one sex to give to the other sex.

Few of these developmental fluctuations are conscious choices for these young people but are the result of a growing reflection on their true self. Although most felt that their fluidity is a natural feature of their self, they knew they could choose whether to tolerate the attractions and whether to engage in sexual or romantic behavior. And, of course, some are more motivated to make changes than others, for unknown reasons.

11

Genderqueer and Nonbinary

I would define myself as genderqueer. There was always this
sort of gendered aspect to my sexuality, . . . [and] those two
things got really blended.
—Jordan, age 27, white, graduate student

Jordan's story will resonate with those who adopt a genderqueer or nonbinary identity, including the queer youths from an LGBTQ resource
center featured in the sociologist Mary Robertson's book *Growing Up
Queer*. Many of the teenagers and young adults used unconventional
gender identities such as "two-spirit," "gender neutral," "some queer,"
"androgynous," "universal," and "genderqueer" that complicate our
notions of gender identity, behavior, and pronouns.[1] These identities
exist along a spectrum of internal and external experiences that are
outside conventional gender binaries. Nonbinary individuals do not
subscribe to gender distinctions such as man/boy/male or woman/girl/
female but identify as neither, both, some combination of both, another
gender altogether, fluctuating between genders, or beyond genders. The
sex and gender psychologist Christina Richards and colleagues summarize genderqueers as having "a gender which is neither male nor female"
and identifying "as both male and female at one time, as different genders at different times, as no gender at all, or dispute the very idea of
only two genders."[2]

   According to Trans Student Educational Resources (TSER), an organization led by trans* youth to promote their well-being, genderqueer is
an internal sense of gender that does not fit socially constructed norms
associated with the biological sex that one is assigned at birth, which is
usually based on physical anatomy (genitalia) or chromosomes. TSER

FIGURE 11.1. The Gender Unicorn. (TSER)

created the graphic "Gender Unicorn," an educationally friendly means to illustrate the complex spectrums of gender and sexuality, used by educational institutions around the world (see figure 11.1). Genderqueer and nonbinary identities do not necessarily stabilize over time and context but frequently fluctuate (gender fluidity) between genders or between having a gender and not having one. According to the *Urban Dictionary*, although "none of these terms mean exactly the same thing—all speak to an experience of gender that is not simply male or female."[3]

The reason why nonbinary baffles some of us is because historically, without giving it a second thought, we assume that everyone is either biologically male or female and a man or a woman—though we have become increasingly aware that not all youths feel that they are the gender that matches their birth sex. Within a binary mind-set, we also anticipate that with biological sex comes matching gender thoughts, feelings, and expressions. That is, we know that some boys feel and act more masculine than other boys and some girls feel and act more feminine than other girls, but not to the extent of acting more like another sex than one's own. Thinking outside these sex and gender boxes is quite daunting, especially in generations older than Millennials. According to the journalist Evan Urquhart, what they cannot fathom are individuals who "feel constrained by a culture that insists that they be either male or female, with all the expectations, assumptions, and stereotypes that come along with choosing one of those identities." Although nonbinaries vary immensely in their gender experiences and preferences, they share, according to Urquhart, "a deep, persistent unease with being associated only with the binary gender assigned to them from infancy."[4] *Healthline* adds that many people experience their gender as "fluid, meaning it can shift and change at any given time," and that genderqueer is one of the most common identities under the transgender umbrella, especially among younger generations. Fortunately for them, their gender identities are "increasingly being recognized in legal, medical and psychological systems and diagnostic classifications in line with the emerging presence and advocacy of these groups of people." They remain, however, marginalized and at risk for victimization and discrimination.[5]

The Transgender versus Genderqueer Umbrella

Although the National Transgender Discrimination report lists "genderqueer," "gender nonbinary," and "gender nonconforming" as identities falling under a much larger transgender umbrella, they differ from trans* youths, many of whom are adamantly nonbinary in identifying as the opposite gender they were assigned at birth. These are individuals whose assigned sex at birth is wrong for them and who later transition (to varying degrees) their gendered self, perhaps including their physical body. This can be especially critical before and after they undergo medical sex or gender transition. By contrast, genderqueers fall under the nonbinary sex/ gender identity umbrella spectrum. They might not necessarily identify as trans* because they feel their gender, whether present or not, is unrelated to their biological sex—which, for them, is beside the point. Many are uninterested in taking gender- or body-altering hormones or surgeries and want others to respect their choice to use genderless pronouns and references such as "they," "per," "xe," "ve," and "ze." The celebrity writer Shondell listed famous people who fall under a genderqueer umbrella, largely because they describe their gender as "half and half," "post-gender," "having the best of both sexes," and "somewhere in the middle." For example, Elly Jackson (of La Roux, a synth-pop act) described her nonbinary look as "androgynous moody bitch."[6]

In *A Guide to Gender*, the author Sam Killermann reverses the trans*/ genderqueer umbrella by proposing that genderqueer is the larger, catch-all umbrella for those who do not identify as cisgender, including individuals who identify as trans*, bigender, and two-spirit.[7] Regardless, the genderqueer umbrella has mushroomed to embrace numerous additional identities, including agender, third gender, trigender, neutrois, transmasculine, transfeminine, bear, butch, femme, boi, genderfree, and androgyne. Many overlap, causing "a barrier to increased understanding and acceptance of genderqueer individuals by those on the outside" of the genderqueer subculture.[8]

One final issue is reconciling sexual orientation labels with a genderqueer identity. Fundamentally, the sex that one is attracted to does not change simply because of one's sense of one's gender—though the label given to that sexual attraction might change. If a cisgender biological female is attracted to males, her sexual orientation is labeled straight; if that same person is nonbinary and sees the self as half male and half female, they will remain attracted to males, but now their sexual orientation appears bisexual or pansexual; if they fluctuate in their gender, then their sexual orientation is fluid. Of course, there are many permutations in these matters.

Prevalence of Genderqueers

"Genderqueer" seldom appears on surveys when individuals are asked about their gender. Rather, they are to check the "female," "male," or, occasionally, "transgender" box. If the women's and gender studies psychologist Janet Hyde and colleagues had their way, individuals would report their gender identity in nonbinary terms: "female," "male," "transgender female," "transgender male," "genderqueer," and "other." Alternatively, and more simply, they could respond to an open-ended question, "What is your gender?" If they indicate a genderqueer self-label, then elaboration would be encouraged, with other labels currently used by nonbinary and gender-nonconforming persons.[9]

The Canadian Trans Youth Health Survey in 2014 used this format, an open-ended text box, to empower youths in a large (N = 324) bilingual study of the health and well-being of trans* and gender-diverse youth (ages 14–25). From the School of Nursing, Hélène Frohard-Dourlent and colleagues reported that the youths "embraced the multiplicity of genders and sexes. Some insisted on differentiating the two terms, while others seemed to collapse them." For the youths, sex consisted of physical characteristics and gender, an internal sense of self. Three identity categories emerged from their text comments: transfeminine/woman/male-to-female, transmasculine/man/female-to-male, and nonbinary/genderqueer. The youths used both social-construction words ("dependent on human interpretation and social context") and the language of bioessentialism ("core," "objective," "unchangeable"). The trans* and gender-diverse youths, counter to conventional wisdom, viewed gender as immutable, sex as malleable ("modifiable via medical interventions"), and both as "beyond binaries." Because the "respondents [had] nuanced, multiple, and at times inconsistent understandings of gender and sex," we need to hear their perspectives.[10]

The reality is that we neither listen to their stories nor include them in research. Thus, the prevalence of nonbinaries is unknown, although most researchers would agree that it is a small number. Two recent studies assessed gender in terms of two types: "ambivalent" (an equal identification with both sexes) and "incongruent" (a stronger identification with the nonnatal sex). In a large Dutch sample, the psychologists Lisette Kuyper and Ciel Wijsen found that 5 percent of those who were born male and 3 percent of those who were born female reported an ambivalent gender (nonbinary). About 1 percent of the population described themselves as having an incongruent gender (trans*).[11] A far lower prevalence was found in a Flemish population by the endocrinologist Eva Van Caenegem and colleagues: 2 percent genderqueer and 1 percent trans*, with few sex differences. Among sexual minorities, however, while male bodies fit this general pattern, the prevalence of gender-ambivalent and gender-incongruent female bodies was more than double the prevalence in the general population.[12] These two studies give conflicting answers as to whether more women or men are nonbinary. With regard to celebrity visibility, certainly more natal females have come out under the genderqueer umbrella: Miley Cyrus, Angel Hare, Grimes, and St. Vincent are examples.[13]

Although we might not understand or fully appreciate genderqueer and nonbinary individuals, listening to their life histories has great merit. Jordan, a genderqueer individual, was certainly forgiving when I slipped in my gender terms during our interview, especially after I profusely apologized. They said, "Don't worry about it." Accepting nonbinary youths for who they are does not mean we have to give up our binary gender world; it just means we should not impose it on everyone. Jordan, for whom standard sexual and gender categories do not apply, can teach us.

Jordan

At different points in life, Jordan has identified as gay, bisexual leaning gay, bisexual, lesbian, fluid, pansexual, and queer and now prefers genderless pronouns and a genderqueer identity. Gender attributes they find sexually attractive have remained stable. Jordan has had sexual and romantic relationships with women and men but is partial to female-bodied individuals and repelled by beefcake males, which explains their lack of pupil dilation to the muscular male actors in the eye-tracking lab experiment; pupil dilation to the shapely female actors was elevated. Jordan is primarily invested in straight relationships (if defined by biological sex), which are also "ostensibly lesbian" (if defined by gender). But to be clear, Jordan believes that "marriage is bullshit." They rated their self as exceptionally high on openness and sensation seeking and slightly elevated on life satisfaction.

Jordon initially warned me that I might not want to interview them, saying, "I don't identify as male" (assigned at birth sex). At several points, they asked for clarification about how I was using "masculine," "feminine," "male," and "female." With considerable animation and humanities-oriented peripheral comments, it was a protracted 90-minute interview, with answers frequently qualified or elaborated. Jordan presented as a blend of masculinity and femininity, and at first glance, it was not altogether obvious as to their assigned natal sex. As the interview progressed, Jordan's core masculinity became increasingly evident in their behavior and personality. With wild, unruly, curly black hair with shaved sides, tight jeans rolled up to midcalf, and a large necklace with matching earrings, Jordan's appearance was a unique blend of counterculture gender.

The youngest of three children born to "old hippies" who are no longer "hippie dippy" in countenance, Jordan grew up in small towns. One cousin was born biologically female and is now a trans* man. As a child and adolescent, Jordan was extremely masculine: baseball, basketball, football, track and field, and wrestling. Most friends were male teammates. Around age 6, Jordan was curious about the "different genitalia of different-bodied people." Jordan's first crush was a childhood (female) friend, and the second, during freshman year of high school, was a gay boy. "We sort of had this flirtatiously kind of thing going on, but nothing ever happened." Their first masturbatory fantasies were about "being with another man or being dressed in drag so to speak": "It often involved me stepping outside of what from hindsight or an external point of view would be the stereotypical male gender role." At 14, Jordan began watching porn, which was not pleasant.

> The actual way that those people were presented was not good at all and totally retarded my development in a different way. There are she-males and trannies, all that kind of shit, . . . [with] people who weren't standard bodied. I mean, it's weird because what I've wondered a lot about recently is how much of me being turned on by pornography involving those people was me being turned on by them or me being turned on by the thought of being them or engaged in things in that particular way. I am okay with being attracted to lots of different types of bodies. I certainly have particular types of male bodies that I am attracted to, particular female bodies that I am attracted to. Being attracted to somebody who happens to have a penis and breasts is not a problem with me. I am past that.

Jordan dated a girl in eighth grade before having their first genital contact with a "modest male friend." They were hanging out at a sleepover with drinking, making out, fondling, and "definitely oral-genital contact." Jordan came out as gay, but, they said, "Nobody thought I was gay because I was so freaking butch." Senior year, Jordan flirted and made out with a girl on the bus after a track-and-field meet, and their "hands definitely went down there on her."

Jordan wondered, "Am I gay, or am I bi as a man?" The answer was no to both because heterosexuality is a part of their life. Though Jordan is not "very monotypic," they are attracted for the most part to women. "For the sense of ease and binary categorization, I would most likely define myself as a woman, and in that context, for simplification, lesbian would be easy."

> It's funny because I do identify myself as a ridiculously masculine trans* feminine person. And it's like, what the fuck does that mean? I tend to be outspoken in a sort of direct way. . . . But sort of going off of the stereo-

type gender norms, I like doing physical activities and heavy-lifting kinds of stuff. I don't shy away from gross or disgusting things. I don't mind blood. I don't mind guts. I don't mind shit. I don't mind mud. Those kinds of things, from a personal perspective, . . . at an innate sort of level, I view them as being masculine in a sort of cultural-imposition level.

This masculinity does not imply that Jordan lacks certain stereotypical traits associated with femininity: "I am incredibly domestic. If I want to be, I really enjoy nesting in particular ways. I am very much in touch with my emotions. I don't mind talking through my emotions."

With Jordan having already established their sexual fluidity from adolescence to the present, gender has always trumped biological sex with regard to what attracts Jordan.

[I am] internalized in, like, the way that different genders are represented in sexual imagery and pornography. Some of it's me, and some of it's me reacting to the images and experiences that I am exposed to. One of my biggest problems for a long time was that interlinking of the fact that I, to some degree or another, don't really find comfort in male[ness] but in general binary gender notions. That was very much tied into my sexual explorations with myself and my sexual fantasies about other people. Interestingly, it took a long time for that to cross over into sexual interactions with other people. And it took until fairly recently for me to actually really break those things apart. It was really like, "Okay, this is me exploring myself."

Jordan's identities are played out to some extent during their sexual fantasies, in which they are both top and bottom, take the lead with both sexes, and are attracted to gender-neutral people. Because Jordan is "rollin' with the punches," they do not think their future will be static but dynamic: "no one else can tell me who I am attracted to."

The most significant romantic event of Jordan's life was a just-ended long-term relationship with Judith. They were equal partners, respected each other, coped with gender and sexual issues, felt safe with each other, and knew they could not be together because each so strongly values independence. Jordan could be in a monogamous long-term relationship or "flying solo"; either is fine.

Responding to my last question, "Is there anything I should have asked?" Jordan emphasized their sexual dilemma.

> Being a queer person is the way that gendered stereotypes work themselves into the bedroom and all that kind of stuff. And wrapped up in that certainly is the attraction of queer people to other queer people. . . . How much of my attraction to other non-stereotypical-gendered people is due to my actual attraction to them or my attraction to the comfort that I feel with them or a mutual understanding. . . . Lots of queer people date queer people even though they ostensibly would be attracted to a much broader range of people.

As Jordan prepared to leave, despite some contentious moments, they thanked me for the interview. "I completely understand and appreciate the need for individual, personal narratives to be important and for people to not be stereotyped."

12

Gender Variance and Gender Toxicity

I thought gender was something you chose every couple of
years. So, at 4, I was going to be a boy, and then I mapped
out the rest of my life regarding what gender I'd be.
—Flora, age 23, white, graduate student

Although genderqueer and nonbinary individuals might resolve the
mismatch between their personal gender identity and personality with
cultural portrayals, even mandates, of the appropriate gender expressions and roles, other youths face gender hurdles that are challenging
to overcome. They differ from nonbinary individuals in that they want
to maintain the gender identity consistent with their biological sex—
but they diverge in two opposite ways. In one case are those who are
coming to terms with gender behaviors and interests that are deemed
by their culture as *inappropriate* for their biological sex (gender nonconformity); in the second case are those who express too much of what
is culturally deemed *appropriate* gender behavior for their biological
sex (toxic masculinity, toxic femininity). The first is linked with not
being sufficiently heterosexual, and the second, with being too heterosexual, displaying traditional gender behavior that is judged unseemly
in today's world.

Although most nonbinary individuals have little to no desire to
change their gender identity or behavior, gender-variant and toxic-
gendered individuals vary considerably in their longing to change. Both
groups tend to view their relative degree of traditional masculinity and
femininity as inherited traits, not easily modified by efforts to change
them. Gender-variant youths who want to change may have tried gay
conversion therapy (to no avail) or gender relearning strategies (to no

avail), largely because of the reactions they suffer from people bent on chastising them for expressing the "wrong" gender. To their detractors (and scientists), gender and sexual orientation variance are linked: tomboy girls become lesbians, and femme boys become gays. If youths express *too much* gender behavior consistent with their biological sex, it may become toxic to others. Extreme allegiance to traditional expressions of gender has primarily focused on toxic masculinity; more recently, the toxic effects of extreme femininity has generated controversy. In either case, "gender toxicity" has become a modern buzzword with ardent social and political animation.

Bridging these areas of research—nonbinary, gender variance, and gender toxicity—has become possible with increasing cultural acceptance of cross-gender behavior and an awareness of gender fluidity. Certainly, there are competing claims: from gender traditionalists who believe we have gone too far and from gender progressives who believe we have not gone far enough. The former long for men who are real men stoic and controlled and for women who know how to please men, raise children, and run the household. The latter are populated by many Millennials and Zoomers who can easily envision an end (or at least major revisions) to gender as we know it today.

Gender Nonconformity/Variance

Over the past several decades, social and biological scientists have focused on one aspect of gender expression and interest: *gender nonconformity*. Gender expression begins during early childhood (some researchers would say from birth) and becomes increasingly apparent during early adolescence. In some cases, especially during the preteen and pubertal years, gender variance can elicit intense and destructive levels of peer bullying and discrimination that have dire psychological and mental health consequences. Nearly every study since the beginning of sexual-minority research—spanning many ages, populations, and cultures and using many different methodologies (child and adult self-reports, observations, experiments)—links gender nonconformity with peer victimization, mental health deficits, and same-sex attractions. Here are a few recent examples from childhood through young adulthood:

- *Elementary children*: Gender-atypical children (withdrawn boys and aggressive girls), compared to gender-typical children, evidenced higher levels of subsequent peer difficulties.
- *Middle school early teens*: Gender-nonconforming girls and boys received more peer homophobic name-calling, resulting in both more social anxiety and more psychological distress.
- *High school seniors*: Gender nonconformity was related to low well-being, regardless of sexual orientation, suggesting that gender-atypical traits are more relevant for psychological health than sexual orientation is.
- *College students*: Adjustment was positively associated with gender-congruent identity, instrumentality, and flexible gender attitudes.[1]

Five conclusions emerged from these studies:

1. Children, adolescents, and young adults who do not conform to gender expectations suffer mental health deficits.
2. These mental health deficits are a direct consequence of receiving peer harassment for their gender nonconformity.
3. Boys get it worse than girls, but both are recipients.
4. The critical instigating factor from the perspective of peers is gender variance and not sexual variance. Peers know who is not acting as a boy or girl; they seldom know who is sexually turned on by the wrong sex.
5. Needed in families and schools are "interventions designed to promote the acceptance of gender nonnormativity" and diversity.[2]

Whether these associations are decreasing over generations, I do not know, but I suspect that is the case. Most youths I interviewed attested to the dramatic decrease in gender-related bullying and the increase in gender and sexual orientation affirmation, especially once they escaped from middle school. Because the prevailing view among sex researchers and the public is that neither gender variation nor sexual variation causes the other but that they emanate from the same biological origin, one indication of attitude changes toward atypical gender expression is data from the Gallup Poll over the past several decades. These data reveal a sharp increase in acceptance of sexual-minority individuals and their moral and legal rights.[3]

Toxic Masculinity

"Toxic masculinity" is when men express traits linked in Western countries with being male "to such an extent that they prove damaging to themselves or a society. Masculine traits include logic, ambition, protection, independence, discipline, and strength among others. Too much of a good thing is not a good thing, and . . . may result in a 'scorched Earth' approach."[4] The damage is primarily to men's physical and mental health and to women and sexual minorities as they lose entitlements to personal, social, and political opportunities and power.

The culture war on men and masculinity was recently reignited when the American Psychological Association (APA) issued its *Guidelines for Psychological Practice with Boys and Men*. Traditional masculinity was depicted as "emotional stoicism, homophobia, not showing vulnerability, [and] self-reliance and competitiveness," all of which permits men to be disproportionally involved in "aggression and violence as a means to resolve interpersonal conflict." Toxic masculinity is lethal when it leads to violence against women (sexual assault, rape), substance abuse, criminal behavior, and suicide.[5] Although the APA report received widespread criticism, it refrained from labeling all masculinity as necessarily *toxic* and from characterizing a singular masculinity. However, masculinity, in its conventional manifestation, is frequently portrayed as essentially antifeminine and as eschewing any sign of weakness, creating "boys and men [who] have been socialized to use aggression and violence as a means to resolve interpersonal conflict." Thus, boys know that they should avoid intimacy with other boys except in a superficial manner and that they should take advantage of opportunities to gain a greater degree of interpersonal, social, economic, and political power in a patriarchal society that glorifies "hegemonic masculinity" and "heterosexist stereotypes." The power achieved is at the expense of women, sexual minorities, and feminine men.[6]

One objection to the APA guidelines came, predictably, from cultural conservatives. Mark Tapson, writing in the *National Review*, countered what he perceived to be an all-out assault on men and masculinity by women, feminists, and liberals. Tapson packed his article with news stories and photos with reference to super-masculine men fighting fires and hurricanes, saving lives, and "simply doing what good men do," which is to act on their masculinity. Men have a "natural responsibility as protectors, stepping up, at risk to their own lives, to help those unable to help themselves. It is this aspect of manhood for which men are never given credit by those deconstructionists in the culture and in academia who view masculinity as an obstacle to their agenda." To Tapson, masculinity is not toxic but a gift to women, sexual minorities, and society at large. Women and gay men should want to marry masculine men because these men are "behaving as a man, a real man."[7]

A second objection came from academic scientists. Lamenting in the *New York Times* the APA's nearly singular focus on the social and cultural determinants of masculinity and its historical amnesia regarding recent progress of masculinity, the psychologist Steven Pinker faulted the guidelines for presenting men as if they were born with a blank state without biological and genetic influences that affect sex differences in gender expression. To Pinker, the report also failed to acknowledge that since the Middle Ages, men have evolved "from a macho willingness to retaliate violently to an insult to the ability to exert self-control, dignity, reserve, and duty. It's the culture of the gentleman, the man of dignity and quiet strength, the mensch." Citing an extensive literature on the healthy lives of individuals who exhibit self-control and who repress rather than vent their anger, Pinker pointed out that repressing emotions is not necessarily bad and that expressing them is not necessarily good. Men who repress emotions "get better grades, have fewer eating disorders, drink less, have fewer psychosomatic aches and pains, are less depressed, anxious, phobic, and paranoid, have higher self-esteem, are more conscientious, have better relationships with their families, have more stable friendships, are less likely to have sex they regretted, are less likely to imagine themselves cheating in a monogamous relationship."[8]

Perhaps all sides would agree that masculinity is not *necessarily* maladaptive or destructive, which raises an obvious point: a singular masculinity does not exist, because there are diverse *masculinities* and the toxic variety may be overdrawn, constituting only a small minority of men's behavior. Supporting this perspective, the social work professor Erin Casey and colleagues investigated patterns of masculine identity among college men. They identified four types:

1. *Normative/Male Activities* (53 percent): average in most respects except very active in sports and gaming
2. *Normative* (35 percent): average in most respects except rarely involved in male group activities such as fraternities or sports teams
3. *Misogynistic* (8 percent): most in fraternities and gaming groups, frequently on sports teams
4. *Sex-Focused* (4 percent): average lifetime of 52 sex partners and 28 one-night stands, one-half used pornography daily[9]

Young men in the misogynistic group were most likely to exhibit toxic masculinity. Relative to the other 92 percent, they adhered to a masculine ideology and sexual script; were hostile to women; and exhibited intimate-partner violence, abuse, and control (e.g., causing a woman to seek medical help for injuries he inflicted, dictating what she can do or see). They rated high on the personality trait of sensation seeking; downplayed the value of monogamy; and, relative to the normative groups, had a large number of one-night stands, lifetime sex partners, paid sexual services, instances of impregnating women, and sexually transmitted diseases. Proportionally, misogynistic men were least likely to be Latinx and most likely to be Asian American. This last finding is consistent with the underlying patriarchal values of some Asian societies.

Given that misogynistic men are overpopulated in traditional masculine bastions, including sports teams and gaming groups, fraternities have had an outsized reputation as a unique fortress for such men. Is this still true, especially in light of the #MeToo movement? The empowerment of women, especially young women, through empathy and solidarity with each other has led many to challenge the toxic masculinity of powerful men who harass and assault them. In a sign of hope that Zoomers are breaking the masculine code, the writer Alexandra Robbins interviewed scores of fraternity men for her article "A Frat Boy and a Gentleman" and was heartened to discover that current generations of young men are "encouraging brothers to defy stereotypical hypermasculine standards and to simply be good people." Many fraternities now routinely welcome gay or bisexual brothers and teach respect for women through programs addressing sexual harassment, assault, and consent. This more inclusive form of masculinity also incorporates attending to the emotional needs and personal doubts of brothers, recognizing sexual uncertainties, and encouraging new ideas about being a man. Robbins acknowledged that both high-risk and low-risk fraternities exist, and considerable education is still needed.[10]

Toxic Femininity

By contrast to toxic masculinity, far less academic and media attention has been devoted to toxic femininity among women. "Toxic femininity" is when a woman, to the detriment of herself, expresses traits linked in many cultures with traditional ideas of being female, such as "passivity, empathy, sensuality, patience, tenderness, and receptivity." Too often these characteristics lead young women to neglect their own needs to attend to or benefit others, particularly men."[11] The resulting cultural outcome has been the loss of women achieving their share of social and political power; for women themselves, the consequence can be depression, exhaustion, and low self-concept.

Some people have questioned whether toxic femininity is a "real thing." The freelance journalist Katie Anthony, in response to her readers, proposed no simple answer, because her take is that femininity is not highly prized and is thus inconsequential—unless it exists in men. Because femininity is inherently toxic ("silent acceptance of violence and domination") in our culture, in her view nontoxic femininity does not exist.

> It's a thing women do to keep our value, which the patriarchy has told us is conditional upon our ability to bear violent domination, . . . [to] feel locked into a performance of their gender bereft of the normal impulses we have toward independence, sexual agency, anger, volume, messiness, ugliness, and being a tough bird to swallow.[12]

Feminine traits are tactics women use to survive oppressive misogyny, or they suffer from *internalized misogyny*.

By contrast, Devon Price, a self-referenced nonbinary social psychologist, finds meaning in the concept of toxic femininity—the origin of which is our strict adherence to the gender binary. "Focusing only on the harm done by men—and the insecurities harbored by men—ignores the broader, systematic nature of the beast. The problem was never just masculinity. It was, and is, inflexible gender roles for men and women alike." To Price, toxic femininity "is just as pernicious as toxic masculinity in how it affects all people regardless of gender." Here is a partial but telling list of toxic femininity:

- A woman won't let herself eat anything but a salad while on a date.
- Every sweater in a woman's closet is thinner and frailer than any in a man's possession.

- A parent insists on piercing the ears of a moments-old baby girl to ensure that she looks ornamented and sufficiently "pretty."
- Having a lengthy and complicated nightly facial-care routine is essential.
- If buying a gift for a woman, one reaches for something soft, sweet, and nonthreatening.

Insecurity persists because the toxic-imbued woman wonders, "Am I appearing adequately alluring and undemanding?" This is not merely sexism but toxic femininity, though both are certainly partners in crime. Price contrasts sexism and toxic femininity in the following way: While *sexism* says that a woman is too frail or docile to play a contact sport, *toxic femininity* says, "You don't want to play football anyway, sweetie, you would look horrible and sweaty in the helmet and pads." Thus, *sexism* focuses on robbing women of status and rights; *toxic femininity* defines womanhood so shallowly that a woman feels degendered and desexed. Both sexism and toxic femininity lead women to feel that they are compressed into "impossibly tight, uncomfortable shapes."[13]

Questions of Toxicity

From a scientific perspective, in nearly every discussion of toxic femininity and masculinity, the causal link between gendered behavior and the hypothesized negative effects are unspecified, meshed, or ignored because they are purported to be "self-evident," at least to the author. Unsubstantiated generalizations are not uncommon, not only regarding the prevalence of toxic gender but also with claims that such behavior is injurious to the individual and their psychological health, to others in relating to the individual, to women or men in general, or to all of the above. Although women are more likely than men to attempt suicide, men are more likely to commit suicide—but are men who display high levels of toxic masculinity more likely than nontoxic men to kill themselves? Is their higher suicide rate the result of their masculine socialization or their male biology (testosterone)? Are intensely masculine men most likely to abuse women and sexual minorities? Are women who throw off toxic femininity less likely to be abused or to gain political and economic power? Do toxic feminine women have more sex?

Regardless of the answers to these questions, the professor of rhetoric and comparative literature Judith Butler argues that attention to gender diversity has been good for both girls and boys by letting them find their way to activities and passions that more fully express who they are and by letting them flourish independent of social dictates about what is gender appropriate. "Indeed, the only prescription that most feminist positions make is to treat people with dignity, to honor the equality of the sexes, to accept gender diversity, and to oppose all forms of violence against people, whether young or old, on the basis of their gender or sexuality."[14]

I agree, but where are the examples of individuals who bridge the gender gaps? Are gay men castigated for not being sufficiently toxic in their masculinity and thus not acting like real men? Are lesbians rebuked because they are not toxic in their femininity or because they display too much toxic masculinity in their personality and behavior toward others? Might people under the bisexual umbrella, who, as a group, are more likely than straights, lesbians, and gays to possess midlevels of gender nonconformity, provide the answer? Are they able to avoid both toxic masculinity and toxic femininity?

Bisexuals and Gender

The psychologists Sara Burke and Marianne LaFrance found that lay conceptions of gender nonconformity varied, with bisexuals generally rated in the middle between straights and gays. Bisexual women were perceived as more masculine and less feminine than straight women and less masculine and more feminine than lesbians. Bisexual men, for their part, were rated considerably less masculine and more feminine than straight men but equally masculine and less feminine than gay men. Bisexuals, however, perceived themselves as similar to straights on masculinity and femininity, rather than in the middle between straights and lesbians/gays.[15]

Who is right? In the most extensive study to date regarding the relationship of gender nonconformity and sexual orientation, regardless of whether information was gleaned from self-reports across the life course or observer ratings of child and adult gender nonconformity, Gerulf Rieger and colleagues found a linear increase in gender nonconformity from exclusively heterosexual to mostly heterosexual, to bisexual, to mostly homosexual, to exclusively homosexual. In particular, "men and women with bisexual orientations appeared neither like heterosexual nor homosexual individuals, at least with respect to their gender-related traits." This linear correspondence between sexual orientation and gender nonconformity was relatively stable over the life course, especially for males, and was believed to have either a genetic or a prenatal origin. According to this research, bisexuals were incorrect in their self-perceptions in the Burke and LaFrance study because they were "in the middle" in their gender expression.[16]

Is this bisexual, bigender uniqueness consequential? Yes, especially for adolescents more than for young adults and for boys more than for girls. Among Dutch adolescents ages 11 to 18, youths with greater levels of same-sex attraction and gender nonconformity—that is, gays and lesbians—were most likely to be the recipients of peer bullying. Being the recipient of homophobic name-calling was more frequently reported by boys than girls—"consistent with the notion that men place more importance on adhering to their gender role than women"—and by younger adolescents than older adolescents. With age, youths were less likely to use overt verbal (name-calling) and physical forms of victimizing, and by late adolescence, most had sufficiently grown up to be accepting of same-sex-attracted peers. Taken together, on average, bisexuals were less likely than their lesbian sisters and gay brothers to be ill treated because they were either less gay or less gender atypical.[17]

The direct link between violating femininity and masculinity standards and mental health is more difficult to prove. Certainly, the detrimental effects of interpreting and coping with a sense of differentness because one does not conform to prescribed heterosexual gender ideologies and sexual scripts affect one's sense of self and place in the world.[18] This is added support to the proposition that sexism and misogyny are more pervasive and incendiary than homophobia and biphobia, largely because parents and their children are outsized contributors to the dissemination and promotion of sexist cultural biases, especially regarding males.[19] Regardless of whether bisexuals suffer the same damaging consequences as gays and lesbians, no one, not even straight youths, receives a free pass if they go against the cultural gender grain.

Although the penalties can be severe, the detrimental cost of being gender variant might well be changing. We are beginning to recognize that the negativity need not be the case; cultural context is not universal, and modern contexts are evolving. In Samoa, *fa'afafine* men report far more childhood gender atypicality (by definition) but are no different from cisgender men on rates of victimization due to bullying.[20] In our Western cultural context, there is growing acceptance of gender-neutral or gender-inclusive pronouns that do not associate a gender with an individual under consideration (see figure 12.1). Use of gender-neutral pronouns has been shown to be effective in several contexts. For example, on the basis of in-depth interviews with 66 queer youths, the health practitioner Camille Brown and colleagues illustrate "how to assess which pronouns to use for a given person, how to use pronouns in different contexts, why respecting pronouns is important to TGD [transgender and gender diverse] people, and flexibility as an integral component of the learning process when it comes to appropriate pronoun use."[21] A second example is the communication professor Minjie Li's experimental study that found "using the transgender subject's preferred pronouns elicited more perceived news content credibility and perceived reporter professionalism."[22]

The Millennial and Zoomer generations have made considerable progress in encouraging girls and young-adult women not to automatically accept the shackles of femininity or, for that matter, of any gen-

1	2	3	4	5
(f)ae	(f)aer	(f)aer	(f)aers	(f)aerself
e/ey	em	eir	eirs	eirself
he	him	his	his	himself
per	per	pers	pers	perself
she	her	her	hers	herself
they	them	their	theirs	themself
ve	ver	vis	vis	verself
xe	xem	xyr	xyrs	xemself
ze/zie	hir	hir	hirs	hirself

FIGURE 12.1. LGBTQ+ Resource Center gender pronouns. (Lesbian, Gay, Bisexual, Transgender, Queer Plus [LGBTQ+] Resource Center)

der. They now have more freedom to be not-straight, to have sex with multiple sexes, and to welcome gender-neutral pronouns and references. This revolution, however, has stalled, but not halted, among boys and young-adult men. This is because, the sociologist Paula England and colleagues speculate, "men's heterosexuality is seen as more precarious and more difficult to uphold than women's heterosexuality." As a result, men are less willing to explore their same-sex attractions or engage in same-sex behavior unless "they are comfortable enough to also take on a gay or bisexual identity." The exceptions, such as dude-sex and bud-sex, are kept secretive, leading England and colleagues to propose that the root of this gender difference is "a broader pattern of asymmetry in gender change in which departures from traditional gender norms are more acceptable for women than men." Although originally the goal was an acceptance of men doing feminine things and a "revalorization of traditionally feminine activities," the message received from the gender revolution "mostly involved women changing by moving into tradition-ally male positions and styles." The revolution did not raise the status of femininity for either sex, especially for men who continue to be devaluated if they embrace femininity. For bisexual men—but not bisexual women—this gender-bending activity entails losing status. Women have more freedom to gender experiment with fewer consequences because their masculinity leads them to fewer social penalties.[23]

Zoomers are building on the Millennials' success on the gender front, stimulated, in part, by celebrities who disclose their sexual and gender nonconformity. Kyrsten Sinema was elected the first openly bisexual US senator, and Nicola Adams, a two-time Olympic gold medalist in boxing and a Member of the Order of the British Empire, are so powerful that they neutralize harassment.[24] Some Zoomer boys are taking the same option of sovereignty. Jake Bain, one of the best football players in the state of Missouri, came out as not being straight, and no one dared question his masculinity or sexuality.[25] Bain is not bisexual, but similar to him, bisexual boys have more options to declare their sexuality if they so choose. This benefits all of us.

PART III
Bisexuals Are Not All the Same

13

Race and Ethnicity Matter

I had to show them that I was Black first, like with the music,
and then that I was bisexual.
—Selena, age 19, Afro-Caribbean and Native American
Indian, student

Although I have included stories of young people from various back-
grounds, I have not systematically acknowledged the impact that race and
ethnicity can have in their lives as bisexual, pansexual, fluid, and nonbinary individuals. In part, this is because few scientists have investigated
possible intersections, and thus little is known, at least from a scientific
perspective. This is alarming to the sociologists Trenton Haltom and
Shawn Ratcliff, who conclude that their results "demonstrated how sexual
identity formation is not solely based on sex or race or class, but that all
three factors offer individually unique insights into sexual minority identity formation."[1] The lives of the young adults I interviewed tell this very
story—beginning with Selena and including Deja, a 21-year-old Black student. Deja reflected on her high school years, when not being straight or
gender appropriate was a stigma: "Anyone who was not liked was called a
faggot. At an all-Black school, Black culture is very homophobic—more
so. Gender roles are very pronounced. The more masculine guys are, the
more cool they are." If Black, Latin, and Asian cultures tend to be biphobic,
we need to know why, even as we also entertain the possibility that they
give their bisexual and gender-nonconforming children developmental
assets that provide them with the ability to lead authentic, fulfilling lives. I
only wish we knew more than what is presented in this chapter.

This scientific silence is consistent with the writer and historian
Ibram X. Kendi's views about race in the United States: the assumption

and superiority of attention given to whiteness. Kendi writes that "racial inequality is when two or more racial groups are not standing on approximately equal footing." In the United States, the unequal balance has always been heavily borne by those who have dark skin, perpetuated since the founding of our first settlements and amplified through slavery, lynching, and the denial of personhood to nonwhites.[2] Racial inequality, widespread throughout US society, exists because of the majority's unexamined but never-ceasing priority given to whiteness, which has certainly affected the plights of African American, Latin, and Asian American youths.[3] Trayvon Martin, 17 years old, nearly 6 feet tall, 158 pounds, and engaged to be married, was murdered, not because he went to the store to buy Skittles but because his skin was dark, he was African American, and he was male.[4] Andrés Guardado, an 18-year-old Salvadoran American male, was shot five times in the back by law enforcement. Before his death, Andrés was working two jobs to pay for his car and to help the family stay afloat after they took a financial hit due to COVID-19.[5] His crime was not having white skin.

Using national survey questions, the sociologist Douglas Hartman and colleagues have suggested that whites are generally unaware of but well connected to their white identity, fail to understand their racial privileges, and adhere to individualistic, color-blind ideals.[6] The Alberta Civil Liberties Research Centre describes whiteness as including the privileges and power that people "who appear white receive because they are not subjected to the racism faced by people of colour." White people assume that they are naturally entitled to certain privileges, whether social, political, economic, or cultural power, as opposed to "those whose exploitation and vulnerability to violence is justified by their not being white." White people are the standard against which all other cultures, groups, and individuals are measured and usually found to be inferior. Whiteness, largely invisible to white people, "perpetuates a lack of knowledge or understanding of difference which is a root cause of oppression."[7]

An antiracist perspective suggests that "racial groups are equals in all their apparent differences—that there is nothing right or wrong with any racial group."[8] Thus, potential differences between dark-skinned and light-skinned bisexual youth do not inherently reside in their skin color but exist because of the former's nonwhite status; both, however, must confront a larger issue of straight privilege. Regardless of skin color, both groups share dual sexual and romantic attractions and thus vary from straight youths in the stigma and discrimination they experience. What is little known or explored is the interaction of bisexual youth of color being denied both white privilege and straight privilege by their ethnic/racial communities. At the very least, because of the presence or absence of whiteness, not all bisexual youths encounter the same hurdles.

Racial- and ethnic-minority youths also face within their own communities similar cultural directives as white youths, to be "normal teenagers," an edict that includes the mandate to be straight and follow gender norms. The African American, Latin, and Asian American bisexual, pansexual, fluid, and nonbinary young men and women I interviewed were painfully aware of cultural attitudes valuing, even glorifying, gender stereotypes and heterosexual marriage; mainstream gender roles and expressions applied to them as well. Many believed they matched them or were close enough; others cared not at all and flaunted cultural stipulations. Some, however, were apprehensive or troubled with reactions they would probably receive if they were known as having any degree of same-sex attraction. Besides being racial/ethnic minorities, they did not want another burden in their life; they must be straight acting and identified. Their anxiety centered around losing the degree of heterosexuality they have while desperately wanting to honor and keep it intact; yet, they did not want to deny their persistent same-sex arousal because of the pleasure it gave them. And, it was, after all, a significant part of who they are.

Against the backdrop of a community historically subjected to racist social values and attitudes and massive discrimination, dark-skinned youths must negotiate with their own families and social institutions, which can readily impede a youth's sexual and romantic trajectories. John Pachankis and colleagues, whose specialty is the mental health problems of sexual-minority individuals instigated and exacerbated by cultural stigma, argue that to comprehend sexual minorities, one must attend "to the local contexts surrounding this important segment of the global population."[9] One of the most threatening and consequential elements in the lives of African American youths is the Black church, which holds specific power to destabilize, complicate, and prolong their sexual identity development.[10] Most Black churches adhere to conservative religious teachings that pose serious challenges for many African American youths regarding accepting, disclosing, and celebrating their multiattracted lives. However, the Black church also teaches families to love, support, and accept children, which can lead some Black youths to recognize and accept their sexuality without necessarily publicly coming out and thus embarrassing their family and community.

The Haitian-born Malachi, introduced earlier, has immediate and extended families that have always attended a Black church and live in conservative areas. Malachi has no plans to come out to them.

> They are very conservative, and when these issues come up, they are very opposed to it. They are socially conservative. . . . So, until I am completely financially secure and independent, I will not tell them. But once I am, then it doesn't matter. My parents will definitely disapprove. . . . My mom has these visions of me bringing home kids and a beautiful wife, so I think it would be more of a shock for her. My dad has been more of the "do whatever you want" kind of person.

When he does disclose to them, Malachi is absolutely certain they would not reject him or his partner, though they would not like his "choices."

Research on sexual and romantic developmental milestones for ethnic- and racial-minority youths and young adults is extremely limited, and thus much of what follows relies on conjectures from sparse data, supplemented with the stories of the youths I interviewed. Of course, not all racial groups are equally progressive with regard to sex-related issues. An online survey of over 20,000 American students at 21 colleges and universities found, "Asians, especially South Asians, appear the most conservative in attitudes and behavior, Latinx students are in the middle, and either Whites or Blacks are generally the most permissive, depending on the issue."[11] I consider the sexes separately among Black youths, primarily because of their unique challenges.

African American Men

The difficulty for an African American young man to identify as bisexual is sometimes compounded by the Black church's teachings about homosexuality, which profoundly affect not only him but also his family and friends. The public-health and adolescent specialist Anthony Morgan and colleagues reported that a 16-year old interviewee, Anthony, had nightmarish difficulties as he wrestled with accepting a bisexual identity and then disclosing it to his family. Since his same-sex sexual debut at age 13, he realized he had both romantic and sexual attractions to girls and boys and then had sex partners of both sexes.[12] Because of the structural location of outlaw sexualities—those that are traditionally low on prestige and high on cultural stigma—multiattracted Black male youths have prodigious struggles as they make their decisions. Anthony did not want to face the potential loss of his own perceived masculinity and hence cultural standing by coming out.

In a small-scale study of 26 young-adult African American gay and bisexual men, predominantly from urban or suburban two-parent middle-class homes, Eric Dubé found that when compared with Latino, Asian American, and white peers, African American young men were the last to become aware of their same-sex sexuality (12 years old), to label their sexuality (almost 17 years old), and to disclose their sexuality (18 years old), especially to parents. They were, however, the earliest to have sex (14 years old) and a relationship (17 years old) with another boy. These data are consistent with other reports that sexual-minority African American male youths tend to engage in sex before labeling their sexual identity. The young men were not blind as to their sexual and romantic arousals but preferred not to label or disclose them. This is evident in the research of Haltom and colleagues with 70 African American youths (sexes combined). Whereas 30 percent privately realized their same-sex attractions prior to age 14 (the highest of the ethnic/racial groups), they had one of the lowest rates of public disclosure, 6 percent prior to age 14.[13] Whatever cultural or familial barriers the young men faced, they did not cause high levels of internalized homophobia or interfere with their ability to integrate either their ethnic or sexual identity. Dubé speculates that the "integration of ethnic and sexual identities is independent of disclosure and internalized homophobia. For many [African American] youths these dual identities may be distinct constructs that do not become integrated or are not even considered necessary to address." Indeed, given their circumstances, they may have made wise decisions about their sexual and romantic developmental trajectories.[14]

National data from the GSS, which has tracked social changes for nearly 50 years, found the prevalence rate for gay and bisexual identification and for same-sex behavior among Black males hovering around 5 percent or less—basically no change from previous years and considerably less than for Black females.[15] More Black men identify as gay than bisexual, the reverse of Black women. The caveat I add regarding same-sex identity and sex is that this is based on *self-reports*, and it is known that some significant percentage of Black males do not disclose these aspects of their lives to parents as well as researchers.

The social work professor Scott Edward Rutledge and colleagues illustrated this problem when they investigated how race is played out in African American communities regarding men on the down low. Several dynamics, unique to African American males, challenge these men not to acknowledge or report their same-sex sexuality.[16] For example, the social work lecturer Thomas Duffin interviewed 33 African American men on the down low who identify as straight, are married or date women, and regularly have sex with men. Though behaviorally bisexual, none identify as bisexual, including 22-year-old Desmond, who adopted a "trysexual" identity. Somewhat confused, his grandmother asked,

"What's trysexual?" Desmond responded, "That means I'm willing to try things that's sexual." "Trysexual" is a term used by other straight-identified African American men on the down low who have sex with men without violating straight norms. In their world, according to Duffin, a bisexual identity is so uncommon as to be nearly undetectable, for three major reasons:

1. The invisibility of bisexuality in their culture: "no history, no shared culture, no norms of behavior, not even a clear definition."
2. Cultural binary mandates: straight or gay with "the bisexual category folded into the homosexual category."
3. The stigmatization of being gay, and hence being bisexual, because it is considered feminine.

With "the effective blending of the two categories [homosexual, bisexual], bisexual identity was seen as undesirable."[17]

The sociologist Elijah Ward has a similar take, listing three explanatory modes for the secretive life of African American bisexual youth: religious beliefs, historical sexual exploitation, and race survival consciousness. "All are intimately related to the history of Black slavery" and to the endemic, corrosive racism in our country. Black homophobia is tied to this racism, primarily from the central role that Black churches have in Black culture. "Indeed, theologically-driven homophobia, aided by black nationalist ideology, supports a strong and exaggerated sense of masculinity within black communities that, along with homophobia, takes a significant but generally unexamined psychic and social toll on people's lives." This hypermasculinity as a living force within African American communities, according to Ward, is central because it emphasizes "strength, toughness, pride, control, poise and emotionlessness. Being cool is expressed in highly stylised yet individualised manners of walking, talking and dressing, and is the key to fitting in with other Black males, especially among youth." Black men, for their part, are to uphold conventional patterns of patriarchy, including sexism and heterosexism—manifested in relating to Black women with exploitation and sexual prowess (see Valerie's story later in this chapter). In part, this may be the result of underlying bitterness, spilling over to contempt and then rage toward white domination and generations of racism that continues to this day.[18]

Black youths, however, have other trajectories available to them if they decide to identify as bisexual. "Others described being less defined by their sexuality, but all described interpersonal pressure to conform to commonly held belief in dichotomous sexuality (e.g., gay or straight) and traditional masculine role expectations (e.g., produce children with a wife)." In the midst of family and religious pressures, Anthony found his way to bisexuality. Although his mother and sister said, "We love you for who you are, gay, straight or not, but you have to look to one person, God." That is, they left his sexuality to the judgment of God. Anthony said, "They were accepting me, but at the same time, they said they like wouldn't condone it. They said I couldn't have a boyfriend"—this probably because it would be too much of a public display.[19]

African American Women

Various media headlines covering the GSS data mirrored the following: "Young people—especially young black women—are more willing to explore their sexuality." The percentage of Black women doing so was nearly three times higher than it was a decade ago and twice what it is among white young-adult women.[20] Bridges and Moore relate a story about Amani, who was thinking about inviting another girl to the prom. Was this the result of trying to be cool or something about her sexuality that was heretofore unknown? The facts were clear to the authors that "Amani is among a growing number of young women of color who self-identify as bisexual or lesbian, which mirrors the progressive spirit of Black teen girls who are organizing and leading protests supporting the Black Lives Matter movement."[21] But, as best as I can determine, few people citing GSS data have given a convincing explanation for the increase over time in Black young-adult women reporting a bisexual identity. Joe Carter, an editor for the Gospel Coalition, believes the cause is pornography. "Viewing of same-sex pornography by black women is affecting their perceptions of same-sex behavior, leading them to increasingly identify with bisexuality."[22] The pornography source is implausible because the reverse causal chain makes more sense: Black women are watching more same-sex porn because they recognize their bisexuality.

A more likely reason is given by Bridges and Moore: "A traditional marriage isn't as necessary as it once was; since women have more educational and economic opportunities, they can afford to be pickier or, possibly, to explore same-sex relationships."[23] Related to this, they note that many potentially available Black men are in jail, and as a result, Black women are increasingly deciding to have children outside of marriage and are achieving progress in education, especially enrolling in college. Although this has not translated to being adequately represented in private-sector jobs, higher salaries, or leadership positions, it has opened them to independent lifestyles—including a bisexual one. Amani may have been motivated to invite a girl to the prom to test the position, "I might be bi." As Bridges and Moore conclude, "We can learn more about, and from, women like Amani about how sexuality intersects with gender, race, ethnicity and age to better understand the shifting landscape of sexual identities and contemporary systems of social inequality."[24] I agree, and Selena and Valerie have taken that step.

Selena

In Selena's high school, there were only three women of color. Selena identifies as multiracial, Afro-Caribbean, and Native American Indian, and it took her a long time to disclose her bisexuality to white friends. "It just is not the thing to do because it looks white European, and that is hard to deal with. I had to show them that I was Black first, like with the music, and then that I was bisexual." Far more difficult was coming out to her mother, who was disappointed that Selena told her godmother before her. "She was the most liberal—we had smoked cigarettes together and had not told Mom." Her mother was worried about AIDS and whether Selena would be hurt.

> She cried—all of this over a week. She was struggling with it—nothing extreme like kicking me out or disowning me. . . . She wants me to be a politician, and she was afraid this would hurt. She wants to protect me. I told her that I'm a Black woman. Can't I handle this one more thing? I'm trying to educate her. She's in a better place but not fully accepting yet. She keeps thinking that she failed some way, perhaps by not having a father around for me.

Selena has not disclosed to other extended family members or to her younger brother.

Valerie

Valerie, age 20, identifies as a Black Jamaican and is currently working to earn enough money to attend a "real college." She is the second youngest of eight children, growing up in an "urban ghetto" with a father who pieced together several part-time jobs and a housekeeping mother. Although Valerie was raised "Christian, apostolic, Bible to the tee," with head cover and long dresses, by age 15, she was developing her own spirituality.

> I was always questioning stuff—the loudmouth, the one who would tell all the family secrets. I questioned what was male/female, race, and not accept things as they are. I was tomboyish in skirts because I was never allowed to go outside. I did play with kids, but I never felt like I had to submit to males. I even beat up the class bully once because I knew that I could, and if not, my brothers would back me up. I mouthed off a lot.

Valerie was harassed daily by both girls and boys because she was smart and androgynous.

Very domineering in my relations with people—assertive, I get what I want, do what I want, don't fear men except for Black men, knock anyone out, don't have to give in to gender things like shaving my armpits (though I do for sexual feelings). My friends say I'm boyish, dykish. I'm feminine because I can really dress up with hats, long dresses, jewelry. . . . Girls are catty, stupid, annoying. Felt more connected to boys.

After one year of college, Valerie dropped out because the education at the community college was too low level.

Valerie is "just now trying to figure it all out." With only scarce childhood memories, one clear day-care recollection has stayed with her. "I wanted to move my cot next to this best friend, and one day I woke up from nap and wished I was napping with her." Valerie's attractions to females have been omnipresent.

I always claimed the right to judge girls and say if pretty or not. I'd judge my brothers' girlfriends, and they'd ask me, and I'd give them an evaluation. This was just before coming out to myself. I realized I could find females attractive, and this was because I was so smart, so I could see things from both sides. I'm like a gay man! I know what I like in a female and what males like in females. I think like a guy, like a fashion designer. . . . So never thought of these attractions as homosexual and not myself.

Things changed when Valerie, with her mother and youngest brother, escaped the father's abuse to live in a suburban apartment for one year. In her white school, it was "cool to be gay or bisexual." Realizing that she understood guys and was frustrated with girls, one day it hit her: "I'm bisexual! Oh shit! I thought I had let down my faith. God was testing me. Was I going to hell?" Valerie usually says "queer"; she doesn't like "lesbian" or "bisexual" because they reinforce categories. "I love women, but it doesn't mean that I don't also like guys."

The first person she came out to was her high school boyfriend.

He thought I was this goddess, and he was real cool. We hung out all the time, and we realized we were attracted to each other. We had a sexual and romantic relationship. I decided I've got to tell him, and I said I was bisexual. And he laughed, bugging out, and said I was so stupid because he was bisexual too! Had been fucking boys since he was 6.

[Next] another friend, and she was very supportive and said, "Don't let the religious stuff get in the way." My very best friend was this girl who loved women but couldn't act on it because she said God made her for guys, so can't act on it. She flipped out. She thinks it's sinful, and she's ashamed of it.

Developing a positive same-sex relationship, however, has been difficult for Valerie. The first was the year she was in college.

We met, and she fell all over me. I was this Black goddess to her. We were opposites: she, white, conservative, dairy farmer; and me, radical, Black, urban, blunt. I was not attracted to her, but she was to me. We acted out the romantic thing to try to make it work. [After a] romantic weekend, we moved very fast! When we got back, I moved in with her. Then we realized we were so different. She was not political, while I have to let everyone know that I'm queer. I had trouble being affectionate with her when around a Black or Latino man, and she couldn't understand this. . . . I just stopped putting energy into it. Ugh! Never good sex between us because she had terrible body image, and it would take her hours to get to the point where she might have an orgasm.

By contrast, Valerie is "very pro-sex": "I love to fuck all the time, probably because I was used by guys." Her first girl sex began when she was 8 years old, with three same-age cousins who initiated it by touching vaginas, kissing breasts, playing out boy-girl things, and penetrating with fingers. "This was just for pleasure, just sex, nice, necessary—not a gay thing, but knew I'd get in trouble if adults found out."

First consensual sex was with Edward, and this was not for sexual plea-sure but for attention. I felt honored that he wanted to use my body. This felt safe, cool, and was an okay trade-off. He protected me from my father and the boys on the street. This was our secret. It authenticated me. He would rub against me, and I would feel his penis. He came. I didn't even know what cum was, and once I asked him what all this sticky stuff was. I bragged about this to my friends. This was just the way sex was.

The first family member Valerie disclosed her bisexuality to was her youngest brother, who was "so cool about it." Valerie believes he might be gay himself. Next was her father. "I thought I'd add to his trauma. He flipped—flipped out. He didn't know what to say. Next morning, he yelled at me: 'Can't be religious and gay.'" They continued to talk, and he is no longer "flipping out but listening—tolerating it, but he still believes it's wrong." With her mother, Valerie wrote a long letter, "which scared her out of her freaking mind." Was Valerie trying to hurt her? Be rebel-lious and evil? "How can you do this to your brothers?" Her mother still claims that she can't sleep at night and that there's a hole in her heart. With Valerie's other siblings, she drops "little bombs," by email or face-to-face. "[One] wanted me to come over and have sex with his girlfriend so that he could join us. I refused."

Valerie is proud to be queer—helped by a college class that "blew away gender boundaries. Fuck the rules! The Bible does not account for lesbians or challenge the gender thing." More troubling is Black culture.

Because I'm a Black woman, I belong to Black men. It is their natural right, they think, to have access to us. He can touch our butt, and this is sanctioned by the Black community. This is perpetuated by rap music. We are their hoes, bitches, prizes. My sexuality challenges Black men directly.

Valerie's task will be a monumental one, but it is not a problem that Black men alone resolve—rather, it is a problem for all men regardless of race or ethnicity and for a culture in all of its manifestations that glorifies manliness and denigrates women. Valerie has taken one step by telling her story and expressing her need to hear and "see more people of color who are queer telling their stories." Aligning herself with other women and men who are equally committed to gender diversity regardless of race or biological sex is the colossal task at hand.

Latino/a Youths

The sociologists Héctor Carrillo and Amanda Hoffman remind us that culture's impact on sexual and romantic development cannot be universally applied to Latin cultures, as the experiences of youths I interviewed illustrate. To Cheryl, a 21-year-old Mexican American student, her ethnicity is critical: "Being Latina has a lot to do with it. Very rigid roles are defined—what a woman and a man are supposed to do. . . . No question, everyone gets married." By contrast, Alejandra, a 23-year-old Cuban American animal trainer, views her ethnicity as present but essentially irrelevant—to the point that she doesn't affiliate herself "with Hispanic groups because that is separatist." Even though individuals within racial or ethnic groups share commonalities, remarkable diversity characterizes each due to factors such as gender, generation, socioeconomic status, history of oppression, country of origin (e.g., from Mexico, Puerto Rico, Cuba, or South America), and, of course, life history. Despite the stereotype of Latin culture as a bastion of religiosity (Cheryl's family) and machismo (see Juan's story later in this section), the church's "influence on social policy is nothing like that of conservative Christian evangelicals in the United States, nor have the rising numbers of Pentecostals been obsessed with homosexuality like their conservative counterparts up north."[25]

Carrillo and Hoffman challenge the idea that commonly held beliefs, such as the traditional male *activo/pasivo* phenomenon of sexual relations, are solely Latino phenomena. The notion that bottoming is "feminine" and therefore more "gay" reflects what is detestable in many misogynist societies and thus has broad purchase across time and place beyond Latin cultures. Besides, modern men of Mexican origin have models available to them other than a heavily gendered style of male homosexuality. Latin young-adult women and men are now less restricted by traditional mandates to marry and raise a family, in part because the power of the Catholic church to affect sexual and romantic attitudes and beliefs has been diluted by recent counterforces such as globalization and immigration. As a result, not only Mexican youths but also Puerto Rican and others of Latin origin in the United States are more willing to adopt nontraditional sexual and romantic trajectories.[26]

The epidemiologist William Jeffries cautions us to be aware of our preconceived white notions about ethnicity, especially interracial and mixed-ethnic individuals. For example, which parts of Selena reflect her African, Caribbean, or Indian heritage? How is it possible to have singular expectations about ethnic and racial influences on her developmental trajectory? Jeffries applies this to Latino men: "It is clear that the 'one drop' rule—that even minuscule levels of homosexual behaviors or attractions constitute one as homosexual—which defines masculinity and sexuality in the United States does not necessarily apply to men of Latin American origin."[27] The South American–born Juan rejects this equation, for personal reasons, though he remains heavily under the power of Latin gender expectations. By contrast, though Puerto Rican Roberto is aware of the same machismo and antigay forces, he says they have little effect on him. Each, however, recognizes that he has more than a drop of same-sex sexuality and femininity and that it is okay to be bisexual.

Eric Dubé reports that the Latin young men he interviewed, compared to other ethnic groups, were relatively early in becoming aware of their same-sex attractions (8 years old), engaging other males in sex (15 years old), labeling themselves as gay or bisexual (15 years old), and disclosing to others (16 years old). He attributes the early onset of these milestones to several factors, including an intensification of gender roles in Latin society. Because the boys from an early age were less likely to conform to traditional gender roles, their same-sex attractions were brought into sharp relief; here was another way in which they felt culturally different.[28]

The difference between the perspectives of Carrillo and Hoffman and of Dubé regarding the degree to which gender roles are traditionally rigid and hence influential in the timing and expression of developmental milestones of Latino youths appears large and difficult to resolve. Perhaps most importantly, Dubé was writing over 20 years earlier and thus reflects earlier generations of Latin culture. Also unknown are the ethnic-group composition and time living in the United States of his research participants, and these and other characteristics matter. My guess is that both reports are true because of the relatively wide diversity among Latin young adults, which is frequently neglected.

The adolescent specialist Omar Jamil and colleagues note this diversity in the developing relationship between the various ways in which ethnic and sexual identities interconnect. They differ, seemingly "independent of each other because neither process [ethnic identity, sexual identity] was referenced in the development of the other." Whereas ethnic identity development focuses on becoming aware of one's ethnic and cultural heritage, "sexual identity development involve[s] finding one's own personally relevant sexual orientation label and connecting to that community."[29] Clearly, no one developmental trajectory is inclusive within or across ethnicity and sexuality. Juan's story is a familiar one: while openly accepting his Chilean heritage, he feels that it conflicts with his long-standing, misinterpreted erotic attractions. He cannot be gay, but he eventually accepts that he might be bisexual by splitting his sexual and romantic attractions.

Juan

Juan, age 20, lived with his parents and older brother in Chile until they relocated to the United States when he was 9 years old. Now a college junior, Juan has a strong Spanish accent and referenced his Chilean heritage several times during the interview. Well dressed for a Saturday morning, he had coordinated the color gray with his shoes, socks, skinny jeans, and tee-shirt stripes. He said that he intends to join a gym and work out because he believes women will be more interested in him if he's muscular. Up front, Juan told me, "I'm nerdy and love math and science." Juan described himself as an introvert, low on curiosity and sensation seeking, and average on masculinity; he likes to be well dressed, clean, and organized. He's not into sports but is masculine: "I think I can be really cold. Stereotypical guys don't express their feelings, and I tend not to express them."

Puberty instigated Juan's first sexual awareness on a family trip to Key West, where he first saw naked people "flaunting their sexuality." He was especially impressed by the male mannequins. "They have big bulges for some reason." Afterward, he goggled on his computer "underwear bulges," not, he said, because of sexual interest but "interest in the male body." The search led to his first masturbatory orgasm, which left him feeling "horrible regret" because Catholicism teaches not to waste sperm that isn't intended to conceive children. Watching porn was also problematic because it led him to fear that he might be bisexual.

> It certainly helped me realize that I am interested in both sexes, and I realized there was something called "bisexual." . . . A lot of people say pornography dehumanizes. I guess for me it has done that in regard to male-on-male relationships. I never feel romantically interested in men. . . . I just kind of see the male body as a sexual object.

In high school, Juan had crushes on an Asian American girl and a Hispanic boy. He felt normal with the girl crush because it was culturally expected; the boy had a nice athletic body, but Juan told no one. "Well, I mean, first of all, both of us are Hispanic, and that's our culture. It's more taboo." Over three-quarters of his adolescent sexual fantasies involved men, and this increased during young adulthood even as his romantic crushes were overwhelmingly directed to women. All potential romantic, but not sexual, interest in guys was either denied or minimized.

Once he begins dating women, he believes his waning sexual desires for them will be correspondingly ignited. This does not imply that his homoerotic desires will subsequently vanquish. He wants attractive men (and their big bulges) in his life because they give him such pleasure.

> I think there's a lot of people who would be at some point willing to try something—let's say a guy with another guy. No one wants to deal with that kind of stigma. I think everyone has a curiosity. . . . If you initiate with the wrong person, it would be bad. I am not gay, and even though I have an inkling to try something, I don't want to seem that way.

Sexually, Juan struggles with his perception that many of his friends believe he is "repressed and gay": "But that's not the case. There are feelings for women I can't let go of." He rated himself as "bisexual leaning gay" but wants to be "bisexual leaning straight." Romantically, he's "straight," which is what he wants. Although having a romantic relationship with a man can't be in the making, he later developed "special feelings" for Sam, his workout partner. Will Juan find the right man to fall in love with, or will he find the right woman who will create the intensity of sexual arousal that he longs for? He "really likes" Asian women (and men) and sees his future with an Asian woman in a sexually monogamous relationship. He believes it's culturally permissible to have guy attractions as long as he does not allow himself to fall in love or be connected with the "pure sex" homosexual world. That world is "a bit seedy or unhealthy and potentially hazardous." Juan doesn't want to be associated with "the flaming or flamboyant homosexual," who churns his stomach. Without the pecs to be accepted by homosexuals, he said, "there is no reason for me to come out and risk stigmatizing myself." At the end of the interview, Juan sought advice on how to ask a potential girlfriend out and what he should do if either of them wants sex.

Six months after the interview, I received an email from Juan requesting "just to talk." He's been dating Cindy for several months. She is a traditional Chinese woman who is willing to make out (on weekends) but will go no further. When Juan tried to touch her breasts, she said it was too soon. When making out, he has frequent erections, but nothing is "ever done with them." Cindy is a virgin and intends to remain so until marriage, which frustrates Juan, but it also relieves him of the onus of initiating sex. With Cindy, he gets fluttering feelings and becomes light-headed; he's in love with Cindy.

The next fall, I received another request from Juan to talk, and we did for nearly two hours. He wanted me to know that he has been working out and has developed upper-body muscles and abs. After apologizing several times for rambling, he said needed to know the difference be-tween a friendship and a romantic relationship, why a drop of gayness makes you not straight but gay, and why straight guys have all the power. Also, Cindy ended their relationship because Juan was spending too much time with his new best friend, Sam. Juan wanted to go all the way with Cindy, or at least make out more, but she always had her studies. He loved cuddling with her; but his erections had become less frequent, and now she never responds to his texts.

What Juan wanted most to talk about, however, was Sam, a Korean American he met in the research lab. They spend nearly every day work-ing out in the gym, with erections. When with Sam, he said, "It'd be sticking straight up." Juan is motivated to work out to make himself more attractive to Sam and to spend more time with him. When together, Sam always talks about hot guys, the size of his penis (which he said takes two hands to hold), "butt sex," and the physique of guys, which leads Juan to believe that Sam might be bisexual. When Sam asked, Juan told him that he's bisexual—the first person he disclosed to. Both are willing to experiment but, for Sam, only if they drink first. Juan emphasized that he's not in love because "Sam is a bit crazy." I asked if he had a Sam crush, and he noncommittally shrugged.

The next I heard from Juan, he was 23 years old and in graduate school. He voluntarily described his sexual orientation as "mostly gay" and his romantic orientation as "nearly always romantically attracted to women." Over three-quarters of his sexual attractions and fantasies involve males, while nearly 100 percent of his crushes and romantic re-lationships are directed toward females—nearly identical to the initial interview. He's still a virgin (no sex with Sam). In the future, he wants equal attractions to both sexes.

> I expressed my feelings [to Sam], and he did not reciprocate. But the friendship still maintained. Throughout that year and beyond, I came to realize my feelings for that guy, in particular, were not exclusively of a sexual nature due to the long periods of time we spent hanging out. More specifically, he could be very close, not physically but in the attention devoted to me.
>
> When I see a guy who's got big muscles (a well-developed body), my eyes certainly dilate, and my attention is caught. . . . However, in think-ing about what exactly attracts me or what I would do with such a guy, my mind comes to a stop. Sure, sexual intercourse would be great, but beyond that, nothing more. . . . I would not enjoy romantic aspects, such as spending time together and being affectionate with each other.
>
> I can't pinpoint what it is that makes me only desire a romantic relation with a woman, perhaps Hollywood or the fact that the overwhelming amount of literature is about heterosexual couples. . . . I noticed when I think about women I'm attracted to, sexual fantasies with them also arise, but my masturbatory habits are still based on 100 percent homosexual con-tent. Nevertheless, I imagine once I am dating a woman again, my sexual drive for women will increase again, not to a fully 50-50 level.

Juan's journey is not over. He worries about the reactions of his par-ents and friends and how to mesh his deep-seated cultural biases about masculinity and marriage with his sexual and romantic desires for both sexes. Men are Juan's "eye candy"—his pupil-dilation scores were decid-edly male oriented—even as he pursues women for romance, sex, and, hopefully, marriage and babies. In four interviews over the course of three years, the themes remained the same: intense sexual interest in men and intense romantic interest in women. Juan continues to struggle with these issues, inhibiting his growth toward the bisexual life that a part of him wants.

Alejandra

Alejandra was raised Catholic in a middle-class Florida home with two sisters. The source of her most difficult life decisions has been having a Cuban father and a white mother, resulting in a split allegiance between the two. Although Alejandra is intellectually committed to her mother's social and politically progressive views, emotionally she is connected to her father's family and their "Cuban passion." In deference to both, Alejandra is bilingual and resists being "militantly Hispanic." She thus honors her father's Hispanic, conservative background without forsaking her romantic and sexual attractions to women, which her mother encourages her to pursue. Alejandra considers herself to be more lesbian than bisexual and more butch than femme—but is not totally in any one sexual or gender camp.

During Alejandra's childhood and adolescence, she knew and even celebrated her physical, behavioral, and personality gender misalignment with her biological sex.

In first or second [grade], I was tall and had short hair with no waist. So once in the mall, my older sister introduced me to others as her younger brother. . . . Once puberty hit, then no problem. In elementary, I played some softball, and in junior high, I did track (sprinter) and basketball (on intramural team). In high school, I did track, doing the shot put. I could have been better, but I did not want to devote that much time to practice. I'd just show up for the meets.

No one has been surprised when I've told them I like women. On a 10-point scale, I'm a 7, a little closer to the masculine side—masculine in that I'm assertive, say and do what I want, don't like dresses, have short hair, felt more in tune with my father at times—helping him out around the house to move things because of my weight and strength. I'm not a huggy-type person. Feminine sometimes, like domestic, like cooking.

Since kindergarten, Alejandra has always had strong relationships with other girls, which felt normal because other girls her age had them as well. Then, during her preteen years, she recognized that her feelings for her loyal best friend was a crush—but, again, her friends appeared to have similar feelings. Alejandra just assumed that she was straight, until her young-adult years, when sexual encounters with men felt like sexual assaults. The first was sophomore year in college, while at a party: "Dancing with a guy I didn't know that well. He was a great dancer, and he was kissing me and feeling my breasts. He wanted me to go to his room. I said no and left. It was like I had been violated." The second encounter was worse, about a year later, and again at a party.

> This guy, I didn't like him physically or personality-wise. He saw me on the couch practically passed out and started kissing me. He had my shirt and bra off and was unzipping my pants. I was lucid enough to know that the way to stop it was to give him a hand job. I did, and then he left. . . . I was violated by him.

Alejandra gave herself "one last chance": "because somewhere in my brain, I felt like this was a last-ditch effort." This guy, too, was "Catholic, Hispanic, very conservative, graduate student, a virgin, and a big mama's boy": "We had things in common, like beer, discussion of religion, moral values. . . . I was trying to like him, but I was suffering over this . . . because it was with a guy."

During this time, Alejandra never questioned her heterosexuality because conservative Cuban culture had no alternative. Sex with men might be bad, but this had little to do with sexual orientation. In college, a number of Alejandra's female friends were attracted to women, and together they had "lots of fun, dating, dancing, really good times": "It was a good path for me. I was attractive to women, and if not, then we could become good friends. I felt more confident with women than with men. I read a lot in women's studies, and I built my resources." Then, a woman entered Alejandra's life, and it was love and first sex with a woman—within hours of meeting.

> I initiated it. It was great, and it went very far. Our parents were gone, so she stayed over the first week. No oral sex the first time—started with lots of kissing. She was doing most of the things because she had her period. I had orgasm, but she did not. Later we talked about this because she said that she seldom had with her female partners because she was always the one who did and not received. We changed that because I felt this was unfair. I felt I had really come into my own. I'm a very sexual person, love to dance, appreciate music, enjoy life, and this had never really all come together with guys.

They talked and emailed every day, but there was a lot of baggage in their relationship, and the seriousness of it bothered both of them. After breaking up, they remained friends, but, Alejandra said, "We left things open-ended. If we were ever in the same place and were not seeing anyone, then we'd be together."

Whatever Alejandra is, she has always been positive about it. "I have no horrible coming-out story. It's because of my personality. I'm confident and feel good about who I am." She has explicitly shared her current committed relationship with her liberal mother.

> I told her that I was dating this woman, and she said she was happy for me and that it was very fine. I told her that it was very strong and that I didn't know if it would happen again. She was very supportive, almost casual, not shocked. She had suspected it. She said, "You don't have to identify yourself, but you do have a choice if you want to be monogamous." That I was shocked by!

Alejandra has never explicitly told her father because, given his Cuban heritage, she said, "It would have been awkward for both of us." However, she added, "[He] welcomes my girlfriend with open arms."

Asian American Youths

Laura, a 21-year-old Chinese American, told me that there is "a term in Chinese which means filial piety—loyalty to parents and do what they want you to do, to be selfless": "Lots of my decisions in life are to fulfill this. Feel guilty when I do not. . . . I owe this to them." Although Laura's view has some cachet across Asian American communities, cultural diversity within Asian American communities spans an array of ethnic groups and national identities living in the United States. Asian American communities include Chinese, Japanese, Korean, Taiwanese, Filipino, and South Asian cohorts. Within each ethnic group, what most influences the trajectories of multiattracted youths and young adults include immigrant generation, language spoken at home, racial identity, and proportion of English speakers in the neighborhood. Tensions between modernity and more conservative, traditional Asian cultural norms (some version of the collectivistic versus individualistic orientation) can be overtly expressed or simply endure as an underlying current. The degree to which one's sexual and romantic life is affected depends, as it does for Latino/a and African American youths, on mainstream acculturation and the larger globalization context.[30]

In Dubé's study, Asian American gay and bisexual young men reported an early awareness of their same-sex attractions (9 years old) but a late onset of sex with males (18 years old), about a year before first disclosure. Dubé gives three reasons for this pattern:

1. Asian American families often adopt a code of silence on the topic of sex, with an implicit understanding that sex should be delayed until marriage or adulthood.
2. Asian American youths frequently report feeling obliged to carry the family name and to produce offspring, which provides a powerful motive to suppress same-sex behavior.
3. Same-sex sexual activities are often perceived by Asian Americans to be consummate with a gay identity. By abstaining from

sexual involvement, they eschew identifying as gay—an act that is thought to bring shame to the youth's immediate and extended family and community.

One downside to the delay in the onset of sexual activity for these youths is a prolonged period of questioning the meaning of their same-sex attractions. The consequence is higher levels of internalized homophobia, leading to "feelings that their same-sex attractions are reprehensible" and hence remaining closeted to family and community members.[31]

Ian

On entering the interview room, Ian, age 18, appeared to be a product of his generation. He had a modern haircut with one earring, wore a V-neck tee-shirt and faded jeans with appropriate kneehole, wore flips, carried a water bottle, held a clipboard close to his chest, and turned on an iPod as soon as the interview was over. He seldom referenced his family's Indonesian origin. Ian appreciates his feminine side: "I like fashion. I like clothes. I like organic food and healthy stuff. . . . I sometimes like acting like a gay stereotype when I am having fun with friends." One guy in high school "wasn't necessarily out, but he was very flamboyant and whatnot. He seemed very comfortable with that. And no one bothered him. He was actually quite popular."

When Ian came out to his mother as bisexual, she said, "Oh no! Those actual people don't exist." Telling his father was more difficult: "[He has a] traditional idea of passing on the family because I am the only son in the family—the whole disappointment." His parents have adjusted, readily accept him, and rarely discuss Ian's "problem."

Laura, Su-Wei, Hei-Ran, and Amy

Several young women I interviewed identified as Asian American, with family connections rooted in East Asia, South Asia, Southeast Asia, or the Pacific Islands. All identified as some version of bisexual, though several thought they might be closer to lesbian by sexual orientation. They hesitated to identify as such or as queer or nonbinary because of their culture and, specifically, their parents' certain objections. Nearly all struggled with a critical issue: whether to come out to their families and communities. Most took the position of one young woman born in Hong Kong:

> My ethnicity held me back. My parents are conservative, and sex is not talked about and in general not much discussion in my household. They're immigrants, and I'm much less Chinese than them. There are no Asian sexual-minority role models. . . . She would say to go the easier way and go with boys. I haven't told her because no need to stress her. We get along pretty well, and I tell her a lot, but I use my judgment.

The anticipated conflict also includes gender issues connected with sexuality. Being something other than straight connotes rejecting traditional feminine gender roles. One young woman was most explicit: "To be femme because Indian culture values beauty in appearance, food, dance." Asian culture, conservative religion, and traditional gender roles thwart or severely delay attempts to disclose to parents.

College senior Laura grew up in an urban suburb and is out to several people, including her older sister. She has no plans to tell either of her parents because of the Chinese influence.

> They want me to grow up and be married [to a Chinese boy] and to have Chinese children, and I don't want to let them down. I identify myself as Chinese American, and it is my biggest source of discrimination. [Mother] had trouble even when [I was] dating the Jewish boy—not have her approval. When I tell her, she'll say that I decided to do this, and I can just as easily decide not to. I have no plans to tell her, but I will eventually. I need to do this. Maybe I'll wait until I have a job and am more independent.

Despite Laura anticipating the negative reactions of her parents, she believes they would never withdraw either emotional or financial support. Laura judges coming out to her parents to be more daunting than coming out as bisexual to her collegiate community. "Comparing being Chinese American with being a bisexual is that I can hide being a bisexual and can choose when to not hide it, so am in more control. This makes it easier."

Su-Wei's parents were born in Taiwan and carry many Taiwanese values. Although Su-Wei has a close relationship with her mother, she sees "no point of telling her": "unless I had a very serious relationship and wanted to settle down with her." Her mother would be furious and disgusted, while her father would be clueless.

> He doesn't care about the world around him. He only knows what Mom tells him. He is the scientist type. He knows it is bad but doesn't care. He would just ignore the subject and wouldn't know how to handle it. Not as close to him. He watches over my studies, and we talk science and engineering things, and he tells bad jokes. We don't talk about anything serious. He'd say, "Go ask your mother."

By contrast, her younger brother—very much a product of youth culture—would accept it. "It would be odd for him, and he'd be uncomfortable but eventually okay."

Recently, Su-Wei returned from an Asian LGBTQ conference with an analysis of Asian queers: "All of them were so sexually repressed. I was the one who was out. The Asian community is tight, and I've managed to escape it. It is hard to come out if in it." Su-Wei fears that an Asian she knows will see her with the queer community on campus and tell her parents. She said she must be internally racist because she's very judgmental about her Chinese friends. "I'm too wild for them. I accept them but don't hang out with them."

For Hei-Ran's Korean Christian family, the issue is less about ethnicity than religion, which has prevented her from disclosing her sexuality. Her mother, born in Korea, is very religious and blames herself for everything.

"Like it's her fault. It would kill her—never forgive herself or me. She'd be shocked. . . . It is wrong because Bible says it's wrong, and send me to therapy." Hei-Ran's father is distant, works 12-hour days. "[He] would not like it but would not disown me." He would simply put it out of his mind.

Amy, an only child in a Chinese American home, is the exception in that she risked telling her parents, perhaps because they were born in the United States, are in professional jobs, and have more exposure to American culture. Amy had been a source of curiosity to her friends in a nearly all-white Long Island community; she learned to adapt early on when her friends would touch her nose and say, "How flat." Smart, independent, and feminine, Amy disclosed to her mother on the drive home from her first college break, freshman year.

> I was fed up with her not knowing me. I told her I was bi in attractions and behavior but lesbian for political reasons. She asked if I was sure and what did this mean—that I wanted to be a boy? She resigned herself and was a little angry. She outed me to Dad. I am very close to her, and so I had to tell her. I felt better because I don't like to hide things. She didn't believe me for the longest time because I had boyfriends, which to her discredited my same-sex romantic relationships.

Things did not go much better with her father. Though he knew it was not an easy choice, he would support and love her.

> He told me it was my business and not to talk about it. He'd like to sweep it under the rug. He is just uncomfortable with it—doesn't want to talk about it. . . . I am close to him, but I can't tell him about my romantic or sexual life. He would not understand such things, and I don't like his views on such things. We can share a lot about careers, ideas, but not about personal things.

Whether working with their cultural context or hometown community or against it, nearly all Asian American young adult interviewees could not ignore it. This is not, however, merely an Asian ethnic or racial issue. White, Latino/a, and African American youths also have a cultural context in which they live, whether economic, class, or regional location. I next take up the impact of regional and social class, because on this topic, there is at least limited research.

14

Bi in the Country

Never thought about it in rural West Virginia. All I knew
was that it was wrong and that I wouldn't be it because was
not the kind of person I was.
—Ida, age 20, white, student

Living on a farm and having limited access to economic resources handicapped Toby and Melissa as they coped with the stress of being neither
straight nor gender conforming. In this, they exemplified the findings
of the sociologists Mieke Thomeer and Corinne Reczek, who mined the
national GSS database. Thomeer and Reczek found sparse economic
resources to be a "central driver of reported happiness disadvantages
for bisexual-identified people, for those with lifelong both-sex partners [read: bisexuals], and for those who transitioned to different-sex
partners [perhaps once bisexual]."[1] Complicating matters is that many
bisexuals living in rural settings are invisible or unwilling to disclose
their sexual status; thus, they are difficult to recruit. Bisexuals who are
out may be unwilling or unable to participate in research studies because
they lack the access, time, or transportation to respond to research
requests. Given that few sex researchers are familiar with rural life, they
have little knowledge about how to overcome these barriers, and thus
they fail to reach rural sexual-minority young people.

What research exists is chiefly speculative, usually based on small-
scale qualitative research from sociological, anthropological, and gender/
sexuality studies perspectives. The conclusion generally reached is that
geographic region and socioeconomic class, separately and in combination, affect the emergence and expression of sexual and romantic trajectories of bisexual, pansexual, fluid, and nonbinary young people. Indeed,

rurality and poverty are so intertwined that it is difficult at times to separate their effects. Although bisexual individuals live in all regions of the United States, the stereotype that sexual minorities migrate to large urban areas has some historical truth. Thus, bisexual research has traditionally focused on large cities because that's where the gay people are. Taking up residence in metropolitan areas gives "sexual outlaws" the anonymity of the masses, avails them of more social and community groups catering to their needs, increases the possibility of finding sexual and romantic partners, and feels safer to them, given the more progressive and accepting spirit in urban areas. The reverse is assumed to be the case for bisexuals living in rural areas, who are more likely than heterosexuals to live in poverty, especially women-headed households and African Americans in same-sex couples. Limited evidence suggests that bisexuals are unwilling to move away from their rural base, perhaps the consequence of having greater ability to hide their sexuality and thus being less likely to experience the brunt of prevailing rural gender norms.[2]

The sociologists Chris Wienke and Gretchen Hill present the conventional depiction of sexual minorities living in rural areas, in contrast not to rural straight individuals but to urban-dwelling sexual minorities. Given the traditional culture of most rural areas, sexual-minority residents experience greater social isolation from other gay people and from the larger rural community. But do these conditions result in feelings of hopelessness, despair, and self-loathing? Supposedly, yes, because the social climate in rural areas is generally hostile toward gay people, with negative attitudes toward homosexuality and bisexuality, few protections with regard to housing and employment, and more acts of verbal and physical violence that harm sexual-minority youths. Without social networks, visible gay neighborhoods, organizations (businesses, health programs, bars), school clubs, and publicly funded and supported community groups typically found in larger cities, it is difficult for teenagers and young adults to achieve pride in their nonstraightness.

Building on these characterizations, Wienke and Hill tested these ideas with the question, Is rural life more detrimental to gay people's well-being than urban life is? They used nationally representative data (NORC) and found little evidence for the conventional wisdom and previous scholarly research that painted a negative picture of rural gay life. Rural living is "no less conducive to gay people's wellbeing, as re-flected in self-reports of happiness, health, and work satisfaction, than are urban areas." One critical benefit is open spaces, providing "places of refuge from the pressures and problems associated with being different" and, for women, places of "safety, freedom from men, and other ben-efits unattainable in the city." Another possibility is that well-adjusted sexual-minority adults do not move from rural to urban areas but stay non-city-dwellers, and those urbanities who move to rural areas do so because they have a positive sense of self.[3]

How do we explain these discrepancies with traditional perspectives—and with those of Melissa and Toby? Several problems limit the usefulness of the NORC findings. One, in the data set, sexual status was determined by self-reports of same-sex behavior, disregard-ing sexual and romantic attractions, sexual identity, sexual-minority virgins, and those who are fearful of reporting same-sex behavior. Two, bisexuals could not be uniquely distinguished from lesbians and gays because the behavioral assessment did not consider those who have sex with both sexes. Three, given when data were collected (1988–2006), most Zoomers and Millennials were excluded, preventing us from knowing whether sexual-minority youths were more likely than adults to escape negative rural influences. Yet, it is no secret from the stories of youths that rural school culture can be brutal to its members who are not straight.

For example, James Morandini and colleagues have examined the role that geography has on the problematic construction and mainte-nance of sexual-minority individuals in Australia. In the sample, those who were living in rural-remote areas (mean age 31) tended to conceal their sexuality from friends, were highly concerned with disclosing their sexuality, and had little LGB-community involvement and few LGB friends. Compared to their inner-metropolitan-area colleagues, gay and bisexual men, but not women, had higher levels of internalized homophobia, with the primary culprit being toxic masculinity, the "emphasis placed on traditional notions of masculinity within rural communities and the severe social sanctions (e.g. bullying and social exclusion) facing men in these communities who are perceived to transgress gender roles."[4]

These findings might well apply to the US heartland. We know that living with multiple sexual and romantic attractions in a rural area differs for women and men, in part because of rural cultural gender expectations.

Rural Women

In the book *Out in the Country*, the communication professor and MacArthur fellow Mary Gray explores being young, queer, and a rural resident. She had difficulty recruiting young women to talk to her because they "were often too busy between work, family, and school commitments." In an email correspondence, Gray elaborated that girls had "the double-bind of being expected to stay closer to home to care for family, having more economic opportunities than their brothers (e.g., home healthcare and retail), but still needing to comply to expectations of normative femininity (they could be less feminine but still were expected to like boys)." That is, they were to be both feminine and masculine, and it was easier being bisexual than lesbian because they were given more latitude if they liked girls *and* boys.[5]

Some adult lesbians in rural areas are highly visible, especially those who return to their hometown with children in tow. Perhaps they are there to care for aging parents or to live as a couple on a farm. They are frequently perceived as more "butch" than local women, a potential positive given that masculinity is highly valued in rural communities. As such, the butch women are given greater leeway to meet the work demands of rural life. Wienke and Hill propose a selection bias in the mental health profile of sexual-minority women who live in rural rather than urban areas. These women may have moved there because of their same-sex marriage, the lower cost of living, and a preferred location to raise children.[6] In addition, several recent media accounts regarding lesbian couples living in rural West Virginia, Texas, and Tennessee have noted that locals commonly adopt a "live and let live" philosophy—two women living together might be less threatening to the rural mentality than two men doing the same. Of course, discretion with regard to publicly touching each other is in order, and an emphasis on family is usually an acceptable reason for tolerance—or blindness.[7] Whether these realities and stereotypes apply to bisexual women who do not live with a same-sex partner or are not butch remains unknown.

The young women I interviewed had fairly consistent negative reactions to growing up in a rural area. They found it "boring, alcoholic," and "very homophobic," which kept them "from realizing it [sexuality] sooner." However, those same conditions could also be positive if they gave the women strength, as it was for one young woman: "Made me want to be a role model for my community." She came out "as okay as possible" in order to inspire other queer, rural girls.

Rural Men

In *Still Straight: Sexual Flexibility among White Men in Rural America*, the sociologist Tony Silva underscores the risks a man encounters if he challenges the centrality of heterosexuality and normative masculinity that is especially prevalent in conservative rural areas.[8] In his article on "bud-sex," Silva notes that "the strong link between heterosexuality and masculinity is especially evident in rural areas, which are often more conservative than urban locales."[9] A rural man is instructed on how to keep within his race and social class; and if he is sexually attracted to other men, then rural norms presume that he is necessarily effeminate, and thus his compromised masculinity will evoke negative reactions within himself and from others. Young men I interviewed noted these deadly stereotypes to be avoided at all costs: "flamboyant in gestures and speaking, more feminine aspects, well dressed"; "hand gestures, voice, and ways of causing body to move, personality and how they act in social situations, the tension like they're feeling something they can't express"; and "aware of fashion, lispy speech, feminine ways of movement."

A rural man does his upmost to internally censor these behaviors, distances himself from any man who displays these characteristics, and, instead, connects with straight men who are particularly rugged in their masculinity so as to be associated with those traits. This last daunting obligation implies that a man, regardless of his sexuality, is expected to live up to cultural standards of gender expression, especially physical labor, toughness, and stoicism: "For rural men with marginalized sexualities, normative rural masculinity is particularly important because it provides them a degree of social acceptance. Many rural gay men even distance themselves from feminine gay men." To comply, a rural man must negotiate among limited options, especially if he wants to engage in bud-sex, belong to heterosexual culture, and disidentify from gay culture. To assist his well-being, he bonds with other men through friends-with-benefits arrangements. Although such a couple is not a romantic pair, they are not necessarily emotionless toward each other.[10]

Of course, rural masculinity is not static but is becoming more flexible across generations. Several men whom Silva interviewed privately reported that they are not totally straight but are "straight-leaning bisexual" or "straight and bisexual." Nearly all are sexually attracted to both sexes, but they publicly identify as straight as a means to strengthen their normative masculinity in rural settings. It is noteworthy in these discussions that no distinction is made between being gay or bisexual because only two lifestyles are recognized: straight and gay. Whether the explicit acknowledgment of bisexuality would change the nature of the discussion is unknown.[11]

Rural Areas in Transition

Because of the generally conservative nature of rural communities, men and women with any degree of same-sex attractions might well decide that the best recourse is to conceal their sexuality or to move to an urban area. To do either, however, might reduce or deny them hope of receiving understanding and support from family and friends or having connections with other sexual-minority individuals or communities, which are, in any case, frequently absent or invisible in rural areas. The psychologist Jennifer Stroup and colleagues examined the challenges and barriers for 41 young bisexual students adjusting to college life in rural areas. In addition to typical adolescent concerns when transitioning to college, sexual-minority teenagers face negotiating their sexuality with roommates and deciding "when, whether, and where to disclose their sexual orientation." Not disclosing could result in forgoing social support, but disclosing could lead to stigma and marginalization, which then elevate psychological distress.[12] In Stroup's study, about half of the respondents experienced discrimination based on their sexuality; this level exceeded what they received because of their gender, physical appearance, or religion. To combat the discrimination, the writer Zachary Zane lists five absolutes:

1. Establish support groups specific to bisexuals.
2. Dispel negative stereotypes associated with being bisexual.
3. Increase bi-visibility so that closeted bisexual learn they are not alone.
4. Increase the number of LGBTQ safe spaces in rural areas to foster a sense of community.
5. Fight against conservative organizations advocating anti-LGBTQ positions.[13]

Despite potential complications, all but 14 percent of Stroup's bisexual youths believed they could be "true to self." They felt accepted—which raises the possibility that despite instances of discrimination, bisexual youths are sufficiently strong to be their authentic self on a rural college campus.

The writer Samantha Allen has a promising outlook on bisexuality in rural America. In the heartland, "public opinion on L.G.B.T. people is finally turning a corner, not just on the coasts but between them as well."

These pockets of acceptance have largely occurred because Millennials are moving south and west and, in the process, helping to change local attitudes. Whether Allen's optimistic analysis that attitudes are changing rapidly in conservative states and that "this country's bright queer future is already here, hiding where too few of us care to travel" proves accurate remains to be seen—perhaps there is change, but is it to the point that rural areas are oases of queer and gender acceptance?[14] Mary Gray is also confident because the internet and the growing number of community resources available to queer youth continue to expand and hence negate the typical attitude that "rural youth lack the resources, capacity, and support to actively foster difference in the seeming homogeneity of their small town."[15]

Toby

Toby saw the interview advertised at the restaurant where he works, and for $20, he wanted to participate. Age 20, a part-time waiter and part-time student at a community college, Toby would clearly impress the fashionable with his intriguing appearance of matched/mismatched colors and fabrics that he pulled off without looking cartoonish. He definitely had the "artistic look," with a notable tattoo, several piercings, and longish, stylistic hair that had been green not so long ago. As a high school sophomore, he "was the first who was dying their hair freaky colors, and this was unique and exciting": "I like green hair. I told my close friends that I liked to be set apart." This was clearly true in his rural, upstate area where he attended a consolidated school in which he feared the negative repercussions meted out to those who failed manly tests. Toby "got grief" because he excelled in soccer, considered a nonmasculine sport, and because he color-coordinated his attire—two strikes against him. The lethal third strike would be any exposure of his slight degree of homoeroticism. As a child, others called him "fag"; but he felt that wasn't right then or now, though he has his doubts, and this bothers him immensely.

Toby's way of coping with his rural culture and leaving jocks behind was to make short films and videos with his best friend, Rip, and to find friends in the drama club. These activities did not, however, fit Toby's imagination of masculinity. He wanted more upper-body strength so that others would know that he isn't anything other than straight. Indeed, he reassured me early in the interview, "I'm really straight, and there have been no changes in that. I'm not gay."

After several child and adolescent romantic flings, the real thing happened for Toby freshman year of high school with a senior girl in his biology class. Within two months, they were dating, and in a note passed during class, she asked if he was sexually active. He wrote back, "I want to be."

> She grabbed my hand and put it under her shirt. I caressed her, and she put her hands down my pants. Parents were in the living room. . . . I was nervous—mostly exhilarating. It was the only time, and then we broke up. I wanted something else but not with her but with someone else. I had a view of myself as being more sexually active.

Sophomore year, Toby met a girl online. They hung out over the summer, beginning a three-year relationship, which he thought would result in marriage until he realized he was losing his passion for her.

> We were sexually active with each other four months into it. Vaginal intercourse was a small event. I thought I'd feel so different but felt the same. Thought I'd feel more masculine and stronger, better. [It] had a huge impact. I lost my virginity and had lots of other firsts. First time in love, and it opened my eyes to a new lifestyle. Amazing.

Although Toby claimed that he had never had a boy crush or sexual experience, 5 percent of his sexual attractions and fantasies include males. Why was he so concerned that others might think he's gay?

> I'm not 100 percent sure that I am [straight]. It is because my outfits match and that I dress well. I can easily approach people with high en-

ergy and spirits. It is frustrating to me because if girls who are attracted to me think that I'm gay, then they won't approach me. I'd have to catch them off guard. Two people have asked me directly, and I say, "No. I like the company of women."

This summer at work, there was this guy. . . . And one day he came in with new haircut, and I said that I liked it. He thanked me, talked a conversation. And every day or so, he came in, and eventually he asked me if I'm gay. I was taken aback, not mad, but I had no idea. But he thought that I was flirting with him. I couldn't tell he is gay—no idea. And I feel badly for him, and he doesn't come by anymore.

What did the stranger pick up on that led him to believe Toby might be a candidate for dating or sex? It was not his matching outfits—after all, Toby was wearing his work uniform.

Toby in his ideal world wants "to choose one lifestyle" because he doesn't "want extra confusion": "I'd not like to be attracted to both sexes and have that solid, my heterosexuality." He has quintessential straight credentials, as indicated by his crushes, sex, and romance with girls and his motel-room weekend escapade when he went through eight condoms with his girlfriend. "Was my sexual peak. Wow! I really like sex." Somewhat confused, I asked why males appear in his sexual fantasies. "Must be my subconscious. Just sort of happens. It is bothersome, and I question myself more." Backtracking once again, Toby relayed another episode, in which he was hanging out with an attractive male friend. "We told each other that we were attracted to each other. I can express my physical attractions—are limits, such as hands on my genitals."

Toby has no regrets about his sexuality because he likes the way things turned out. Is he totally straight? I was doubtful given his desire not to have "extra confusion," his belief that everyone is a little bit bisexual, and the fact that he's only "pretty sure" he won't experience a gay lifestyle that interests him. If he's bisexual, then it's because everyone is bisexual, to varying degrees, due to their "subconscious fantasies."

On a follow-up interview a year later, Toby's prediction that in the future he'd be 100 percent straight faltered. He moved out of his hometown community into a college-town apartment where he has greater freedom. Now 21, Toby's same-sex attractions doubled to 10 percent, with a small percentage of sexual fantasies, sexual contacts ("masturbated on a webcam while watching someone else do the same"), and infatuations devoted to guys. When asked about his sexuality, Toby didn't say "mostly straight"—which would be in line with his percentages—but "bisexual leaning straight."

When Toby reflected on what he believes are traditional views about the sexual and romantic relationships of young men, his response is revealing.

> Young men are complex sometimes, and their actions do not always have straightforward, simple motives. Young men like sex, but we are not all out there always looking for a new sexual partner. And if we are, maybe it is because we are exploring ourselves, our own sexual preferences, and how we most enjoy to have sex and find the right person or persons compatible with our needs and desires. Maybe we also just want to learn, to become more "sexually mature." And some of us may believe that to do so, we need to experience multiple partners.

As Toby becomes further removed from his rural background, his Kinsey score reflects where he is—but not necessarily where he will end up. Although he wants an open relationship in his future, is this to free him up to have sex with women *and* men? Toby doesn't yet have a label for what is emerging from the fluidity of his subconscious to conscious awareness.

Melissa

Melissa, a 21-year-old college student, was more combative than Toby in resisting her rural culture. She grew up in a small, rural Iowa town where "everyone is white and Christian," and the prevailing moralistic flavor bothered her because it was "against Blacks, gays, etc." Anyone who came out as anything but straight would "get beat up," and she didn't want to be any more hated than she already was. What made her unpopular was her masculinity. She built things, was analytical and mathematical, ran track, and was intelligent, strong, and success oriented (science/engineering). Melissa often played alone and was treated as an adult by adults. At first, her friends were girls, but she became "disgusted with girls, tossing their hair and falling all over boys": "So, I made friends with boys." She would not be subordinate to or dependent on boys but "in charge": "because I like being equal."

Melissa noted that her first same-sex attractions were in first grade, but she ignored them until two years previous. "I thought I'd always be heterosexual, with close, intense female friends." She had girl crushes and "late sex" with Quinn. It had been a goal of hers to have a sweetheart and sex before graduating from high school. Her pattern had been dating boys for a month or so before breaking up with them, but Quinn was better than most.

> It was this nice, okay kid who was a bit different in high school. I was a political dork in my high school and so intimidated others. This was just fine with me. I wanted to have sex. . . . Quinn was also a virgin. It was uneventful. It happened, and I was just there. It was a little painful. He came and I didn't.

Once in college, Melissa realized that "the boy thing" didn't entice her anymore: "I wouldn't be pursuing them." The eureka moment came when she walked into a café: "It suddenly hit me, and I realized this. It happened when this woman and me held our glances a bit longer, and then we talked. I went home, and this was a big cathartic breakdown." Now, she's "happier than ever before—such a release, this bonding with gay people."

I call myself bisexual—not comfortable with the dyke thing. I don't make rash decisions. I've been thinking about it, no real angst about it. All of this made sense to me all at once. This was not because of love, because I had dated boys in high school and here. At some point, it didn't make sense, that I just wasn't into the standard heterosexual thing. When I came to college, I was moving away from the boy thing. I was lonely in relationships with them.

This happiness has not netted Melissa either sex or romance with another woman, which she eventually wants, but not if it interferes with her career plans to be an engineer.

I've had big crushes. I have this crush on this girl, and when I do, I am really hung out. Seems like this is all I need, to have a crush and not the relationship. Maybe because I am so career oriented. I won't dress up and flirt, which was why not had sex with a girl yet. I've felt more an option for me in the last two years, but I've not had the time lately because of classes and doing pottery. I'm lazy when it comes to relationships. I'll wait until someone likes me. I don't mind being single.

Most of Melissa's collegiate friends know Melissa's sexuality, but not her back-home friends or anyone in her family. Melissa is 99 percent sure that her parents would have no problem because they are "hippy, liberal parents" who are pro-gay.

Don't know why I haven't, except no deadline works. Don't know what to tell them, and I don't want to think about it. She knows everything about me. So, I've tried hinting. I'll say little things, like I took a women's study class, and when they bought my little brother trucks, I told them they ought to buy boy dolls, unless she was afraid he'd grow up to be gay. She bought the dolls and told me, "I don't care what my kids are as long as they are happy."

The same holds for her father, who imposed no curfew on Melissa.

> He is less talkative yet is loving. Full support of me, but we don't just chat like Mom and I do. Doesn't know the details of my life, which is fine with me, but it does scare me a little. He thinks I'm perfect, and I'm afraid it will annoy him. Don't know him as well—more weird. I would tell him at the same time, because if I didn't, he'd know within two to three seconds because Mom would tell him—no secrets in our family. I'd tell in passing, no big deal, no hugging. They should know, and I have guilt because they deserve to go through the same process I've been through in questioning my sexuality and thinking about it. It's not fair to them. They deserve a mourning period. He'll be the hardest. He will probably make jokes about it.

Both of Melissa's younger sisters will be fine with it. So, too, will her maternal grandmother—the kingpin, with "Democrat," "Catholic," and "Kennedys" "stamped on her forehead": "Very strong woman who ran her house, but she has old views on gender issues. A woman should feed her man. If I told her, she'd say, 'Don't know what you're saying!'" Two of her children never married, leading Melissa to believe she may have a gay aunt and uncle. Melissa herself wonders if she is on the road to being "totally gay."

PART IV

Beyond a Singular Bisexuality

15

Bisexualities

What Needs to Change

If someone finds out you are bisexual, they will think differently about you and not want to be around you because they
judge you.
—Toby, age 20, white, waiter and student

Although most of the young people I interviewed were positive about
their own sexual, romantic, and gender selves, some pockets of resis-
tance were apparent. Most had come to terms with themselves but were
largely unhappy with the world and its view of what it means to be bisexual, pansexual, fluid, or nonbinary. From these interviews and my own
reading, in this chapter I explore changes that need to be implemented
before we can conclude that our work is done.

Bisexual Is Not One Thing

In a "state of the union" proclamation at the turn of the 21st century, the
bisexual activist and writer Paula Rodríguez Rust reminded us of three
critical issues echoed by the youths I interviewed:

1. Bisexuality is excluded from our awareness because being straight
   is considered the normal developmental path.
2. Bisexuality must be understood on its own terms—"not merely as
   a combination of heterosexuality and homosexuality, but as a form
   of sexuality that offers the possibility for greater understanding of
   sexuality in general."

3. Within the basic rubric of bisexuality is an exceptionally broad range of sexual, romantic, and gender characteristics.[1]

Here, I focus specifically on the third: there's more than one way *not to be* straight or gay. The various ways that bisexuality, writ large, has been experienced by the young adults I quote in these pages is evidence of this fact. Several pioneers in the field of bisexuality, including Rodríguez Rust and Fritz Klein, advised us not to treat all bisexuals as if they constituted a single group—there is a diversity of ways in which bisexuals have little in common with each other in their attractions, sexual behaviors, romantic relationships, gender expressions, identities, and personality traits. If we ignore this multiplicity of bisexuality, we court danger, creating misinformation regarding bisexuals' prevalence, characteristics, and mental health. Yet, this cautionary warning remains largely ignored today.[2]

The corrective for science is to listen to youths and young adults as they talk about their unique encounters with bisexuality. In their voices, new visions of bisexualities become clear, which is necessary if we are to erase the caricature of a singular bisexuality. I propose not a perfect or even ideal solution to the complexity of bisexuality, but if we have to have sexual identities, let them be complicated and open to change over time. Here is my tentative characterization of bisexuals:

1. *Primary bisexuals*: Have an active degree of arousal, behavior, and/ or identity motivated by fervent, passionate, and deep-seated attraction to both sexes and, perhaps, genders, to varying degrees
2. *Closeted bisexuals*: Similar to primary bisexuals but are not out for a variety of personal, political, or cultural reasons (e.g., unsafe to come out, internalized biphobia)
3. *Transitional/transient bisexuals*: Identify themselves as bisexual as a phase, a pause, on their way to coming out as gay, lesbian, or something else
4. *Situational bisexuals*: Engage in same-sex behavior in particular settings such as prisons, gangs, prep schools, convents, and frater-

nities/sororities for a variety of reasons (experimentation, pleasure, power dynamics, exchange of resources such as money or drugs) that may or may not be related to sexuality

5. *Sensation-seeking bisexuals*: Experience high levels of sexual curiosity and sex drive, which motivate them to engage in many sexual activities regardless of their sexual orientation
6. *Clinical bisexuals*: Identify as bisexual secondary to clinical pathology, such as bipolar illness, obsessive-compulsive disorder, or borderline personality disorder, rather than their sexual/romantic attraction
7. *Queer bisexuals*: May or may not be bisexual by orientation but identify as such for political or cultural reasons

This is not the universe of bisexualities, but it probably encompasses a majority of the bisexual composite as we know it. Tomorrow this might not be the case, especially if we consider the wide variation in gender identities and expressions.

By blending these fundamentally distinct varieties of bisexuals as if they were a unified whole, we risk misunderstanding bisexuality. Particular features thought to characterize bisexuals might be prominent for some and not others. For example, openness to new experiences might best typify sensation-seeking and primary bisexuals; mental health problems, clinical and transitional bisexuals; and susceptibility to minority stress and stigma, transitional bisexuals. Because in most data sets bisexual-identified individuals constitute a relatively small group (less than 4 percent), it is relatively easy (and likely) to recruit a biased sample that distorts what it feels like to have multisexual attractions. For example, if the sample of bisexuals is solicited from a clinical caseload, an online support group, a political or social action group, or a friendship network with a snowball method, a number of clinical and political bisexuals might be likely to volunteer. If they constitute as little as 15 percent of the total, they will probably have profound effects on reports of negative mental health outcomes.

Obliterating Stereotypes

Recognizing that there is not a singular bisexual would help neutralize the colossal and destructive stereotypes surrounding bisexuality. Eighteen-year-old Zane said that his friends told him that bisexuals are "confused," "can't make up their minds," and are "slutty." Some young adults I interviewed had to overcome external biphobia and their own internalized confusions. Few, however, experienced the severe negative repercussions described on many bisexual websites; few witnessed gay or bisexual bashings in their middle or high school. For example, in Caleb's Jewish high school, one "colorful" boy was celebrated:

> He didn't hang out in a crowd and didn't put himself in situations where he would get bullied. And even if he did, he would be like, "Okay, you are a Neanderthal. I am going to move on with my life." The other kids were a little more flamboyant, and so if they got bullied, their girlfriends quickly yelled at them [the bullies] and it never happened again. . . . Every girl wanted a gay best friend.

Several writers catalogue major bisexual stereotypes prevalent in our culture:

- Bisexuals are merely gays or lesbians who deny "their true sexuality either because they are going through a transitional phase of coming out, because they are afraid to face their own or others' homophobia, or because they are unwilling to shoulder the burden of being a member of an oppressed minority."
- Bisexuals engage in sexual behavior with both sexes because they are experimenting and not because they are truly attracted to both sexes.
- Confused, conflicted, and indecisive, individuals settle on a bisexual label because they do not know what else to use if they want to straddle the middle.

- Driven by sexual impulses, bisexuals shop around for sex partners, and when a sexual situation presents itself, they go for it. This promiscuity dominates their lives because monogamy cramps their style.
- Bisexuals are merely trying to fit in with a stylish or contemporary label, suitable until they enter the real world after high school or college graduation.

Bisexuals are, according to these stereotypes, promiscuous, lying, or in denial.[3]

The health and clinical psychologists Christina Dyar and Brian Feinstein prefer the word "binegativity" to "biphobia." They define "binegativity" as "hostility toward bisexual people, stereotypes that bisexuality is an unstable and illegitimate sexual orientation, and stereotypes that bisexual individuals are sexually irresponsible (e.g., unfaithful in relationships, have sexually transmitted infections)." They found that such attitudes are higher among older generations, low-income and uneducated individuals, and political and religious conservatives—some of whom disbelieve that bisexuals exist, especially male bisexuals.[4]

The psychologists and women's/gender studies professors Megan Yost and Genéa Thomas reported that in their study, women were less negative than men in their attitudes about bisexuality, consistent with the general trend that women are less conservative and more progressive on social issues. Men expressed significantly greater prejudice toward bisexual men than toward bisexual women because to them, bisexual women do not challenge but support the patriarchal order. To men, bisexual women are free-spirited women and are thus perceived to be open to having new sexual experiences with the men themselves. Besides, what women do with other women is erotic but not, in men's eyes, really sex because no penis-vagina penetration occurs. Thus, woman-woman sex does not erase a woman's prized virginity, something only a man can take away.[5]

The law school professor John Sylla's perspective is that it matters less to the patriarchy what women do because they are considered "a form of property first under control of their fathers and later bartered to come under ownership and dominion of a husband . . . [and] not seen as real equal people." In a *Stanford Law Review* discussion, the legal scholar Kenji Yoshino presented the case for why the "category of bisexuality has been erased in contemporary American political and legal discourse . . . [and] how bisexuals have increasingly contested their own erasure." This erasure has historically fixated on bisexual men, in part because their greater degree of gender nonconformity is judged by straight men to be unmanly, an embarrassment to men everywhere. Men should solely desire sex with women, not with men. Male bisexuality has been more frequently questioned, stigmatized, and even criminalized than has female bisexuality—in religious, cultural, and legal canons over many centuries.[6]

Brian Dodge and colleagues suggest two major reasons why women are more positive than men in their sexual attitudes. One, because society at large monitors women's sexual behavior to define and control them, women are less prone to pose similar regulations on the lives of sexual minorities. Two, because women are more likely than men to identify as bisexual and fluid, they are less judgmental about others who are as well. How do we change men to be less sexist? According to Dodge and colleagues, the best way would be to loosen the gender expectations we have regarding "heteronormative norms and stereotypes." This will be difficult because gender and sexual stereotypes are stubbornly impervious to change. If men were to recognize within themselves their sexual, romantic, and gender spectrum points, we might gain considerable ground in correcting negative attitudes and behaviors toward male bisexuality. In the process, we would improve men's attitudes and behavior toward gender- and sexual-nonconforming men and women and hence reduce sexism, misogyny, and, hopefully, violence.[7] One way to reduce this sex-difference dilemma would be to become less controlling of women's sexuality and more supportive of gender nonconformity among men, including their gender and sexual fluidity. We are some distance away from these two solutions.

How pervasive are these stereotypes? Sara Burke and Marianne LaFrance have found that straight men and women like bisexuals less than they like gays and lesbians, because of a host of negative stereotypes they have about bisexuals: "less likely to prefer one partner at a time, more likely to cheat in relationships, to care more about sex than emotional commitment, or to have an STD, more likely to be promiscuous or deceptive, and less likely to be warm, sincere, competent, intelligent, decisive, loyal to friends, or dependable." On the other hand, gay and lesbian participants liked bisexuals more than straights liked bisexuals, yet they excluded bisexuals from their own group and viewed bisexuals as more unstable individuals. Although some bisexuals held these negative views about other bisexuals, most did not. Rather, they rejected the characterization of bisexuals as "uniquely indecisive, prone to nonmonogamy, focused on sex, or likely to cheat."[8]

As we become more aware of diverse sexual and gender expressions and identities, stereotypes toward multiattracted individuals are easier to debunk. Although it is true that about one-half of gay men pass through a bisexual phase on their way to a gay identity, perhaps because "they thought that others would accept them more readily as bisexual than as homosexual" or "they wanted a future with a wife and children," it is important to realize that in reality, few bisexually identified men and women are transient bisexuals.[9]

On the optimistic side, a marked positive shift across the board is occurring during the past decade among the Zoomer and Millennial generations. Dodge and colleagues attribute this in part to the lessening of "stringent masculinity expectations [that] are changing rapidly in youth populations in the U.S. and elsewhere." In the United States, this trend has extended to every demographic group, including most religious groups, political parties, and young people, which does not imply that the work is done, because some bisexual individuals do not enjoy the benefits of these positive shifts. Thus, the need to develop intervention approaches to promote positive attitudes remains.[10]

Are Bisexuals Sick or Healthy?

The young people I interviewed had heard stories about the poor mental health of bisexuals—though few believed that these stories applied to them or their friends. Time and time again, researchers have documented the disproportionate and pervasive tendency for the bisexual population to be facing serious mental, physical, and social health issues. Yet, is it fair to generalize from these research samples to the overall state of bisexuals? On principle, I would say no, but if these are the only bisexuals available to study, is it better to include them as representing bisexuals than to have no one at all? My answer would be mixed.

One example of the gap between the reality of bisexual lives and science is a highly cited literature review a decade ago that established, "LGB people are at higher risk of mental disorder, suicidal ideation, substance misuse, and deliberate self-harm than heterosexual people."[11] This conclusion has been highly influential, leading a National Institutes of Health–funded research paper to conclude that bisexuals suffer "dramatic disparities in depression, anxiety, stress, and other health outcomes . . . in comparison to their heterosexual and homosexual counterparts."[12] This judgment was reinforced by the public-health professor Lori Ross and colleagues, who pooled 52 eligible studies for a meta-analysis and found a consistent pattern of higher rates of depression and anxiety among bisexual people compared to heterosexuals and lesbian/gay people.[13] Ignored in this presentation is an overlooked or ignored fact: in many of these studies, bisexuality was defined as an identity and not as sexual or romantic attractions or behaviors. Aren't these bisexuals a biased subset of the larger bisexual population? Would removing the "I'm bisexual because of my mental illness" clinical bisexuals eliminate the difference? Would recruiting a representative sample of multiattracted individuals reduce disparities in mental health outcomes between bisexuals and other populations? I believe so, but it is difficult to determine because researchers ignore the highly heterogeneous nature of the bisexual population.

Other problems also plague the existing bisexual research. Bisexuals are frequently grouped with lesbians and gays as if they were the same thing—they are not and should be separated. Another problem is that women constitute the overwhelmingly proportion of most bisexual samples (usually between 65 percent and 85 percent of the total). Thus, bisexuals' health should not be compared to that of straight men, as is typical, but to that of straight women. Other oddities also exist, especially with regard to how bisexuals are defined. For example, a study of nearly 15,000 15-year-old adolescents from eight European countries defined bisexuals as "ever being in love with both girls and boys," and not based on sexual attraction, behavior, or identity (probably because of the subjects' minor status and hence a hesitation on the part of the researchers to ask sexual questions). The "both-gender love" youths were more likely than "opposite-gender love" youths to engage in "cigarette smoking, alcohol consumption, drunkenness, and cannabis use." This sounds familiar. Neglected, however, is that the second-largest group (13 percent), who registered "healthy," had never been in love. Is it possible that some in this group have multiple romantic and sexual preferences but experienced difficulty finding a "same-gender love" partner in middle or high school? In addition, another "healthy" group was the nonresponding group, which was larger than either the same- or both-gender group. Might these individuals include youths who refrained from revealing their same-sex love attraction on the survey (perhaps wondering if it would really be anonymous)? If these possibilities are true, have the authors excluded from their bisexual group not only most of its members but also its healthiest? If they were to reconsider their definition of bisexuality, would they backtrack their overarching conclusion that the vulnerability of 15-year-old bisexuals is "a universal phenomenon"?[14]

Ross and colleagues propose that three contributing factors suppress bisexual mental health: "experiences of sexual orientation-based discrimination, bisexual invisibility/erasure, and lack of bisexual-affirmative support."[15] I agree that these factors exist, and we must commit ourselves to correcting them. But I have doubts that these three lead to the apparent extreme mental and physical health disparities between bisexuals and other youths. Rather, the haunting, troubling results stem from the failure of scientists to include individuals along the full spectrum of bisexuality and to assess the positive aspects of multiattracted individuals' lives.

Positive Bisexual Lives

When we clump all multiattracted individuals together as if they were one cohesive group, we focus too narrowly on what is wrong and neglect what is right about their bisexual lives. By doing this, the prospect of getting at the truth is eradicated, and whatever is found has to be, in the words of the sociologists and educators Erich Steinman and Brett Beemyn, "simplistic, incomplete, and sometimes clearly inaccurate." Steinman and Beemyn, in contrast to the aforementioned surveyors, accentuate the diversity of bisexuals with regard to their "relative attraction to men and women, the frequency and gender mix of romantic and sexual relationships, the primacy of each gender in terms of organizing one's life and commitments, and other social and sexual differences."[16] Recognizing this reality implies that any global characterization of bisexuals has to be a miscalculation. Youths know this; sex researchers, not so much.

As a result, I have been highly critical of research in this regard because of its ill-conceived, counterproductive, and inaccurate "suffering suicidal script" that seemingly documents the unhappiness, suffering, vulnerability, and even death among sexual-minority youth. Such a portrait does not represent normative LGBTQ experiences, and endlessly repeating this false claim might actually promote the very self-destructive behavior it is intended to overcome. Predisposing vulnerable youth to lose faith in the possibility of a positive future for themselves does not lead to good mental health. We must rectify this negative prominence because it is emblematic of the larger dominant paradigm in research with minorities: to emphasize the negative rather than the positive aspects of life.[17]

There is another cost to doing bad research, articulated by the sociologist Audrey Bryan, who has also had misgivings about the abundance of "harrowing narratives of LGBTQ experience and identity," which "position LGBTQ youth as universally at risk of mental health difficulties, including self-harm and suicidality." By focusing on these "dramatic, easily identifiable moments of homophobic violence," we neglect "a deeper analysis of the normalization and taken-for-grantedness of heterosexuality which enables such violence to flourish." Bryan argues that "the framing of queer youth as victims in need of help, tolerance and inclusion results in a preoccupation with protecting LGBTQ students from harm, as opposed to a preoccupation with heteronormativity as a hegemonic cultural system which must be actively challenged and dismantled."[18] In our educational policies and practices, we should be challenging the assumed (and hence dominant) sexual and gender-based paradigms if we want to nurture school cultures that affirm diversity in sexual and gender identities.

In response to the overwhelming negative preoccupation of research on bisexuality, the Institute of Medicine recommended that we increase knowledge about the true prevalence of bisexuality, document the breath and diversity of bisexual individuals, and counter the pervasive presentation of bisexual individuals as psychologically disturbed and distressed. What should garner our attention is bisexuals' resilience, strength-based capacities, and resources such as supportive networks, self-esteem, and coping skills. From a positive psychology perspective, the goal should be to provide a more balanced understanding of bisexual lives. "We must acknowledge that there are positive aspects of being a member of a sexual minority and, conversely, that heterosexuality may also carry health risks."[19]

What are the developmental assets of bisexuals? Do they have unique internal strengths and external supports? Though these are nearly always ignored, examples exist. Coupled bisexual men report higher levels of emotional intimacy than straight men do, which indicates that the sexual and emotional intimacies in men's romantic relationships are not limited by their sexual orientation. Those who have a bisexual, bi-affectionate, or queer identity score significantly higher than straight young adults do on cognitive flexibility, authenticity, and empathy and, more generally, do not differ from straight individuals in quality of life, lifestyle, health indicators, friendship quality, perceptions of school climate, academic orientation, and peer victimization. Depending on one's perspective of what is an advantage, strength, or talent, bisexual women and men have more sex partners than straight undergraduate and graduate students do.[20]

Speculating further, the political scientist Ellen Riggle and colleagues offers a long list of potential positive aspects of sexual minorities, including bisexual, pansexual, and fluid individuals: belonging to a community, creating families of choice, forging strong connections with others, serving as positive role models, developing empathy and compassion, living authentically and honestly, gaining personal insight and a sense of self, involving oneself in social justice and activism, freeing oneself from gender-specific roles, exploring sexuality and relationships, and enjoying egalitarian relationships. To the best of my knowledge, few researchers have taken up the challenge to document these realities among individuals under the bisexual umbrella.[21]

Bisexual advocates argue for more bisexual communities to combat biphobia, bisexual erasure, and daily microaggressions that result in depression and unhappiness. I totally agree, but they must also provide the positive message delivered by young people: being bisexual is okay and sometimes fantastic. What is most related to mental health is to feel that one's sexuality is neither bad nor wrong and to accept it. Well-being is difficult to realize if the only thing one hears about bisexuality is its problems and pathology. If we were to listen to the life stories of bisexual individuals and their positive life trajectories, this gap between the reality of bisexual lives and science would be resolved. However, first we must give up our belief that having any degree of same-sex attraction is the most compelling thing to know about a person. I disagree. Few people state the most obvious fact we know about bisexuals: the vast majority of them are psychologically healthy, and they seldom think about or attempt suicide, are depressed or anxious, engage in self-harm, or have a diagnosable mental health problem. Why this point is seldom made baffles me. Perhaps it is the result of funding sources (little money available for investigating positive attributes), disciplinary fidelity (public health, sociology of deviance, social work, clinical psychology), and the investigator's own personal history (having grown up facing pain, rejection, stigma).[22]

We must also challenge the assumption that the most appropriate reference group for mental health outcomes consists of straight males, as if male heterosexuality had laid claim to be the *healthiest* (see the discussion of toxic masculinity in chapter 12). Combining several lines of research on neuropsychological differences between the sexes (elicited from multimodal brain-imaging data and external behavior) reveals that sexual-minority men, more so than straight men, share numerous commonalities with women on behavioral, cognitive, and personality characteristics, including internalizing psychological conditions. Thus, from a sex-inversion perspective, we should consider straight women rather than straight men as the basis for comparison when exploring female-typical health issues such as levels of self-esteem, depression, interpersonal sensitivity, emotion-focused ruminative coping modality, and reporting style.[23] In addition, when sexual-minority men and women are the recipients of prejudice and discrimination, the assumption has been that masculinity (stoicism, belligerence, self-assertion) had license to claim and define the *healthiest* response, rather than femininity (gentleness, empathy, sensitivity). Thus, any sign of mental health problems among bisexual individuals must be evaluated in light of whom they are being compared to: straight men or women?

Finally, we can never forget a basic message in these pages: the vast majority of multiattracted individuals under the bisexual umbrella are excluded from research that supposedly represents and characterizes bisexuality. Left out are mostly straights and mostly gays; those who are bisexual solely in romantic domains; portions of those who have a nonexclusive sexual or romantic identity such as pansexual, queer, kinkster, trans*, and nonbinary; and those who are unsure, questioning, or nonresponders.

In or Out of the Closet?

Young people with multiple sexual or romantic attractions can usually choose the degree to which they are out or not about their bisexuality. Who is included in the bisexual population due to their visibility vexes those who explore an issue raised by John Pachankis a decade ago: Given the ease with which many bisexuals conceal their sexuality, is it better for their mental health to come out and face possible stigma and discrimination or to remain hidden but risk threats to their authenticity? Counter to those who believe that it is better to hide their stigmatized sexuality so as to avoid harassment or violence, Pachankis found that those who have "a concealable stigma also face considerable stressors and psychological challenges. The ambiguity of social situations combined with the threat of potential discovery makes possessing a concealable stigma a difficult predicament for many individuals." If they have access to social support to help them navigate the stress of being out of the closet, then it is better to be out about their sexuality.[24]

Other researchers remind us that youths who are out might be risking their health and even their life. Using a population-based Canadian government survey, Travis Salway Hottes and colleagues found, contrary to the idea that being out is good, that disclosure of sexual identity was associated with a higher rate of suicide ideation among bisexual men. The authors speculate that disclosure may have resulted in increased contact with "interpersonal stigma, which accumulate[s] to produce mental distress." Being more open laid bare bisexuals to stigma and discrimination from both heterosexual and gay/lesbian individuals. Other researchers in the United States, Australia, and the Netherlands agree, citing potential outcomes such as drug use and mental health problems—at a time when being accepted by peers is crucial. The negative effects of being out and bullied are less severe for Black bisexual high school students than for white, Hispanic, and mixed-race/ethnic bisexual youths. On the basis of five years of YRBS data from nearly 20,000 high school students who identify as bisexual, the clinical psychologist Brian Feinstein and colleagues speculate that Black bisexual youth experience greater resilience due to their history of coping with racism and their higher level of religiosity; they are also less likely to be out and thus less susceptible to victimization—that is, concealing their sexuality protects them.[25]

In general, because bisexual youths are less likely than lesbians and gays to transgress cultural gender norms, they are better able to conceal their sexuality and thus to protect themselves from experiencing stigma and harassment. But, as Pachankis suggests, are they more likely to suffer mental health problems because by concealing their stigmatized sexuality, they live with a more "inauthentic self" and hence suffer from low self-esteem, depression, anxiety, and suicidal ideation?[26] I do not ultimately know the answer to whether it is better to conceal or not to conceal, because the research has a fatal design flaw: findings are based on samples that do not reflect the general population of multiattracted individuals but are biased by those who are willing to expose to researchers the nature of their sexuality.

The answer to whether it is better to be in or out of the closet is extremely complicated because the decision to be out is based on a host of factors, such as personality characteristics, gender expressions, family support, friendship networks, regional location, and historical time—plus, by accident. That said, there are several take-aways from the research. First, the reason why publicly identifying as bisexual rather than merely having bisexual attractions is more highly associated with negative mental health outcomes is probably exposure to a greater degree of stigma and victimization. Second, self-identified bisexuals may be more out because they are unable to conceal their sexuality, with a higher level of gender nonconformity and willingness to act on their homoeroticism than those who are closeted. Unable or unwilling to hide, they receive the full negative brunt of not being sufficiently gender appropriate based on prevailing cultural norms. Third, a critical causal factor in these patterns might be an individual's prior susceptibility to mental health problems that correspond to the psychologist Avshalom Caspi's p factor (psychopathology).[27] That is, perhaps bisexual individuals with preexisting mental health problems are more prone to identify as bisexual and to disclose their sexuality to others and are thus less apt, able, or willing to hide their sexuality. Given that in general, bisexual individuals in research samples are drawn disproportionately from *clinical* and *political* subgroups, they are both more out and more likely to suffer mental health problems. Perhaps it is not their bisexuality that is the problem but their high p factor that leads them to be "pulled" out of the closet, rather than to come out on their own volition. The relative importance of the p factor, gender nonconformity, sexual/romantic attraction, and harassment is unknown, but my bet is the order just listed flows from most to least critical.

What is clear is the pertinence of Travis Salway Hottes and colleagues' ominous warning that bisexual concealment produces "misclassification, or information bias, in studies that attempt to estimate and investigate mental health burdens in sexual minorities." The result has been repeatedly shown in these pages: if individuals do not register their bisexuality, the resulting underreporting of multiattracted individuals is not likely to be random, leaving those who are willing to disclose as a unique subset of bisexuals. This is critical because, as Pachankis points out, concealment complicates efforts to reduce forms of inequality that are built into the system and that underestimate the "size of the global closet." By omitting significant numbers of the true bisexual population, our knowledge about bisexuality is distorted and, if it is based on troubled subpopulations, can give bisexuality, with its alleged high levels of mental health problems, a "bad name" in the eyes of youths who are coming to terms with their own sexuality. It can divert, misapply, or deny interventions that benefit some but not others, and it can complicate attempts to understand health disparities among bisexuals. Plus, it snubs those who fall outside traditional bisexual categories but reside under the bisexual umbrella. Pansexual, mostly straight, fluid, questioning, kink, trans*, mostly gay, nonbinary, and queer individuals are negated in principle as well as in reality.[28]

Listening to Youths

The simplest means to expand our understanding of bisexuality as it morphs across time and place is to listen to young people who are living it. Yet, similar to the medical sciences, the behavioral and social sciences have become not descriptive but mechanistic, not observational but explanatory, and not anecdotal but statistical.[29] If we do not heed the voices of youths, we will lose our way about what it means to have multiple attractions.

Niobe Way and Deborah Tolman have shown us how to do it. Talking with adolescent boys, the developmentalist psychologist Way discovered, contrary to what we believe, that by nature, boys express and seek deeply fulfilling emotional connections and love with each other, but as they grow into manhood, they are told to nix these relationships and lose the intimacy with their male friends because it is time to "man up." They become emotionally stoic, lonely, and isolated as the liabilities of toxic masculinity encourage their independence and aggressiveness. This *crisis of connection* plagues them throughout young adulthood and probably beyond. Though Way interviewed straight boys, are bisexual boys better able to preserve the quality of their adolescent friendships in a manner that is healthy for their development? Are they under the same spell of cultural masculinity and to the same degree? We do not know, but bisexual boys would be at a momentous advantage if they were able to sustain their intimate friendships and crushes with both sexes—though this might depend on whether they are closeted and thus feel pressure to conform to typical masculinity norms.[30]

Building on the work of the psychology and social justice professor Michele Fine, the social welfare professor Deborah Tolman and colleagues point out that adolescent girls' sexual desire is a *missing discourse* "in both the literature on teen sexuality and within the walls of schools and sex education classrooms." To address this shortcoming, Tolman and colleagues interviewed eighth-grade students to elicit narratives about their sexual and romantic relationships. The protocol consisted of open-ended questions such as the students' reasons for wanting or not wanting a girlfriend or boyfriend and their experiences with physical intimacy within and outside the context of a romantic relationship. Then they were asked, "Could you tell me a story about something that's happened in your relationship [or about how it started or a special time] that can help me understand what it's like for you?" Follow-up questions yielded "co-constructed narratives about these experiences with romantic relationships." The girls benefited by "considering aspects of their lives that they had not given much thought to in any previous context."[31]

These conversations are rare between researchers—or parents, for that matter—and youths, which is why we know so little about the bisexual lives of Zoomers and Millennials. We need both quantitative data, with their statistical lines of code, and, chiefly, qualitative data that listen to how youths think, feel, and interpret their sexual, romantic, and gender lives. I would suggest that before any scholar constructs their research design, they should first talk with the individuals who will be participants in the study about the topic of interest—and more. As Tristan Bridges and Mignon Moore note regarding their interviews with young women of color, "[They] shed light on the processes through which they understand their sexuality, take on new sexual identities, and experiment with or experience different sexual identities over time."[32] Besides, this is the most enjoyable aspect of research.

If we had talked to bisexual, pansexual, fluid, and nonbinary young people, many research errors noted in this book would have been prevented. We would have refrained from lumping all multiattracted individuals together, acknowledged that bisexuality exists on a spectrum, recognized that those along the spectrum might share little in common with each other, and celebrated the importance of gender in their lives.[33] Despite the evidence presented earlier in this chapter, we would have doubted the inevitable mental health problems of bisexual youths. Many do not experience a stigmatized existence—especially those who have supportive families and friends and possess pleasing personalities, self-confidence, life satisfaction, and resilience. Rather, if we were to go back to the source, the roots of the social and behavioral sciences, then we would ask multiattracted individuals about their lives, especially how recent cultural shifts have affected them.

For some young adults, being bisexual is a prized possession, according to the sociologist Max Morris, himself a Millennial. The sexual-minority college men he interviewed in the United Kingdom had special stature in their peer culture precisely because of their same-sex attractions. After coming out, Nathan discovered that he and his fellow classmates became "really close-knit": "so we're all open and honest with each other." Bradley observed, "Honestly, no one is fussed anymore" about what sexuality you are. How do straight youths benefit from having bisexual friends? They are graced with "touch-based interactions between members of the same sex," such as "kissing, cuddling, and spooning, which was seen as indicative of their strong friendships." Straight guys might jokingly call these "bromances," an acceptable same-sex relationship; young women might refer to their special person as a "passionate friend." Whether these are code words for romantic orientation and hence for bisexuality is beside the point. They have a right to call it by whatever works for them.[34]

Similar to Morris's UK young men, many bisexuals I interviewed articulated the advantages of being bisexual. They had more sex and dating opportunities ("you don't need a cell phone but a phone book!") and had it easier than lesbians and gays because they had the ability to hide. Being bisexual opened "a new market, a new world of opportunities and world of experience"; they had more people "to mesh with" and were not as "boring as straights." I think we should be celebrating their resourcefulness and life satisfaction.

16

Postidentity Revolution

I think this is sort of the age of bisexuality. . . . It's a thing on
its own.[1]

—Woody Cook, age 19, white, model

A silenced bisexual teenager in the 1980s, Gen X's Charles Blow, the journalist, commentator, and author of *Fire Shut Up in My Bones: A Memoir*, grew up in a rural Louisiana town where being a Black bisexual man was certainly not a prestigious thing to be or proclaim. Blow writes, "[Although] the word *bisexual* was technically correct, I would only slowly come to use it to refer to myself, in part because of the derisive connotations. But, in addition, it would seem to me woefully inadequate and impressionistically inaccurate." It was a scandalous concept to others and also an inadequate moniker to Blow because it "reduced a range of identities, unbelievably wide and splendidly varied, in which same-gender attraction presented itself in graduated measures, from a pinch to a pound, to a single expression."[2] In this regard, Charles Blow was prescient of the Zoomers to come.

A slightly younger Gen Xer, Andrew Gillum, was almost governor of Florida and a rising political star until he was discovered in a compromising sexual situation with a male escort. *Slate* reporter Christina Cauterucci notes the historical significance of Gillum: "In politics and pop culture, bisexual women are far more visible than bisexual men." Although Gillum had remained closeted for personal and political reasons—similar to many Gen Xers—once he named his sexuality, he also had to overcome the "suspicion American culture directs at Black male sexuality." Although, as Cauterucci notes, it was not exactly the "triumphant, linear narrative many of us have come to expect from political coming out stories," it nevertheless was progress.[3] Will the Zoomers do better?

Many of the young adults I interviewed would resonate with Blow's misgivings about the assumption that bisexuality means a transient identity, "a pit stop or a hiding place." And, similar to Gillum, they could agree that being bisexual does not necessarily mean forgoing a traditional marriage or a political career. The Gen X words that nearly all Zoomers could easily revere are those of Billie Joe Armstrong, lead vocalist of the punk band Green Day: "Bisexuality is a very beautiful thing." Gen Xers have frequently battled to achieve acknowledgment, acceptance, and support—Zoomers have less so, because it's now easier for them to be self-accepting, perhaps because during the interim, attitudes have become notably more positive as new generations of youth live comfortably with multiple attractions and identities. Zoomers have a new way of talking about their sexual, gender, and romantic lives. But are we listening? Do we care? I hope so.

The young adults I listened to occupy the full range of bisexuality, from the cusp of straightness to the cusp of gayness to those who feel the two edges of the continuum are foreign to them. They know they are somewhere in the vast middle—not necessarily equidistant from the poles, just somewhere in the interior of the spectrum. Those on the border, the mostly straights and the mostly lesbians/gays, seldom desire to convert to heterosexuality or homosexuality because there is just too much pleasure in women-loving-men, men-loving-women, women-loving-women, and men-loving-men to love only a single sex. True, some near the cusp of gayness are a little shaky because a part of them has dreams of being *culturally normal*—that is, being straight—and they are not yet ready to abandon their fantasies or their delusions. At least once or twice in their life, some have wished for a straight miracle because they thought life would be so much easier; and maybe it would have been, but then it would not be them. They do not want to limit their future options to one sex or to sacrifice their personal blend of sexual and romantic complexity. These twists and turns characterize many of the interviews. Even if I could pin them down, some left room in their future to squirm out of strictures to their attractions and behaviors. Rigid rules and unyielding expectations seldom existed—and this was the magic of the interviews. Listening to the developmental trajectories of multiattracted youths and young adults is an electrifying experience.

If we don't ask questions, not only will we get multiattracted youths' life wrong, but we will also systematically underestimate their number, overestimate their pathology, and ignore their assets. Simplistically counting the ratio of sex partners with each sex is probably meaningless; it is the quality and not the number of sexual encounters that matters most. Besides, such calculations snub the lives of asexual bisexuals, virgin bisexuals, gendered bisexuals, and romantic bisexuals. We routinely privilege sex over romance, as if romantic orientation is irrelevant when understanding bisexuality. Again, youths tell us a very different story about what is most consequential in their lives when it comes to their sexuality. Their young lives reveal that scientific approaches to their lives are frequently misguided, detrimental, or injurious to them and their bisexual brothers and sisters.

Generational Transformations

I believe Charles Blow's teenage experience some 40 years ago, and yet things have changed. Though recalcitrant stereotypes unmistakably persist, leading some young people to struggle for self-acceptance and support from others, many others thrive by overcoming the erasure and denial. The Zoomer Emma González became one of the most visible bisexual women in the United States, with millions of Twitter followers, though her visibility is less about her bisexuality than her political activism following the shooting at her Parkland, Florida, high school. At the time, Emma focused on calming the people around her, and three days later, she "mustered remarkable resilience and courage when she transformed her anguish and heartbreak into unabashed activism." Emma founded March for Our Lives, a nonprofit, nonpartisan organization advocating for stricter gun laws, and she is a feminist because she believes in "equality of the sexes (and all genders)." As to her own sexuality, Emma is rather nonchalant, even in the face of taunts. She told *Variety*, "A lot of people say 'dyke' in terms of negative statements against me. Technically it's for lesbians. I'm not a lesbian; I'm bisexual. I like guys and girls. There's confusion with the fact that definition isn't widely known. But it's fine, I guess. We'll get there." And then she moves on to other issues, such as registering young voters.[4]

Another Zoomer, the 19-year-old model Woody Cook, discovered the significance of bisexuality for himself: it answered troubling aspects of himself. He disclosed his bisexuality not as an adult but as a 15-year-old and in the process gained clarity and authenticity. While growing up, Woody "had all these thoughts," and he "just shook it off." But while at a party, he heard a classmate say, "It's great being gay." His reply even shocked himself: "'Yeah, I'm gay too. I'm bisexual.' I just said it as a laugh at the time." The next day, Woody woke up to a big question: "'Why did I say that?' And then, the more I thought about it I thought, 'Oh my god, that explains everything!' And then it was that miracle moment, where my entire life had been really conflicted, and I suddenly realised that was it." Woody does not care what sex someone is and is laid back about his sexual orientation. His interviewer, Cecile Harris, elaborated on the "no big deal" revelation. "Not to him, not to his friends. . . . Love who you want. Be who you want. 'Is this the age of bisexuality?' we wonder together. A generation so accepting that everyone, more and more, is now able to be exactly who they are—without the restrictions and insecurities of previous generations."[5] Similar to Emma González, Woody Cook simply accepts his bisexuality for what it is. Neither is shutting up about their sexuality—but neither is making a huge production of it either. They take whatever time they need for self-reflection to reach a more holistic and acceptable self.

This *age of bisexuality* is not exactly without antecedent. Fifty years ago, the poet and songwriter Rod McKuen refused to label himself: "I think the straights, gays and bi's all do themselves a tremendous disservice by putting themselves into any kind of category. I don't believe that there are only three kinds of sexuality."[6] Pansexual, fluid, and nonbinary youths have taken this one step further by embracing a new world of bisexuality. Indeed, it is even happening in China. Among over 50,000 young adults from nearly 2,000 universities across China, just over 10 percent identify as bisexual or pansexual, 7 percent say they are unsure or list another sexuality (possibly some version of bisexuality), and 5 percent say they are gay. The adult world is also transforming itself, as a majority of the Chinese population supports marriage equality. These same trends are recorded across other countries and cultures of the world.[7]

In the United States, the singer and actor Ben Platt disclosed to his family that he is gay when he was 12 years old, and Miley Cyrus came out as pansexual to her mother at age 14. Emma González and Woody Cook publicly came out as bisexual during adolescence. These announcements no longer generate gasps of amazement, as many youths are coming out as bisexual, as noted by the British Office for National Statistics in the 16-to-24-year-old cohort—more than those who say they are gay or lesbian combined.[8] Yet, despite this visibility, bisexual youths continue to face, as my interviewee Jacob pleaded in frustration, the burden to explain what bisexual means. This needs to change, and it will if we grasp the messages youths are delivering:

1. One can have a slight or major component of bisexuality—that is, there is a spectrum of sexuality, romance, and gender—with the capacity for fluctuation over time and context.
2. A singular bisexual identity is inadequate to reflect the unbelievable kaleidoscope of gender, romantic, and sexual identities.
3. The prevalence rate of bisexuality is considerably higher than national estimates when we count the uncounted and the miscounted multiattracted individuals.
4. Zoomers identify as pansexual, fluid, genderqueer, nonbinary, questioning, no label, and many more.

5. Most bisexuals lead normal, healthy, fulfilling lives with authenticity and hope for the future.

We need to listen to their stories and their lives to appreciate their experience in this time of considerable disruptions about what we thought we knew about romance, gender, and sexuality.

The severe limitations of current scientific research on bisexuality contribute to a shockingly low count of bisexuals and trivialize their psychological well-being. We need to recalculate our numbers and our conclusions because 90 percent of multiattracted individuals are neglected in our counts. Perhaps we miss those who are the happiest and the healthiest. Our disregard of their positive attributes and their joys of having multiple attractions mystifies and dismays me. I believe the young adults would laugh (hysterically) at the 3.1 percent prevalence rate that national studies report. Indeed, 11.5 percent of Zoomers report that they are bisexual. Whether they would disagree with my 25+ percent estimate, I cannot say.

The far more important task is finding out what life is like for today's youths, as Max Morris did when he interviewed middle- and working-class boys ages 16 to 18 in the United Kingdom. The majority had positive experiences being openly bisexual: "an enriching coming out process, accepting friends, and inclusive school [environment]." Whatever sustained harassment they experienced declined over time, and none felt marginalized or victimized. It is very likely that this would also hold for bisexual girls.[9]

Zoomer participation in the postidentity revolution is easily mapped on social media platforms, with the inclusion of the usually recalcitrant heterosexual boy. One such example is the straight boy and his homies who embrace "homiesexuality." Though anyone can be homiesexual, TikTok and YouTube have been besieged with young men stretching the bounds of male gender and, by implication, male sexuality. The journalist Alex Hawgood writes about this startling trend, "Ostensibly heterosexual young men spooning in cuddle-puddle formation, cruising each other on the street while walking with their girlfriends, sharing a bed, going in for a kiss, admiring each other's chiseled physiques and engaging in countless other homoerotic situations served up for humor and, ultimately, views." Is this their version of a bromance or passionate friendship, though more explicitly sexual than in previous generations? Though homiesexuals are admittedly "feigning gay as a form of clickbait"—girls are the primary audience for the boys' antics—they might also be signaling their need for deeply fulfilling, carefree male connection, as noted by Niobe Way, and, I would add, for physical bonding with each other. A 16-year-old boy told Hawgood, "In the new generation everyone is fluid and so men have become less hesitant about physical stuff or showing emotions. It would seem ridiculous if you were not OK with it." Perhaps these youths are mostly straight (bisexual) or gender flexible; at the very least, they're showing a softer masculinity that is sensitive, erotic, affectionate, and kind. Perhaps Gen Alphas (born in the early 2010s) will also embody it. That is what we want, right?[10]

Although it is difficult to fully track the genesis and evolution of this dramatic shift in the way youths treat each other, surely it is related to the radical decline of cultural *homohysteria*. According to the sociologists Mark McCormack and Eric Anderson, this is the fear, especially among straight men and women, that they will be publicly perceived as gay, lesbian, or bisexual if they violate established boundaries of sexuality and gender. As homohysteria falls off across Western societies, including family and friends, benefits accrue to everyone in "the social inclusion of gay male peers; the embrace of once-feminized artifacts; the increased emotional intimacy and physical tactility; the erosion of the one-time rule of homosexuality; and the rejection of violence."[11]

It is no longer unusual for Zoomers and now even some Alphas to come out as bisexual while still living at home, a rare occurrence in older generations. Many are seldom bullied or harassed but are accepted by those who respect and admire them for being true to their sense of self. All stand to gain when straight-oriented men and women reject negative attitudes and stereotypes to honor bisexual, pansexual, nonbinary, and fluid individuals and their lives. And, perhaps, more than a few will recognize their own fluidity, acknowledge their place on sexual and romantic spectrums, and welcome their "little bit of gayness" as a good thing.

Postidentity Epoch

Just barely below the surface of these transformations is another revolution—clamoring for visibility, if we knew where to look. It is rooted in the progressive attitudes and perspectives of youths and young adults. For example, according to a 2019 Pew Research Center report, Zoomers, born after the mid-1990s, are one of the most socially and politically liberal age groups in US history, similar to Millennials except they are more open to social change along a range of ethnic, sexual, and trans* issues. Nearly 90 percent believe that same-sex marriage is a good thing or does not matter; 60 percent agree that forms should include gender options other than "man" and "woman."[12] Given this progressive shift, which has only become magnified during the present time, and the widespread confusion with the latest terms and identities, the time is right to rethink our notions about sexual, romantic, and gender matters.

Three broad-based options are open to youths. One, they can continue to adopt one of the standard sexual identities: straight, bisexual, or gay/lesbian. Of course, what exactly these mean to them might differ from our own understanding. We should ask. A young woman I interviewed publicly identifies as lesbian to connote sisterhood with other feminists who love women, although she remains sexually attracted to men and women, depending on their gender expression. Another young woman identifies as bisexual because she is only sexually attracted to women but falls in love with men.

A second option is available to those who find traditional identities too restrictive or too off-putting: invent their own identity. We could help by expanding the list we give them to choose from. A year ago, Susan Brooks emailed me regarding the Pinnacle Foundation, which provides educational scholarships and mentoring to disadvantaged LG-

BTIQ youths in Australia.[13] She had a request: "We are trying to increase scholarship applications from Lesbians so would appreciate an update on what conspires few women to identify as Lesbian." After several email conversations, she advised board members,

> Recent longitudinal analysis of our scholars' sexual and gender identities has demonstrated that the use of the acronym LGBTIQ . . . is now "out of step" with contemporary attitudes because of the increase in applicants who see themselves outside of this terminology. . . . Young women today see the term "lesbian" as outdated and for some it implies a particular lifestyle or political position. For others, it sounds too "clinical" while others feel that they are not ready to see themselves as solely loving women.

Application options for sexual orientation are now "straight," "queer," "nonbinary," "pansexual," and "asexual." I would have added several more, such as "fluid," "questioning," and "unsure"—but it's a beginning.

Implementing an open-ended option was provided in a national online study, with the recruitment assistance of the singer and actor Lady Gaga. With a sample of over 19,000 high school students, Arielle White and colleagues explored a critical question: when students were given an "other" option to the sexual identity question, followed by an open-ended response box, over 5 percent wrote in a variety of nontraditional identities. The most frequent were, in order, "pansexual," "asexual," "unsure," "questioning," "demisexual," "queer," "no label," "panromantic," "bicurious," "confused," and "biromantic."[14] How many would have chosen "bisexual" if forced to select one of the traditional three identities or would have left the question unanswered is unknown—and that is okay. When given the opportunity, they can provide their own words.

A third option occurring in many young lives, regardless of sexuality, is a minimization, if not an elimination, of the necessity to label oneself with a culturally defined, simplistic sexual identity. Because youths are not always convinced that sexuality or romance is set for life, they pursue diverse pathways to explore and understand their lives. Let's be clear: they are not forsaking sex or love but are rather refuting culturally authorized labels that do not correspond to the complexity of their lives. To them, the mere construction of categories reifies labels across time and place and, most importantly, exaggerates artificial differences between them and their friends. Besides, if mainstream straight youth are not required to assume a sexual identity, why should they?[15] One ideal alternative is simply to be descriptive, similar to the singer Rita Ora, who has said, "I have had romantic relationships with women and men throughout my life."[16] Another is to choose an identity taken from an expanding list of accessible identities. The Millennial actors Bex Taylor-Klaus and Ezra Miller are "nonbinary"; Jake Choi, "sexually fluid"; and Nico Tortorella, "gender fluid." This development leaves established identity terms, such as "bisexual," with sundry and perplexing meanings that do not easily map onto the experiences of Alphas, Zoomers, and Millennials. We need to ask young people about their preferences and to develop better, open-ended measures of sexuality and romance. If we did, their answers would trigger a radically new perspective—which might well happen with the upcoming Alpha generation.

All options can lead youths to reside in a postidentity revolution.

The Future

I was first sensitized to the meaning of these generational changes after interviewing sexual-minority youth for an earlier book, *The New Gay Teenager*. At that time, I speculated that we were entering a *postgay* epoch: "Teenagers are increasingly redefining, reinterpreting, and renegotiating their sexuality such that possessing a gay, lesbian, or bisexual identity is practically meaningless. Their sexuality is not something that can be easily described, categorized, or understood apart from being part of their life in general." This suggested to me a radical shift, not just in words but in understanding the breadth of their sexual, romantic, and gender lives. "They are in the forefront of what can be called a postgay era, in which same-sex attracted individuals can pursue diverse personal and political goals, whether they be a desire to blend into mainstream society or a fight to radically restructure modern discourse about sexuality."[17]

This assessment was initially challenged by the sociologist Stephen Russell and colleagues because they believe that terms such as "gay," "lesbian," and "bisexual" are still relevant and that these youths face severe minority stress and stigma. I agree with the psychologist Phillip Hammack and colleagues that some youths feel comforted or empowered with a traditional, well-recognized sexual identity. Nothing I have said would challenge this perspective. Of course, I never said traditional sexual identities had disappeared or argued, as Russell and colleagues quoted me as saying, that "LGB identities are no longer a source of stigma for adolescents." These authors and many others represent the current zeitgeist: highlight the distress and complications rather than the joys of having same-sex attraction. Indeed, revolutionary evidence is apparent even in Russell and colleagues' study. They asked high school students to select a sexual identity: "Gay/Lesbian, Straight/Heterosexual, Bisexual, Queer, Questioning, and Write-In." Of the nonheterosexual youths, nearly one-third chose or wrote in one of the following descriptions: questioning, queer, pansexual, asexual, everything, open, anything, no-label, don't like labels, no comment, curious, flexible, still deciding, no idea, I wish I knew, not thinking about it, heteroflexible, bisexually gay, supergay, normal. To me, this is a strong *affirmation* of a change-in-the-making from traditional gay, lesbian, and bisexual identities. In the decade since my previous book, although my presumption of sexual identity's transience was perhaps overdrawn, it is clear that we have entered an antiestablishment sexual identity period. The postgay is becoming a progressive, insurgent *postidentity* era.[18]

One serious unease that I have wrestled with is whether these developments are durable over time. That is, are they in perpetuity or merely youthful indiscretions, an example of youths' rebellion against the status quo and their parents' generation? Is the postidentity epoch merely a fleeting moment in time before societal pressures to be monosexual, to settle down, and to practice monogamy take effect? The cultural message received by some youths is, "Let go of your weird identities and genders and be *normal*." Even if a youth caves, these regressive forces are ultimately ineffective in suppressing or altering a youth's prevailing erotic and romantic arousal and attraction, which are more private and less susceptible to being chosen than adopting an identity or engaging in sexual or romantic behavior.

I believe in this durability because I am convinced by biology that sexual, romantic, and fluid orientations are primarily about genetics, either a polygenic characteristic of individuals that is constant across time and context or a function of the prenatal environment and its hormonal effects on the brain. I previously cited Brendan Zietsch's genetic research in these matters. Additional evidence comes from a 2005 BBC internet survey of nearly 200,000 individuals from 28 countries. The relatively stable rates of bisexuality "observed across nations for both women and men suggest that *non-social* factors likely may underlie much variation in human sexual orientation"; these factors are unrelated to "gendered social norms across societies."[19] Thus, what varies is the willingness to express, name, acknowledge, and celebrate sexual and romantic attractions. I cannot yet answer questions of longevity with regard to identity and behavior, at least with Zoomers, because they are still in what adults call the "indeterminate" phase of youthful experimentation with gender, love, and sex. Is the social cachet for everyone to be bisexual or whatever is the contemporary obligatory thing to be—maybe it's pansexual, fluid, nonbinary, or trans*—a mere footnote to the modern record? We will see, but I would bet against that idea.

With Millennials, however, we are on firmer ground regarding stability because the limited evidence suggests that these changes may be permanently a part of their lives. Throughout this book, I have cited a number of studies supporting a postidentity revolution. If one is inclined to disbelieve those studies, I now reference one of the most frequently cited national data sets: Add Health. The once adolescents (Wave 1) are now in the oldest segment of the Millennial generation. At Wave 3 (2002), they averaged 22 years of age, and at Wave 4 (2009), 29—that is, they moved from the last vestiges of adolescence into young adulthood. At Wave 3, 94 percent of the men and 85 percent of the women identified as straight; their self-reported sexual behavior and attraction were comparable. Seven years later, as young adults, changes were evident. While some nonstraight youths joined the ranks of straights (for reasons unknown but perhaps to conform to societal expectations), nearly 50 percent more men and over 200 percent more women left straightness for a nonstraight identity. The vast majority of these men (75 percent) and women (88 percent) "became" mostly straight—that is, they became bisexual because they recognized their small degree of same-sex attractions or behavior. Thus, with age, more did not join heterosexuality, as predicted by the "become normal" advocates, but left it. It was multiattracted identities that gained the most. It is possible that Zoomers are recognizing their bisexuality earlier than Millennials and that they will be *more likely* during young adulthood to move toward alternatives to the straight box. Perhaps they are more willing to create their own identities to fit their life trajectories—and Alphas might do so at an even higher rate and at an earlier age.

It is worth noting that it is women, not men, who are leading these revolutionary changes. Men are following, not yet closely but persistently—as homiesexuals illustrate. Perhaps in the near future, men will more fully embrace and enact this element of feminine freedom, fulfilling Marlo Thomas's message 50 years ago of "free to be you and me," which welcomed the value of being comfortable with one's identity. My guess is that the trends will be magnified if the reference point is not to sexual but to romantic identity, attraction, and behavior. This component of lives might be easier for males to acknowledge—to say, "I have a crush on my best friend" rather than "I have sex with my best friend"— perhaps reducing toxic masculinity throughout our culture. As I mentioned earlier, the most serious obstacle to the *new man* and the *strong woman* is sexism and misogyny, not biphobia—though the latter certainly contributes to what many youths feel is harmful to them.

As might be expected, social media comes to our aid. The actors 31-year-old Evan Rachel Wood (*Westworld*), 25-year-old Brigette Lundy-Paine (*Atypical*), and 32-year-old Tyler Blackburn (*Pretty Little Liars*) have lived the life exemplified by many postidentity young adults, regardless of gender and sex, fêted in this book. Since age 12, tomboy Wood has been drawn to girls and boys. "I thought women were beautiful but because I was born that way I never once stopped to think that was strange or anything to fear." The girl attractions were buried because of antigay hate speech in her North Carolina community. Now, she is open about her sexuality, hoping that her story will help young people come to terms with themselves.[20]

Brigette Lundy-Paine came out by phone to her mother once she began dating her first girlfriend. "And then after that it was kinda like, 'Oh, I don't have to really tell anybody else.' I just date who I want and not have to put up with it." She identifies as queer and says that her task is to figure out if she "ever will date a straight guy again": "It's all about testing the waters."[21]

So, too, Tyler Blackburn battled social pressure to remain binary (either gay or straight). The pressure emanated from older LGBTQ people who believe that bisexuality is "a cop-out or bullshit or the easy way out or something": "and that always stuck with me because I felt the pressure from all sides to have [my sexuality] figured out." Blackburn confesses that he just wanted to say, "Please just let me be gay and be okay with that, because it would be a lot fucking easier." But he knew he was unquestionably in the "gray zone." Similar to many Millennials and Zoomers, Blackburn is a step beyond simple bisexuality—which tires him. "I just want to live my truth and feel OK with experiencing love and experiencing self-love." He says, "We're at a place where fluidity is spoken about in such a beautiful way that it doesn't make me feel as pressured to have it figured out. My goal above everything is to feel as happy as possible. As free as possible."[22]

Because all three actors detest being placed in an identity box, they are postidentity. That is, they are exactly where they should be—the here and now. Given the postidentity revolution we are entering, even "bisexual" as a label or identity has become passé to some people. To a significant degree, Millennial celebrities are foreshadowing the death of sexual identities for the Zoomer and Alpha generations. During the past several years, a number of assorted personalities have come out in a manner at odds with previous generations. They use evocative, postidentity descriptions.

- Paris Jackson (age 22, model): "I don't feel like there is a label for my sexuality that fits."
- Ronan Farrow (age 32, journalist): Confirms he is a part of the LGBT community but doesn't like labels.
- Alyson Stoner (age 27, dancer, actor): "Am attracted to men, women, and people who identify in other ways."
- Felix Jaehn (age 26, DJ): "Sometimes I was more interested in girls, sometimes more interested in boys."
- Lucas Hedges (age 23, actor): "Not totally straight, but also not gay and not necessarily bisexual."
- Janelle Monáe (age 34, singer, actor): "Being a queer black woman in America—someone who has been in relationships with both men and women—I consider myself to be a free-ass motherfucker."
- Kehlani (age 25, singer): "Not bi, not straight. i'm attracted to women, men, REALLY attracted to queer men, non binary people, intersex people, trans people. lil poly pansexual."[23]

The actor Lee Pace (*The Hobbit*, *Guardians of the Galaxy*) responded to a reporter's question about his sexuality by not using "bisexual" in reference to himself but describing his behavior: "I've dated men. I've dated women. I don't know why anyone would care." In this, Pace's views are shared by many Zoomers and Millennials.[24]

Final Hope

Science has obviously not recruited representative samples of multiattracted individuals and, as a result, has misrepresented how many—the millions uncounted—who fall under the bisexual umbrella but do not necessarily identify as bisexual. Where is the research that helps us understand the developmental history of 20-year-old Malachi? He transitioned from a "straight" childhood to a "bisexual leaning straight" adolescence to an "equal attraction" young adulthood to his now "pansexuality." We know little about his and others' developmental histories, their characteristics, their joys of life, and their contributions to our world. A bisexuality does not exist—but *bisexualities* do.

I'm also optimistic because I believe the Zoomers' messages are permeating our culture. A young mother recently wrote to me that she is choosing to raise her son pansexual—not as an identity but to be open to loving all, the full spectrums of sex and gender. She closed her email with the essence of this book: "But I can't help but wonder how society would be if we all just stopped worrying about our own identities so much and just be. Love ourselves. Love each other. And be open to any possibilities." She's a Millennial, which gives me additional hope that her thoughtful, profound statement will become the norm as we raise our Zoomers and Alphas.

That mother's perspective is shared, I believe, by many youths, which we would know if we troubled ourselves to listen to their voices. They say that many theories about them are misguided and detrimental and injurious to them and their brothers and sisters. We need our family members, friends, educators, clinicians, and others who care for them to listen. Although we have frequently lost our way, we must return to the source about what it means to have multiple attractions. These youths give me hope. I will close with the words of two of them:

We've come to a new age where sexuality is so much less of a thing. I mean, it can still be a thing and a lot of people still care, but there are enough people who don't care. I feel like it's the time for everyone to be liberal about it. If everyone is really open about it, then there is nothing that the people who don't like it can do. (Woody Cook, age 19, model)[25]

Something that really made me want to run is when someone came up to me to tell me they were part of the LGBTQ community, but they were too afraid to tell anyone. I felt my heart break for them. I want to help all the kids who feel like that to feel free to be who they are. (Ella Briggs, age 11, 2019's Connecticut's Kid Governor)[26]

May Woody and Ella foretell our future.

ACKNOWLEDGMENTS

I thank the multiattracted young men and women—the bisexuals, pan-sexuals, fluids, and nonbinaries—who shared their sexual and romantic histories with me. They are the inspirational foundation of this book, joining the other young adults who participated in two prior books. They epitomize the transformations of the Millennial generation in matters of sex and love and motivate and encourage Zoomers to move further along the spectrum to the possibility of being open, honest, and revolutionary in their commitment to lead authentic sexual, romantic, and gender lives.

Having worked with several publishers during my professional life, I am thrilled to be working with the wonderful people at the New York University Press. Their catalogue well represents the progressive spirit of the young adults I interviewed. In particular, working with Ilene Kalish, my acquisition editor, has been every writer's dream: enthusiastic, supportive, and speedy; she has added considerable wisdom and knowledge through the final edits of this book. Sonia Tsuruoka has been the patient, knowledgeable professional that writers must have to guide their book through the publication process. Production editor Alexia Traganas has been timely and extremely helpful in keeping me on track. Copyeditor Andrew Katz has been kind but firm in his suggestions; he understood what I was trying to say even when I did not. These people—and others behind the scenes—have been nothing short of amazing, and they well typify the NYU Press tradition of excellence. They have been a pure delight to work with.

My Sex & Gender lab's post-doc scientist, Gerulf Rieger (now at the University of Essex), provided invaluable technical, theoretical, and personal support during this process. Collaborator professors Mark Mc-

Cormack (University of Roehampton) and Kara Joyner (Bowling Green State University) helped steer me in good directions; James Rounds, director of the EEG and Psychophysiology Lab at Cornell University taught us how to gather physiological data; and graduate students Matthew Stief, Sarah Merrill, and Zhana Vrangalova and undergraduate research assistant Brian Martin Cash were essential to collecting data, coding data, understanding data, managing the lab, and telling me when to self-correct.

I am especially grateful to Fritz Klein (founder) and John Sylla (chairman and chief executive officer) of the American Institute of Bisexuality and to Dean of Human Ecology Alan Mathios, for financial support during the past four years. My home department, Human Development, and Cornell University have been willing to let me pursue my dreams. John Sylla might well be the most important person in bisexual research today—not only for funding so many projects but also for his critiques and encouragements. He knows bisexuals.

Finally, I am able to write because I have one of the most loving and supportive husbands in the universe, Kenneth Miles Cohen.

METHODOLOGICAL APPENDIX

Men

Among the 206 young men I interviewed, 28 identified as bisexual. I excluded from this book the 40 mostly or primarily straight young men and the 21 mostly or primarily gay young men because their stories were included in earlier books. All were participants in one of two research projects, which, in all respects, followed the ethical guidelines mandated by Cornell University, where I was employed.

Friends and Lovers Study

From April 2008 through April 2009, 160 young men across a range of sexualities between the ages of 17 and 27 (mean = 20.0) volunteered for my Friends and Lovers study. The research was advertised as an interview study with young men about their friends and lovers since they were "a child, teenager, and now." By participating, they contributed to an understanding regarding the sexual development of young men of all sexual orientations from earliest memories to the present time.

Of the young men in the study, 70 percent identified as white, with the rest identifying as Asian American (13 percent), African American (7 percent), Latino (6 percent), or Native American (3 percent). Most (72 percent) were university students, and the others were enrolled in a local community college or were employed. Their academic majors were widely distributed across the social sciences, biological/life sciences, engineering, and humanities. The most desired career trajectories were, in order, finance, marketing, or business; teaching (schoolteacher or professor); medicine (medical doctor or in the medical field); law;

264 | METHODOLOGICAL APPENDIX

and engineering. Nearly three-quarters reported that they were either middle or upper middle class. Two in ten reported that their families are working class or lower middle class. Two-thirds were raised in a small or medium-sized town or suburb or a small city. Nearly one-third grew up in an urban area, and a few were from rural/farming communities.

Fliers were posted in freshman and sophomore residence halls and college cafés. The study was advertised on online newsletters and a fraternity email list. Advertisement cards were hand distributed by undergraduate research assistants, and on occasion, participants gave the advertisement cards to their friends. If young men wanted to participate, they notified me directly. These potential participants were sent details regarding the project's purpose and design, including time commitment and payment of $20. They were required to complete an informed-consent form and were provided with a list of interview times. Once interviews were scheduled, participants were sent a preinterview survey requesting basic demographic data (age, education, major, citizenship, ethnicity, social class, community size, and career objectives) and their high school and college activities, clubs, and organizations. They were informed that they should bring a completed hard copy of the informed consent with them to the interview.

Interviews were held in a private location in an academic building on campus and lasted from 40 to 135 minutes, with an average of 73 minutes. At the beginning of the interview, each young man completed a questionnaire about the percentage of his sexual attractions, sexual interactions (genital contact), infatuations/crushes, sexual fantasies, and romantic relationships that was directed to males and females when he was a child, an early adolescent, an adolescent, and now, as well as the percentages for each in his ideal future. Interviews were not recorded, in compliance with Human Subjects Committee mandate at the time, so their quotes are not literally verbatim (but they are extremely close) or as extensive as those of the young men in the next section's study. I took extensive notes with a shorthand technique I developed to record nearly every word, and I transcribed these notes immediately after each interview.

Eight individuals who volunteered for the study did not respond to further email contact to establish an interview time. Thus, 93 percent of the young men who contacted me completed the research. Of the young men who were sent a questionnaire, 100 percent returned it, and 100 percent of those who set up an appointment completed the interview. Three did not show at the appointed time but contacted me and rescheduled.

The participants were paid a $20 incentive for their time. All but one agreed to be contacted in succeeding years to participate in longitudinal follow-up questionnaires, interviews, or experiments. Of the 160 young men, eight identified as bisexual and are featured in this book: Casey, Dave, Donovan, Ian, Jordan, Kenworthy, Toby, and Zane (all pseudonyms).

Personality and Sexuality Study

Dr. Gerulf Rieger, a postdoctoral fellow in my Sex and Gender Lab, and undergraduate research assistants recruited 229 participants in 2012. Of these, 109 were young men between the ages of 18 and 32 (mean: 21.9). The research was broadly advertised as a lab-based study investigating issues of sex, gender, and personality. The primary purpose was the assessment of sexual orientation through pupil dilation and eye-tracking techniques.

At the time, 66 percent of the men were undergraduate college students, and an additional 17 percent had completed their undergraduate education and were employed. Others were in graduate school (9 percent), completed some college and dropped out (6 percent), or finished high school (2 percent). Seventy-five percent identified as white, and the rest identified as Asian American (12 percent), Latino (5 percent), mixed ethnicity/race (5 percent), and African American (4 percent).

Advertisements for the study were placed on a Facebook page, posted in several residence halls and fraternities, and advertised on websites catering to members of athletic teams. To increase recruitment of sexual minorities, the study notice was also posted on a Craigslist forum oriented toward sexual minorities. Participants contacted the lab by email, and written informed consent was obtained once they arrived at the university lab. After they finished the physiological portion of the study, an online questionnaire using an internet-based survey tool was administered, which included a 7-point sexual orientation identity scale. At the conclusion of the questionnaire, they could indicate a willingness to participate in an interview to track their "sexual and romantic development from first memories to the present day." All but four agreed to be contacted.

Of the 109 men, 46 scheduled a follow-up interview for an additional incentive of $20. Nineteen identified as bisexual, nine of whom are featured in this book: Caleb, Gene, Jacob, José Luis, Juan, Malachi, Sawyer, Roberto, and Zach (all pseudonyms).

Informed consent to record interviews was allowed by the Human Subjects Committee under particular guidelines. One, a signed consent was secured from all participants. Two, all participants were given the opportunity to have the recorder turned off at any point during the interview; one individual asked for a temporary halt (while discussing a family secret). Three, all participants were given the option to have the transcript deleted at the conclusion of the interview; none so requested. A paid research assistant who was not otherwise involved in the study and was living in Florida transcribed the recordings, which are a source of quotes used in this book. Quotes have been altered to mask personal identifying details and to delete extraneous, repetitive information. Due to the tape recording, individual life stories of these young men are considerably more extensive than those of the Friends and Lovers participants.

Women

Parallel with the Friends and Lovers study of men, 78 women between the ages of 17 and 25 (mean: 20.8 years) responded to advertisements for an interview study with "young women who are attracted to other women romantically, physically, or sexually." The title of the study, "Then I Kissed Her," was a recommendation made by undergraduate women research assistants as a means of soliciting women who have some degree of same-sex desire. The women were diverse in sexual identification, social class, religious affiliation, and size of hometown community but less so in educational level and regional distribution. The young women were recruited through announcements in college classes on gender and sexuality, fliers sent to campus social and political organizations, and advertisements placed in a community newsletter and in public places (bar, bookstore, café) for sexual minorities in rural upstate New York communities. To broaden the sample, postings were made on several internet electronic mailing lists for sexual-minority women. This multiple recruitment strategy was undertaken to draw participants along the spectrum of same-sex attractions. For example, campus political organizations tend to include individuals who openly identify their sexuality; college courses on gender often draw students who are beginning to acknowledge their same-sex attractions.

To volunteer, participants contacted the principal investigator by email. Special efforts were made to include individuals who were not comfortable openly identifying as lesbian or bisexual by assuring them that such identifications were not necessary to participate. All interviews were confidential and were neither audiotaped nor videotaped (in compliance with the Human Subjects Committee). Because of the recruitment strategy, the response rate cannot be calculated because it is unknown how many potential participants who knew about the study and who met selection criteria did not volunteer. Nine percent of the women who contacted the investigator did not return phone or email messages or failed to show up for the appointment. Because of human-subjects guidelines, no attempt was made to discover how individuals found out about the study or their reasons for refusing to participate.

Due to the interview protocol, which included potentially "uncomfortable," sexually oriented questions, a woman professor was scheduled to conduct the interviews. She, however, opted out because she feared that the nature of the research would negatively impact her tenure review. Given this last-minute change, the Human Subjects Committee requested three procedural changes. One, I was to conduct the interviews to safeguard compliance with Cornell standards/procedures. Two, to increase the comfort of all potential women recruits with having a male interviewer, they were given the option of an in-person or phone interview. Three, due to the committee's privacy concerns, personal descriptions of the young women were not recorded. Most directly, these stipulations affected my ability to describe the women participants or record their life histories in detail comparable to the men participants.

Of the 78 women, 32 (41 percent) chose the phone option. In-person interviews were conducted in a faculty office or a place chosen by participants that afforded privacy and confidentiality. The purpose and procedures of the research project were explained, questions were answered, and consent was secured in accordance with the guidelines of the university's Committee on Human Subjects. There were no demographic differences between those who were interviewed in person and those were interviewed by phone except that the women interviewed by phone were more likely to identify as lesbian. The participants were paid a $20 incentive for their time.

Interviews ranged between 30 to 75 minutes (median: 45 minutes). Initial questions requested that participants give their age, ethnicity, hometown community location and size, family social class, and current sexual identity label (open-ended format). The remainder of the interview focused on milestones of sexual and romantic development, from earliest memories of same-sex attractions to current feelings about one's sexual and romantic self. Extensive notes were taken, and these were transcribed.

The women identified as lesbian/bi-lesbian (45 percent), bisexual (33 percent), or questioning/unlabeled (22 percent). All but the first group are included in this book. For the sample as a whole, 78 percent identified as white; the rest identified as Asian American (13 percent), African

American (7 percent), or Latina (3 percent). Their academic majors were widely distributed across the social sciences, biological/life sciences, engineering, and humanities. Over three-quarters reported that they were either middle or upper middle class. Two-thirds were raised in a small or medium-sized town or suburb or a small city. Nearly one-fourth grew up in an urban area, and one in ten were from rural/farming communities. Nearly one-half grew up in the Northeast, and one-quarter were from the South. Of this group, 24 are featured in this book: Alejandra, Alicia, Amy, Cheryl, Deja, Eden, Elizabeth, Emma, Flora, Harper, Hei-Ran, Ida, Jen, Kristin, Laura, Leila, Madeline, Melissa, Rachel, Selena, Sierra, Stacey, Su-Wei, and Valerie (all pseudonyms).

Reflections on Methods

Although the young adults I interviewed are diverse in many respects (social class, personality, religion, ethnicity, geographic region), I do not claim that they are representative of their generation in their basic personal and social lives. Ideally, I wanted more African American, Latin, and Native American young adults to volunteer. My physical location in a rural college town probably handicapped my ability to recruit these individuals; it also limited the number of interviewees who grew up in large urban areas, had few socioeconomic resources, and were not attending college. On the other hand, social class diversity was enhanced with the monetary incentive—several participants were obviously quite happy to receive the money. I purposely did not advertise in psychology classes, to enhance disciplinary diversity, and made it clear that individuals from all sexualities were welcome.

Any study such as this one will, by definition, omit those who do not want to share, for whatever reasons, their sexual and romantic development with a stranger—thus, they are underrepresented. This might be particularly true for women who would have been interviewed by a male academic. Despite these limitations, the young women and men who did participate were enthusiastic participants in the research.

NOTES

PREFACE

1. For Dr. Kenneth Altshuler, bisexuality was merely a resting stop on the way to "compulsive homosexuality." He defined bisexuality as having "equal frequency and pleasure with either sex, and therefore an equal preference and relatively random choice in the sex of their partner." K. Z. Altshuler, "On the question of bisexuality," *American Journal of Psychotherapy, 38* (1984), 484–493, quote p. 493. Dr. Ruth believed that most who claim to be bisexual or who lead a bisexual lifestyle are in reality "not sure" and will eventually fall into one category or the other. See Peppermint, "Dr. Ruth has decided that bisexuals . . . aren't," *LiveJournal* (October 18, 2005), https://inki.livejournal.com.

2. My early books presented the vitality and assets of sexual-minority youths during their developmental trajectories: *Gay and Lesbian Youth: Expressions of Identity* (Washington, DC: Hemisphere, 1990); *". . . And Then I Became Gay": Young Men's Stories* (New York: Routledge, 1998); and *"Mom, Dad. I'm Gay.": How Families Negotiate Coming Out* (Washington, DC: American Psychological Association, 2001). Eventually, I summarized the literature in *The New Gay Teenager* (Cambridge, MA: Harvard University Press, 2005), quote p. 169. The latest relies more on the actual words of youths: *Becoming Who I Am: Young Men on Being Gay* (Cambridge, MA: Harvard University Press, 2016) and *Mostly Straight: Sexual Fluidity among Men* (Cambridge, MA: Harvard University Press, 2017).

INTRODUCTION

1. C. Harris, "Son of the beach," featuring Woody Cook at PRM Models, *Boys by Girls* (January 28, 2019), www.boysbygirls.co.uk.

2. The stories in Way's 2011 book are a fascinating read: *Deep Secrets: Boys' Friendships and the Crisis of Connection* (Cambridge, MA: Harvard University Press, 2011). The quote is from an interview she did with the *New Yorker*: Vanna Le, "Ask an academic: The secrets of boys" (March 15, 2011), www.newyorker.com.

3. This review is from L. Dunham, "The enduring spell of *The Outsiders*," *New York Times Magazine* (September 5, 2018), www.nytimes.com.

4. Celebrities coming out as something other than straight are frequently reported on social media and in the press. A. Kacalasee, "National Coming Out Day: 17 celebrities who came out this year (so far)," *NBC News* (October 11, 2018), www.nbcnews.com.

1. BISEXUALITY NOW

1. Lisa Diamond is the most visible scientist documenting the fluidity of women. See her book *Sexual Fluidity: Understanding Women's Love and Desire* (Cambridge, MA: Harvard University Press, 2008) and her article "Sexual fluidity in male[s] and females," *Current Sexual Health Reports, 8* (2016), 249–256, doi:10.1007/s11930-016-0092-z.

2. With a life in biology, Anne Fausto-Sterling has recently focused on how the environment affects biology. See her important book *Sex/Gender: Biology in a Social World* (New York: Routledge, 2012) and her article "Gender/sex, sexual orientation, and identity are in the body: How did they get there?," *Journal of Sex Research, 56* (2019), 529–555, doi:10.1080/00224499.2019.1581883.

3. They made their case in the opening introduction to the special issue: E. Steinman & B. Beemyn, *Journal of Bisexuality, 1* (2001), 1–14, quote p. 5.

4. See, respectively, B. K. Stewart, "Here's why bisexuality in girls is totally on the rise," *Teen Vogue* (January 11, 2016), www.teenvogue.com; S. Schmidt, "10 years after 'I Kissed a Girl,' Rita Ora's single stirs debate over portrayals of bisexuality," *Washington Post* (May 6, 2018), www.washingtonpost.com; and maxcw99, "Cobra Starship—I Kissed a Boy (music video) Parody of Katy Perry—I Kissed a Girl," YouTube (November 22, 2008), www.youtube.com/watch?v=-oi4yKFOLcg. Additional support for this sex difference is in A. S. Arriaga & M. C. Parent, "Partners and prejudice: Bisexual partner gender and experiences of binegativity from heterosexual, lesbian, and gay people," *Psychology of Sexual Orientation and Gender Diversity, 6* (2019), 382–391, doi:10.1037/sgd0000337.

5. The average age of sexual attractions is around age 8. R. C. Savin-Williams, *The New Gay Teenager* (Cambridge, MA: Harvard University Press, 2005). This was first noted by M. K. McClintock & G. Herdt, "Rethinking puberty: The development of sexual attraction," *Current Directions in Psychological Science, 5* (1996), 178–183, quote p. 180, doi:10.1111/1467-8721.ep11512422.

6. A. B. Suleiman, A. Galván, K. P. Harden, & R. A. Dahl, "Becoming a sexual being: The 'elephant in the room' of adolescent brain development," *Developmental Cognitive Neuroscience, 25* (2017), 209–220, quote p. 209, doi:10.1016/j.dcn.2016.09.004.

7. This diversity and unpredictability of developmental trajectories were highlighted in the English Avon Longitudinal Study, which followed over 5,000 youths between the ages of 11 to 15. See the primary source: G. Li & J. T. Davis, "Sexual experimentation in heterosexual, bisexual, lesbian/gay, and questioning adolescents from ages 11 to 15," *Journal of Research on Adolescence* (October 10, 2019), doi:10.1111/jora.12535, with earlier supporting evidence in A. P. Smiler, L. B. W. Frankel, & R. C. Savin-Williams, "From kissing to coitus? Sex-of-partner differences in the sexual milestone achievement of young men," *Journal of Adolescence, 34* (2011), 727–735, doi:10.1016/j.adolescence.2010.08.009.

8. These are detailed in two chapters: L. M. Diamond & R. C. Savin-Williams, "Adolescent sexuality," in R. M. Lerner & L. Steinberg (Eds.), *Handbook of Adolescent Psychology* (3rd ed., pp. 479–523) (New York: Wiley, 2009); and R. C. Savin-Williams, "Developmental trajectories and milestones of sexual-minority youth," in J. Gilbert & S. Lamb (Eds.), *Cambridge Handbook of Sexual Development: Childhood and Adolescence* (pp. 152–175) (New York: Cambridge University Press, 2018).

9. There are many sources for where adolescents receive sex information, and usually parents are low on the list. Here are a few of the better articles: M. Epstein & L. M. Ward, "'Always use protection': Communication boys receive about sex from parents, peers, and the media," *Journal of Youth and Adolescence, 37* (2008), 113–126, doi:10.1007/s10964-007-9187-1; R. Evans, L. Widman, K. Kamke, & J. L. Stewart, "Gender differences in parents' communication with their adolescent children about sexual risk and sex-positive topics," *Journal of Sex Research, 57* (2020), 177–188, doi:10.1080/00224499.2019.1661345; L. Widman, S. Choukas-Bradley, S. W. Helms, C. E. Golin, & M. J. Prinstein, "Sexual communication between early adolescents and their dating partners, parents, and best friends," *Journal of Sex Research, 51* (2014), 731–741, doi:10.1080/00224499.2013.843148.

4. GENERATIONAL REBELLION

1. This issue is explored in greater detail in two chapters I wrote: "The new sexual-minority teenager: Freedom from traditional notions of sexual identity," in J. S. Kaufman & D. A. Powell (Eds.), *The Meaning of Sexual Identity in the Twenty-First Century* (pp. 5–20) (New Castle, UK: Cambridge Scholars, 2014); and "Identity development among sexual-minority youth," in S. J. Schwartz, K. Luyckx, & V. L. Vignoles (Eds.), *Handbook of Identity Theory and Research* (pp. 671–689) (New York: Springer, 2011).

2. J. M. Jones, "LGBT identification rises to 5.6% in latest U.S. estimate," *Gallup News* (February 24, 2021), https://news.gallup.com.

3. Results reported in J. Berona, S. D. Stepp, A. E. Hipwell, & K. E. Keenan, "Trajectories of sexual orientation from adolescence to young adulthood: Results from a community-based urban sample of girls," *Journal of Adolescent Health, 63* (2018), 57–61, doi:10.1016/j.jadohealth.2018.01.015; and in T. Fu, D. Herbenick, D. Dodge, C. Owens, S. A. Sanders, M. Reece, & J. D. Fortenberry, "Relationships among sexual identity, sexual attraction, and sexual behavior: Results from a nationally representative probability sample of adults in the United States," *Archives of Sexual Behavior, 48* (2019), 1483–1493, doi:10.1007/s10508-018-1319-z.

4. The report is the American Psychological Association, *Answers to Your Questions: For a Better Understanding of Sexual Orientation and Homosexuality* (Washington, DC: Author, 2008), 1, www.apa.org.

5. The classic Kinsey Scale is described in A. C. Kinsey, W. B. Pomeroy, & C. E. Martin, *Sexual Behavior in the Human Male* (Oxford, UK: Saunders, 1948).

6. The most well-known is Fritz Klein's Sexual Orientation Grid: *The Bisexual Option: A Concept of One-Hundred Percent Intimacy* (New York: Arbor House, 1978). Others include R. L. Sell, "Defining and measuring sexual orientation: A review," *Archives of Sexual Behavior, 26* (1997), 643–658; and M. G. Shively & J. P. DeCecco, "Components of sexual identity," *Journal of Homosexuality, 3* (1977), 41–48.

7. This unique study involved many specialists and trainers: M. S. Friedman, A. J. Silvestre, M. A. Gold, N. Markovic, R. C. Savin-Williams, J. Huggins, & R. L. Sell, "Adolescents define sexual orientation and suggest ways to measure it," *Journal of Adolescence, 27* (2004), 303–317, quotes pp. 311–312, doi:10.1016/j. adolescence.2004.03.006.

8. This critical review is seldom cited but should be more frequently: M. Wolff, B. Wells, C. Ventura-DiPersia, A. Renson, & C. Grov, "Measuring sexual orientation: A review and critique of U.S. data collection efforts and implications for health policy," *Journal of Sex Research, 54* (2017), 507–531, quote and summary p. 526.

9. Two recent innovative research studies using this method are A. E. White, J. Moeller, Z. Ivcevic, & M. A. Brackett, "Gender identity and sexual identity labels used by U.S. high school students: A co-occurrence network analysis," *Psychology of Sexual Orientation and Gender Diversity, 5* (2018), 243–252, doi:10.1037/ sgd0000266; and M. P. Galupo, J. L. Ramirez, & L. Pulice-Farrow, "'Regardless of their gender': Descriptions of sexual identity among bisexual, pansexual, and queer identified individuals," *Journal of Bisexuality, 17* (2017), 108–124, doi:10.1080 /15299716.2016.1228491.

10. These various names and concepts in the popular press can be found at A. Tsoulis-Reay, "Are you straight, gay, or just . . . you?," *Glamour* (February 11, 2016), www.glamour.com; and J. Wortham, "On Instagram, seeing between the (gender) lines," *New York Times Magazine Tech and Design Issue* (November 16, 2018), www.nytimes.com.

11. A. C. Salomaa & J. L. Matsick, "Carving sexuality at its joints: Defining sexual orientation in research and clinical practice," *Psychological Assessment, 31* (2019), 167–180, quotes pp. 175, 168, doi:10.1037/pas0000656.

12. Among scholars who are open to alternative ideas are L. M. Diamond, "Toward greater specificity in modeling the ecological context of desire," *Human Development, 48* (2005), 291–297; S. W. Gangestad, J. M. Bailey, & N. G. Martin, "Taxometric analyses of sexual orientation and gender identity," *Journal of Personality and Social Psychology, 78* (2000), 1109–1121, doi:10.1037//0022-3514.78.6.1109; N. Haslam, "Evidence that male sexual orientation is a matter of degree," *Journal of Personality and Social Psychology, 73* (1997), 862–870; R. C. Savin-Williams, *The New Gay Teenager* (Cambridge, MA: Harvard University Press, 2005); R. L. Sell, "Defining and measuring sexual orientation: A review," *Archives of Sexual Behavior, 26* (1997), 643–658.

13. AVEN, "Overview," www.asexuality.org.

14. The authors' perceptive and spot-on critique of research is A. C. Salomaa & J. L. Matsick, "Carving sexuality at its joints: Defining sexual orientation in research and clinical practice," *Psychological Assessment, 31* (2019), 167–180, quote p. 167, doi:10.1037/pas0000656.

15. L. Villarosa, "Chirlane McCray: From gay trailblazer to politician's wife," *Essence* (May 9, 2013), www.essence.com.

16. This question was asked by N. McConaghy, "Heterosexuality/homosexuality: Dichotomy or continuum," *Archives of Sexual Behavior, 16* (1987), 411–424; and McConaghy, "Unresolved issues in scientific sexology," *Archives of Sexual Behavior, 28* (1999), 285–318. One answer came from N. Haslam, "Evidence that male sexual orientation is a matter of degree."

17. This dilemma is still with us: C. L. Muehlenhard, "Categories and sexuality," *Journal of Sex Research, 37* (2000), 101–107, doi:10.1080/00224490009552026.

18. Life stories of these young men are in R. C. Savin-Williams, *Mostly Straight: Sexual Fluidity among Men* (Cambridge, MA: Harvard University Press, 2017); R. C. Savin-Williams, *Becoming Who I Am: Young Men on Being Gay* (Cambridge, MA: Harvard University Press, 2016).

19. M. Wolff, B. Wells, C. Ventura-DiPersia, A. Renson, & C. Grov, "Measuring sexual orientation: A review and critique of U.S. data collection efforts and implications for health policy," *Journal of Sex Research, 54* (2017), 507–531, quote p. 510, doi:10.1 080/00224499.2016.1255872.

20. I discussed these issues in R. C. Savin-Williams, "An exploratory study of the categorical versus spectrum nature of sexual orientation," *Journal of Sex Research, 51* (2014), 446–453, doi:10.1007/s10508-013-0219-5; and R. C. Savin-Williams, "Sexual orientation: Categories or continuum? Commentary on Bailey et al.," *Psychological Science in the Public Interest, 17* (2016), 37–44, doi:10.1177/1529100616637618. Also see S. K. Yeskis-West, "Middle sexualities and what people say about them," *Odyssey* (March 7, 2017), www.theodysseyonline. com; and P. Moore, "A third of young Americans say they aren't 100% heterosexual," *YouGov* (August 20, 2015), https://today.yougov.com.

5. WHO IS BISEXUAL?

1. Summarized from Bisexual Resource Center, "Frequently asked questions," http://biresource.org.

2. General Social Survey, home page, http://gss.norc.org.

3. Among researchers who have used these data include M. L. Hatzenbuehler, A. Bellatorre, Y. Lee, B. K. Finch, P. Muennig, & K. Fiscella, "Structural stigma and all-cause mortality in sexual minority populations," *Social Science & Medicine 103* (2014), 33e41, doi:10.1016/j.socscimed.2013.06.005; M. B. Thomeer & C. Reczek, "Happiness and sexual minority status," *Archives of Sexual Behavior, 45* (2016), 1745–1758, doi:10.1007/s10508-016-0737-z. This same identity question has been used by others, including the Oregon Healthy Teen Survey and the European

Union Agency for Fundamental Rights. See M. L. Hatzenbuehler & K. M. Keyes, "Inclusive anti-bullying policies and reduced risk of suicide attempts in lesbian and gay youth," *Journal of Adolescent Health 53* (2013), S21eS26, doi:10.1016/j. jadohealth.2012.08.010; J. E. Pachankis & R. Bränström, "How many sexual minorities are hidden? Projecting the size of the global closet with implications for policy and public health," *PLoS One, 14*(6) (2019), e0218084, doi:10.1371/ journal.pone.0218084.

4. Centers for Disease Control and Prevention, "Behavioral Risk Factor Surveillance System," www.cdc.gov.

5. B. K. Gorman, J. T. Denney, H. Dowdy, & R. A. Medeiros, "A new piece of the puzzle: Sexual orientation, gender, and physical health status," *Demography, 52* (2015), 1357–1382, doi:10.1007/s13524-015-0406-1.

6. T. Lea, J. de Wit, & R. Reynolds, "Minority stress in lesbian, gay, and bisexual young adults in Australia: Associations with psychological distress, suicidality, and substance use," *Archives of Sexual Behavior, 43* (2014), 1571–1578, doi:10.1007/ s10508-014-0266-6.

7. National Institute on Alcohol Abuse and Alcoholism, "National Epidemiologic Survey on Alcohol and Related Conditions-III (NESARC-III)," www.niaaa.nih.

8. W. B. Bostwick, C. J. Boyd, T. L. Hughes, & S. E. McCabe, "Dimensions of sexual orientation and the prevalence of mood and anxiety disorders in the United States," *American Journal of Public Health, 100* (2010), 468–475, doi:10.2105/ AJPH.2008.152942.

9. Few use all of the measures, but Bostwick et al. is an exception

10. Add Health, "Social, behavioral, and biological linkages across the life course," https://addhealth.cpc.unc.edu. For definitions of terms, see R. C. Savin-Williams, K. Joyner, & G. Rieger, "Prevalence and stability of self-reported sexual orienta-tion identity during young adulthood," *Archives of Sexual Behavior, 41* (2012), 103–110, doi:10.1007/s10508-012-9913-y.

11. For a critical discussion, see R. C. Savin-Williams & K. Joyner, "The dubious assessment of gay, lesbian, and bisexual adolescents in Add Health," *Archives of Sexual Behavior, 43* (2014), 413–422, doi:10.1007/s10508-013-0219-5.

12. For a critical discussion, see D. Cornell, J. Klein, T. Konold, & F. Huang, "Effects of validity screening items on adolescent survey data," *Psychological Assessment, 24* (2012), 21–35, quote p. 12, doi:10.1037/a0024824.

13. C. R. Li, D. R. Follingstad, M. I. Campe, & J. K. Chahal, "Identifying invalid responders in a campus climate survey: Types, impact on data, and best indica-tors," *Journal of Interpersonal Violence* (May 13, 2020), doi:10.1177/0886260520918588.

14. There are many examples and critiques: J. R. Cimpian, J. D. Timmer, M. A. Birkett, R. L. Marro, B. C. Turner, & G. L. Phillips II, "Bias from potentially mischievous responders on large-scale estimates of lesbian, gay, bisexual, or questioning (LGBQ)–heterosexual youth health disparities," *American Journal of*

Public Health, 108 (2018), S258–S265, doi:10.2105/AJPH.2018.304407; J. R. Cimpian & J. D. Timmer, "Large-scale estimates of LGBQ-heterosexual disparities in the presence of potentially mischievous responders: A preregistered replication and comparison of methods," *AERA Open* (November 18, 2019), doi:10.1177/2332858419888892; X. Fan, B. C. Miller, K. E. Park, B. W. Winward, M. Christensen, H. D. Grotevant, & R. H. Tai, "An exploratory study about inaccuracy and invalidity in adolescent self-report surveys," *Field Methods, 18* (2006), 223–244, doi:10.1177/152822X06289161; D. Cornell, J. Klein, T. Konold, & F. Huang, "Effects of validity screening items on adolescent survey data," *Psychological Assessment, 24* (2012), 21–35, doi:10.1037/a0024824; J. Lopez & D. S. Hillygus, "Why so serious? Survey trolls and misinformation," *SSRN* (March 6, 2018), doi:10.2139/ssrn.3131087; J. P. Robinson & D. L. Espelage, "Inequities in educational and psychological outcomes between LGBTQ and straight students in middle and high school," *Educational Researcher, 40* (2011), 315–330, doi:10.3102/0013189X11422112.

15. S. E. McCabe, T. L. Hughes, W. Bostwick, M. Morales, & C. J. Boyd, "Measurement of sexual identity in surveys: Implications for substance abuse research," *Archives of Sexual Behavior, 41* (2012), 649–657, doi:10.1007/s10508-011-9768-7; see also R. C. Savin-Williams & K. M. Cohen, "Prevalence, mental health, and heterogeneity of bisexual men," *Current Sexual Health Reports, 10* (2018), 196–202, doi:10.1007/s11930-018-0164-3.

16. L. M. Carpenter, *Virginity Lost* (New York: New York University Press, 2005), chapter 2.

17. A. W. Blum, K. Lust, G. Christenson, & J. E. Grant, "Links between sexuality, impulsivity, compulsivity, and addiction in a large sample of university students," *CNS Spectrums* (April 15, 2019), 1–7, doi:10.1017/S1092852918001591.

18. Judy Wieder, "Coming clean," *Advocate* (January 24, 1995), www.advocate.com.

19. S. Freud, *Three Essays on the Theory of Sexuality* (London: Imago, 1905).

6. STRAIGHTS HAVING SEX WITH EACH OTHER

1. Dan Savage, "Savage love: Crossing over," *Stranger* (November 26, 2009), www.thestranger.com.

2. A. Hoy & A. S. London, "The experience and meaning of same-sex sexuality among heterosexually identified men and women: An analytic review," *Sociology Compass* (June 1, 2018), e12596, quote p. 12, doi:10.1111/soc4.12596.

3. G. Phillips II, L. B. Beach, B. Turner, B. A. Feinstein, R. Marro, M. M. Philbin, et al., "Sexual identity and behavior among U.S. high school students, 2005–2015," *Archives of Sexual Behavior, 48* (2019), 1463–1479, doi:10.1007/s10508-019-1404-y.

4. The term "gal-pal sex" was suggested by Tony Silva in email with the author (January 28, 2019). For information on sex differences, see L. M. Diamond, "Sexual fluidity in male and females," *Current Sexual Health Reports, 8* (2016), 249–256, doi:10.1007/s10508-017-0967-8.

5. Interview in N. West, "I went to Skirt Club, a lesbian sex party for straight women," *Autostraddle* (August 9, 2017), www.autostraddle.com.

6. See Pham's fascinating and innovative research: J. M. Pham, "Institutional, subcultural, and individual determinants of same-sex sexual contact among college women," *Journal of Sex Research, 56* (2019), 1031–1044, quotes pp. 1031, 1041, doi:10.1080/00224499.2019.1607239.

7. A. Tunell, "Inside Skirt Club, the secret, worldwide sex party for bisexual women," *Cosmopolitan* (December 27, 2018), www.cosmopolitan.com.

8. J. Budnick, "'Straight girls kissing'? Understanding same-gender sexuality beyond the elite college campus," *Gender & Society, 30* (2016), 745–768, quotes pp. 751, 761, 763, doi:10.1177/0891243216657511. Also relevant is A. Chandra, W. D. Mosher, & C. Copen, *Sexual Behavior, Sexual Attraction, and Sexual Identity in the United States: Data from the 2006–2008 National Survey of Family Growth* (National Health Statistics Reports No. 36) (Washington, DC: US Department of Health and Human Services, March 2011), doi:10.1007/978-94-007-5512-3_4.

9. Pham, "Institutional, subcultural, and individual determinants," 1041.

10. Ward's books include *Not Gay: Sex between Straight White Men* (New York: New York University Press, 2015), quotes pp. 25, 27; and *The Tragedy of Heterosexuality* (New York: New York University Press, 2020). Also see her comments in an interview with J. Singal, "Why straight men have sex with each other," *The Cut* (August 5, 2015), http://nymag.com.

11. Silva's stories and perspectives are presented in his book *Still Straight: Sexual Flexibility among White Men in Rural America* (New York: New York University Press, 2020); and his articles "Bud-sex: Constructing normative masculinity among rural straight men that have sex with men," *Gender & Society, 31* (2017), 51–73, quote p. 51, doi:10.1177/0891243216679934; and "'Helpin' a buddy out': Perceptions of identity and behaviour among rural straight men that have sex with each other," *Sexualities, 21* (2018), 68–89, doi:10.1177/1363460716678564.

12. H. Carrillo & A. Hoffman, "'Straight with a pinch of bi': The construction of heterosexuality as an elastic category among adult US men," *Sexualities, 21* (2018), 90–108, quotes pp. 94, 95, doi:10.1177/1363460716678561.

13. My last book was devoted to them: R. W. Savin-Williams, *Mostly Straight: Sexually Fluidity among Men* (Cambridge, MA: Harvard University Press, 2017).

14. For this perspective, see W. L. Jeffries, "A comparative analysis of homosexual behaviors, sex role preferences, and anal sex proclivities in Latino and non-Latino men," *Archives of Sexual Behavior, 38* (2009), 765–778, doi:10.1007/s10508-007-9254-4.

15. A. Kuperberg & A. M. Walker, "Heterosexual college students who hookup with same-sex partners," *Archives of Sexual Behavior, 47* (2018), 1387–1403, doi:10.1007/s10508-018-1194-7.

16. Examples in Savin-Williams, *Mostly Straight*.

17. I believe Flanders has it right. C. E. Flanders, M. E. LeBreton, M. Robinson, J. Bian, & J. A. Caravaca-Morera, "Defining bisexuality: Young bisexual and pansexual people's voices," *Journal of Bisexuality, 17* (2017), 39–57, quote p. 39, doi:1 0.1080/15299716.2016.1227016; C. E. Flanders, "Under the bisexual umbrella: Diversity of identity and experience," *Journal of Bisexuality, 17* (2017), 1–6, quote p. 4, doi:10.1080/15299716.2017.1297145.

7. WHY ROMANCE MATTERS

1. Stated in an email sent to Sexnet@listserv.it.northwestern.edu (August 13, 2010).

2. M. T. Walton, A. D. Lykins, & N. Bhullar, "Beyond heterosexual, bisexual, and homosexual: A diversity in sexual identity expression," *Archives of Sexual Behavior, 45* (2016), 1591–1597, quote p. 1596, doi:10.1007/s10508-016-0778-3. Also relevant is M. P. Galupo, R. C. Mitchell, & K. S. Davis, "Face validity ratings of sexual orientation scales by sexual minority adults: Effects of sexual orientation and gender identity," *Archives of Sexual Behavior, 47* (2018), 1241–1250, doi:10.1007/s10508-017-1037-y.

3. S. Cacioppo, F. Bianchi-Demicheli, C. Frum, J. G. Pfaus, & J. W. Lewis, "The common neural bases between sexual desire and love: A multilevel kernel density fMRI analysis," *Journal of Sex Medicine, 12* (2012), 1048–1054, quote p. 1049. See also H. Fisher, *Why We Love: The Nature and Chemistry of Romantic Love* (New York: Henry Holt, 2004); and E. Hatfield & R. L. Rapson, "The neuropsychology of passionate love," in E. Cuyler & M. Ackhart (Eds.), *Psychology of Relationships* (pp. 519–543) (Hauppauge, NY: Nova Science, 2009). The second quote is from H. Devlin, "What do you get when you fall in love?," *The Guardian* (February 11, 2019), www.theguardian.com.

4. Greater details in E. Hatfield & S. Sprecher, "The Passionate Love Scale," in T. D. Fisher, C. M. Davis, W. L. Yaber, & S. L. Davis (Eds.) *Handbook of Sexuality Related Measures: A Compendium* (3rd ed., pp. 469–472) (Thousand Oaks, CA: Taylor & Francis, 2009).

5. S. J. E. Langeslag, P. Muris, & I. H. A. Franken, "Measuring romantic love: Psychometric properties of the Infatuation and Attachment Scales," *Journal of Sex Research, 50* (2013), 739–747, quote p. 747, doi:10.1080/00224499.2012.714011.

6. D. A. Hill & J. A. R. A. M. Van Hooff, "Affiliative relationships between males in groups of nonhuman primates: A summary," *Behaviour, 130* (1994), 143–149, material summarized from p. 148.

7. B. X. Kuhle & S. Radtke, "Born both ways: The alloparenting hypothesis for sexual fluidity in women," *Evolutionary Psychology, 11* (2013), 304–323, quote p. 304, doi:10.1177/147470491301100202. For a somewhat different view, see M. Apostolou, "Are women sexually fluid? The nature of female same-sex attraction and its evolutionary origins," *Evolutionary Psychological Science, 4* (2018), 191–201, doi:10.1007/s40806-017-0128-2.

8. M. Apostolou, email correspondence with the author (October 22 and 23, 2018).

9. M. R. Kauth, *The Evolution of Human Pair-Bonding, Friendship, and Sexual Attraction: Love Bonds* (New York: Routledge, 2021), doi:10.4324/9780367854614. The quote is from the publisher's description of the book.

10. A. B. Barron, & B. Hare, "Prosociality and a sociosexual hypothesis for the evolution of same-sex attraction in humans," *Frontiers in Psychology, 10* (2020), 2955, doi:10.3389/fpsyg.2019.02955.

11. J. F. Benenson, & H. Abadzi, "Contest versus scramble competition: Sex differences in the quest for status," *Current Opinion in Psychology, 33* (2020), 62–68, quote p. 62, doi:10.1016/j.copsyc.2019.07.013.

12. Three examples are F. Klein, B. Sepekoff, & T. J. Wolf, "Sexual orientation: A multi-variable dynamic process," *Journal of Homosexuality, 11* (1985), 35–49, doi:10.1300/J082v11n01_04; R. L. Sell, "Defining and measuring sexual orientation: A review," *Archives of Sexual Behavior, 26* (1997), 643–658, doi:10.1023/A:1024528427013; M. G. Shively & J. P. DeCecco, "Components of sexual identity," *Journal of Homosexuality, 3* (1977), 41–48, doi:10.1300/J082v03n01_04.

13. In my book *Becoming Who I Am: Young Men on Being Gay* (Cambridge, MA: Harvard University Press, 2016). Also see J. S. Morandini, A. Blaszczynski, I. Dar-Nimrod, & F. K. Barlow, "Sexual vs. romantic orientation in gay/bisexual men: Developmental trajectories, discordance, and implications for adjustment," poster at the annual meeting of International Academy of Sex Research, Toronto, ON, August 9–12, 2015.

14. The measures are, in order, from J. Berona, S. D. Stepp, A. E. Hipwell, & K. E. Keenan, "Trajectories of sexual orientation from adolescence to young adulthood: Results from a community-based urban sample of girls," *Journal of Adolescent Health, 63* (2018), 57–61, doi:10.1016/j.jadohealth.2018.01.015; M. Becker, K. S. Cortina, Y. M. Tsai, & J. S. Eccles, "Sexual orientation, psychological well-being, and mental health: A longitudinal analysis from adolescence to young adulthood," *Psychology of Sexual Orientation and Gender Diversity, 1* (2014), 132–145, doi:10.1037/sgd0000038; G. Priebe & C. G. Svedin, "Operationalization of three dimensions of sexual orientation in a national survey of late adolescents," *Journal of Sex Research, 50* (2013), 727–738, doi:10.1080/00224499.2012.713147; Galupo, Mitchell, & Davis, "Face validity ratings of sexual orientation scales"; Morandini et al., "Sexual vs. romantic orientation in gay/bisexual men"; Savin-Williams, *Becoming Who I Am*.

15. P. Nardi, *Gay Men's Friendships: Invincible Communities* (Chicago: University of Chicago Press, 1999).

16. S. Robinson, A. White, & E. Anderson, "Privileging the bromance: A critical appraisal of romantic and bromantic relationships," *Men and Masculinities, 22* (2019), 850–871, doi:10.1177/1097184X17730386; E. Anderson, *Inclusive Masculinity: The Changing Nature of Masculinities* (New York: Routledge, 2009).

17. L. M. Diamond, "What does sexual orientation orient? A biobehavioral model distinguishing romantic love and sexual desire," *Psychological Review, 110* (2003), 173–192, quote p. 177.

18. R. F. Jaramillo, "Why can't men say 'I love you' to each other?," Modern Love, *New York Times* (May 10, 2019), www.nytimes.com.

19. Famous examples are given in "Bromance alert! 21 famous celebrity besties," *MSN Entertainment* (March 20, 2017), www.msn.com.

20. Robinson, White, & Anderson, "Privileging the bromance," 850.

21. Examples in Nardi, *Gay Men's Friendships*; R. Brain, *Friends and Lovers* (New York: Basic Books, 1976), 39–40; Diamond, "What does sexual orientation orient?"

22. Robinson, White, & Anderson, "Privileging the bromance," 866.

23. L. M. Diamond, "Passionate friendships among adolescent sexual-minority women," *Journal of Research on Adolescence, 10* (2000), 191–209, quote p. 191, doi:10.1207/SJRA1002_4.

24. Dillon is featured in my book *Mostly Straight: Sexually Fluidity among Men* (Cambridge, MA: Harvard University Press, 2017).

25. B. Hawn, "Bromance parody," YouTube (December 7, 2014), www.youtube.com/watch?v=-7bJnTIcUEg&list=RD-7bJnTIcUEg&start_radio=1&t=25.

8. HOW MANY BISEXUALS ARE THERE?

1. B. Dodge & T. G. M. Sandfort, "A review of mental health research on bisexual individuals when compared to homosexual and heterosexual individuals," in B. A. Firestein (Ed.), *Becoming Visible: Counseling Bisexuals Across the Lifespan* (pp. 28–51) (New York: Columbia University Press, 2007), 29.

2. Arousal measures have included pupil tracking and dilation, vaginal secretions, and areas where the brain lights up in fMRIs. See M. L. Chivers, "The specificity of women's sexual response and its relationship with sexual orientations: A review and ten hypotheses," *Archives of Sexual Behavior, 46* (2017), 1161–1179, doi:10.1007/s10508-016-0897-x; M. L. Chivers, G. Rieger, E. Latty, & J. M. Bailey, "A sex difference in the specificity of sexual arousal," *Psychological Science, 15* (2004), 736–744, quote p. 741; M. L. Chivers & J. M. Bailey, "A sex difference in features that elicit genital response," *Biological Psychology, 70* (2005), 115–120, doi:10.1016/j.biopsycho.2004.12.002.

3. Agreeing with this perspective is R. H. Farr, L. M. Diamond, & S. M. Boker, "Female same-sex sexuality from a dynamical systems perspective: Sexual desire, motivation, and behavior," *Archives of Sexual Behavior, 43* (2014), 1477–1490, doi:10.1007/s10508-014-0378-z.

4. B. Carey, "Straight, gay or lying? Bisexuality revisited," *New York Times* (July 5, 2005), www.nytimes.com. The research study is G. Rieger, M. L. Chivers, & J. M. Bailey, "Sexual arousal patterns of bisexual men," *Psychological Science, 16* (2005), 579–584, quote p. 582.

5. A. M. Rosenthal, D. Sylva, A. Safron, & J. M. Bailey, "Sexual arousal patterns of bisexual men revisited," *Biological Psychology, 8* (2011), 112–115. The same findings were also documented with Australians: J. S. Morandini, B. Spence, I. Dar-Nimrod, & A. D. Lykins, "Do bisexuals have a bisexual viewing pattern?," *Archives of Sexual Behavior, 49* (2020), 489–502, doi:10.1007/s10508-019-01514-y.

6. J. E. Rullo, D. S. Strassberg, & M. H. Miner, "Gender-specificity in sexual interest in bisexual men and women," *Archives of Sexual Behavior, 44* (2015), 1449–1457, quote p. 1449, doi:10.1007/s10508-014-0415-y.

7. E. Slettevold, L. Holmes, D. Gruiaa, C. P. Nyssena, T. M. Watts-Overall, & G. Rieger, "Bisexual men with bisexual and monosexual genital arousal patterns," *Biological Psychology, 148* (2019), 107763, doi:10.1016/j.biopsycho.2019.107763.

8. J. Jabbour, L. Holmes, D. Sylva, K. J. Hsu, T. L. Semon, A. M. Rosenthal, et al., "Robust evidence for bisexual orientation among men," *Proceedings of the National Academy of Sciences, 117*(31) (2020), 18369–18377, doi:10.1073/pnas.2003631117.

9. A. Ganna, K. J. H. Verweij, M. G. Nivard, R. Maier, R. Wedow, A. S. Busch, et al., "Large-scale GWAS reveals insights into the genetic architecture of same-sex sexual behavior," *Science, 365* (2019), eaat7693, doi:10.1126/science.aat7693.

10. J. Budnick, "'Straight girls kissing'? Understanding same-gender sexuality beyond the elite college campus," *Gender & Society, 30* (2016), 745–768, doi:10.1177/0891243216657511.

11. Data from A. Chandra, W. D. Mosher, & C. Copen, *Sexual Behavior, Sexual Attraction, and Sexual Identity in the United States: Data from the 2006–2008 National Survey of Family Growth* (National Health Statistics Reports No. 36) (Washington, DC: US Department of Health and Human Services, March 2011), doi:10.1007/978-94-007-5512-3_4.

12. Consistent with recent usage by gender and transgender activists, communities, and scholars, I use *trans** to refer to the range of individuals who identify in transgender terms.

13. W. B. Bostwick, C. J. Boyd, T. L. Hughes, & S. E. McCabe, "Dimensions of sexual orientation and the prevalence of mood and anxiety disorders in the United States," *American Journal of Public Health, 100* (2010), 468–475, doi:10.2105/AJPH.2008.152942.

14. E. O. Laumann, J. Gagnon, R. T. Michael, & S. Michaels, *The Social Organization of Sexuality: Sexual Practices in the United States* (Chicago: University of Chicago Press, 1994).

15. E. Mishel, "Intersections between sexual identity, sexual attraction, and sexual behavior among a nationally representative sample of American men and women," *Journal of Official Statistics, 35* (2019), 859–884, doi:10.2478/jos-2019-0036; C. E. Copen, A. Chandra, & I. Febo-Vazquez, *Sexual Behavior, Sexual Attraction, and Sexual Orientation among Adults Aged 18–44 in the United States: Data from the 2011–2013 National Survey of Family Growth* (National Health

Statistics Reports No. 88) (Washington, DC: US Department of Health and Human Services, January 2016).

16. L. L. Lindley, K. M. Walsemann, & J. W. Carter Jr., "The association of sexual orientation measures with young adults' health-related outcomes," *American Journal of Public Health, 102* (2012), 1177–1185, doi:10.2105/AJPH.2011.300262; R. C. Savin-Williams, K. Joyner, & G. Rieger, "Prevalence and stability of self-reported sexual orientation identity during young adulthood," *Archives of Sexual Behavior, 41* (2012), 103–110, doi:10.1007/s10508-012-9913-y; R. S. Geary, C. Tanton, B. Erens, S. Clifton, P. Prah, K. Wellings, et al., "Sexual identity, attraction and behaviour in Britain: The implications of using different dimensions of sexual orientation to estimate the size of sexual minority populations and inform public health interventions," *PLoS One, 13*(1) (2018), e0189607; J. Richters, D. Altman, P. B. Badcock, A. M. A. Smith, R. O. de Visser, A. E. Grulich, et al., "Sexual identity, sexual attraction and sexual experience: The Second Australian Study of Health and Relationships," *Sexual Health, 11* (2014), 451–460, doi:10.1071/SH14117; G. Priebe & C. G. Svedin, "Operationalization of three dimensions of sexual orientation in a national survey of late adolescents," *Journal of Sex Research, 50* (2013), 727–738, doi:10.108 0/00224499.2012.713147; L. M. Greaves, F. K. Barlow, C. H. J. Lee, C. M. Matika, W. Wang, C. J. Lindsay, et al., "The diversity and prevalence of sexual orientation self-labels in a New Zealand national sample," *Archives of Sexual Behavior, 46* (2017), 1325–1336, doi:10.1007/s10508-016-0857-5.

17. R. C. Savin-Williams & K. Joyner, "The dubious assessment of gay, lesbian, and bisexual adolescents in Add Health," *Archives of Sexual Behavior, 43* (2014), 413–422, doi:10.1007/s10508 013 0219-5

18. T. Fu, D. Herbenick, D. Dodge, C. Owens, S. A. Sanders, M. Reece, & J. D. Fortenberry, "Relationships among sexual identity, sexual attraction, and sexual behavior: Results from a nationally representative probability sample of adults in the United States," *Archives of Sexual Behavior, 48* (2019), 1483–1493, doi:10.1007/ s10508-018-1319-z.

19. R. C. Savin-Williams & K. M. Cohen, "Prevalence, mental health, and heterogeneity of bisexual men," *Current Sexual Health Reports, 10* (2018), 196–202, doi:10.1007/s11930-018-0164-3; also see in the United States, G. Li, A. M. Pollitt, & S. T. Russell, "Depression and sexual orientation during young adulthood: Diversity among sexual-minority subgroups and the role of gender nonconformity," *Archives of Sexual Behavior, 45* (2016), 697–711, doi:10.1007/ s10508-015-0515-3, and in Britain, Y. Xu, S. Norton, & Q. Rahman, "Adolescent sexual behavior patterns in a British birth cohort: A latent class analysis," *Archives of Sexual Behavior* (January 6, 2020), doi:10.1007/s10508-019-01578-w.

20. J. T. Goldbach, H. F. Raymond, & C. M. Burgess, "Patterns of bullying behavior by sexual orientation," *Journal of Interpersonal Violence* (November 10, 2017), doi:10.1177/0886260517741623.

21. R. C. Savin-Williams *Mostly Straight: Sexually Fluidity among Men* (Cambridge, MA: Harvard University Press, 2017); R. C. Savin-Williams, *Becoming Who I Am: Young Men on Being Gay* (Cambridge, MA: Harvard University Press, 2016).

22. Savin-Williams & Cohen, "Prevalence, mental health, and heterogeneity."

23. A. Ghaziani, "The closet," *Contexts, 16* (2017), 72–73, doi:10.1177/1536504217732060.

24. J. J. Mohr, D. Skyler, S. D. Jackson, & R. L. Sheets, "Sexual orientation self-presentation among bisexual-identified women and men: Patterns and predictors," *Archives of Sexual Behavior, 46* (2017), 1465–1479, doi:10.1007/s10508-016-0808-1; T. Bridges & M. R. Moore, "Young women of color and shifting sexual identities," *Contexts, 17* (2018), 86–88, quote p. 88, doi:10.1177/1536504218767125.

25. Savin-Williams, *Mostly Straight.*

26. Research reported in D. M. Doyle & L. Molix, "Disparities in social health by sexual orientation and the etiologic role of self-reported discrimination," *Archives of Sexual Behavior, 45* (2016), 1317–1327, doi:10.1007/s10508-015-0639-5; R. C. Savin-Williams, "An exploratory study of exclusively heterosexual, primarily heterosexual, and mostly heterosexual young men," *Sexualities, 21* (2018), 16–29, doi:10.1177/1363460716678559; J. Jabbour, K. J. Hsu, & J. M. Bailey, "Sexual arousal patterns of mostly heterosexual men," *Archives of Sexual Behavior, 49* (2020), 2421–2429, doi:10.1007/s10508-020-01720-z.

27. A. E. White, J. Moeller, Z. Ivcevic, & M. A. Brackett, "Gender identity and sexual identity labels used by U.S. high school students: A co-occurrence network analysis," *Psychology of Sexual Orientation and Gender Diversity, 5* (2018), 243–252, doi:10.1037/sgd0000266.

28. Qazi Rahman, Department of Psychology, King's College, London, email correspondence with the author (March 17, 2019); Savin-Williams & Joyner, "Dubious assessment of gay, lesbian, and bisexual adolescents." For suggestions on how to alleviate these problems, see J. R. Cimpian, J. D. Timmer, M. A. Birkett, R. L. Marro, B. C. Turner, & G. L. Phillips II, "Bias from potentially mischievous responders on large-scale estimates of lesbian, gay, bisexual, or questioning (LGBQ)–heterosexual youth health disparities." *American Journal of Public Health, 108* (2018), S258–S265, doi:10.2105/AJPH.2018.304407.

29. Priebe & Svedin, "Operationalization of three dimensions of sexual orientation"; M. L. Hatzenbuehler & K. M. Keyes, "Inclusive anti-bullying policies and reduced risk of suicide attempts in lesbian and gay youth," *Journal of Adolescent Health, 53* (2013), S21eS26, doi:10.1016/j.jadohealth.2012.08.010; A. Campbell, F. Perales, & J. Baxter, "Changes in sexual identity labels in a contemporary cohort of emerging adult women: Patterns, prevalence and a typology," *Journal of Sex Research* (August 27, 2020), doi:10.1080/00224499.2020.1814092; Mishel, "Intersections between sexual identity, sexual attraction, and sexual behavior."

30. A. W. Blum, K. Lust, G. Christenson, & J. E. Grant, "Links between sexuality, impulsivity, compulsivity, and addiction in a large sample of university students," *CNS Spectrums* (April 15, 2019), 1–7, doi:10.1017/S1092852918001591.

31. Greaves et al., "Diversity and prevalence of sexual orientation self-labels"; L. M. Greaves, C. G. Sibley, N. Satherley, & F. K. Barlow, "Investigating inappropriate and missing sexual orientation question responses in a New Zealand national survey," *Psychology of Sexual Orientation and Gender Diversity, 6* (2019), 284–295, quote p. 293, doi:10.1037/sgd0000328. Also see B. K. Gorman, J. T. Denney, H. Dowdy, & R. A. Medeiros, "A new piece of the puzzle: sexual orientation, gender, and physical health status," *Demography, 52* (2015), 1357–1382, doi:10.1007/s13524-015-0406-1.

32. Mishel, "Intersections between sexual identity, sexual attraction, and sexual behavior," 876.

33. J. P. Calzo & A. J. Blashill, "Child sexual orientation and gender identity in the Adolescent Brain Cognitive Development Cohort Study," *JAMA Pediatrics, 172* (2018), 1090–1092, doi:10.1001/jamapediatrics.2018.2496.

34. K. S. Elkington, M. L. Wainberg, M. Ramos-Olazagasti, C. Chen, A. Ortin, G. J. Canino, et al., "Developmental trends in sexual attraction among Puerto Rican early adolescents in two contexts," *Child Development* (July 20, 2019), doi:10.1111/cdev.13286.

35. Mishel, "Intersections between sexual identity, sexual attraction, and sexual behavior," 876.

36. J. E. Pachankis, "The psychological implications of concealing a stigma: A cognitive-affective-behavioral model," *Psychological Bulletin, 133* (2007), 328–345, doi:10.1037/0033-2909.133.2.328.

37. T. S. Hottes, D. Gesink, O. Ferlatte, D. J. Brennan, A. E. Rhodes, R. Marchand, & T. Trussler, "Concealment of sexual minority identities in interviewer-administered government surveys and its impact on estimates of suicide ideation among bisexual and gay men," *Journal of Bisexuality, 16* (2016), 427–453, doi:10.1080/15299716.2016.1225622.

38. Mel2718, "Bisexual erasure," *Urban Dictionary* (October 16, 2011), www.urbandictionary.com.

39. Various social media outlets have tracked these developments: T. Daley, "Something I want to say . . . ," YouTube (December 2, 2013), www.youtube.com/watch?v=OJwJnoB9FKw&t=1s; H. Dresden, "Tom Daley identifies as queer, 'not 100 percent gay,'" *Out* (April 24, 2018), www.out.com; S. Hattenstone, "Tom Daley: 'I always knew I was attracted to guys,'" *The Guardian* (July 18, 2015), www.theguardian.com; J. Tabberer, "Dustin Lance Black says Tom Daley's 'head still turns for girls' as they discuss marriage," *Gay Star News* (December 4, 2017), www.gaystarnews.com.

40. Andrew Sullivan, "What's a bisexual anyway? Ctd," *The Dish* (December 9, 2013), http://dish.andrewsullivan.com.

41. M. R. Yost & G. D. Thomas, "Gender and binegativity: Men's and women's attitudes toward male and female bisexuals," *Archives of Sexual Behavior, 41* (2012), 691–702, quote p. 699, doi:10.1007/s10508-011-9767-8.

42. A discussion of these issues is in R. Magrath, J. Cleland, & E. Anderson, "Bisexual erasure in the British print media: Representation of Tom Daley's coming out," *Journal of Bisexuality, 17* (2017), 300–317.

43. Hottes et al., "Concealment of sexual minority identities."

44. J. E. Pachankis & R. Bränström, "How many sexual minorities are hidden? Projecting the size of the global closet with implications for policy and public health," *PLoS One, 14*(6) (2019), e0218084, doi:10.1371/journal.pone.0218084.

45. Pew Research Center, "A survey of LGBT Americans" (June 13, 2013), www. pewsocialtrends.org.

46. J. Taylor, J. Power, E. Smith, & M. Rathbone, "Bisexual mental health: Findings from the 'Who I Am' study," *Australian Journal of General Practice, 48* (2019), 138–144, doi:10.31128/AJGP-06-18-4615.

47. See a discussion of many of these issues as applied to men in E. Anderson & M. McCormack, *The Changing Dynamics of Bisexual Men's Lives: Social Research Perspectives* (New York: Springer, 2016).

9. PANSEXUALITY

1. American Institute of Bisexuality, home page, www.americaninstituteofbisexuality.org; see also bi.org, "What Bi Looks Like," https://bisexual.org.

2. Bisexual Resource Center, "About," http://biresource.org; other definitions are available at the Urban Dictionary's website: "Pansexuality," www.urbandictionary.com.

3. C. K. Belous & M. L. Bauman, "What's in a name? Exploring pansexuality online," *Journal of Bisexuality, 17* (2017), 58–72, quote p. 68, doi:10.1080/15299716.2016.1224 212; C. E. Flanders, "Under the bisexual umbrella: Diversity of identity and experience," *Journal of Bisexuality, 17* (2017), 1–6, quote p. 4, doi:10.1080/15299716.2017.1297145; M. P. Galupo, J. L. Ramirez, & L. Pulice-Farrow, "'Regardless of their gender': Descriptions of sexual identity among bisexual, pansexual, and queer identified individuals," *Journal of Bisexuality, 17* (2017), 108–124, quote p. 122, doi:10.1080/15299716.2016.1228491.

4. Galupo, Ramirez, & Pulice-Farrow, "Regardless of their gender," 122.

5. J. S. Morandini, A. Blaszczynski, & I. Dar-Nimrod, "Who adopts queer and pansexual identities?," *Journal of Sex Research, 54* (2017), 911–922, quotes p. 911, doi:10.1080/00224499.2016.1249332.

6. E. Lenning, "Moving beyond the binary: Exploring the dimensions of gender presentation and orientation," *International Journal of Social Inquiry, 2* (2009), 39–54, quote p. 48.

7. E. Grinberg, "What it means to be pansexual," *CNN* (August 1, 2017), www.cnn.com.

8. Belous & Bauman, "What's in a name?," 68.

9. R. Setoodeh, "Miley Cyrus on 'The Voice,' Donald Trump and coming out," *Variety* (October 11, 2016), http://variety.com.

10. N. Briese, "Panic! at the Disco's Brendon Urie comes out as pansexual," *US Weekly* (July 6, 2018), www.usmagazine.com.

11. O. Gettell, "Andrew Garfield calls for a pansexual Spider-Man," *Entertainment Weekly* (September 8, 2015), https://ew.com.

12. L. M. Greaves, C. G. Sibley, G. Fraser, & F. K. Barlow, "Comparing pansexual and bisexual-identified participants on demographics, psychological well-being, and political ideology in a New Zealand national sample," *Journal of Sex Research, 56* (2019), 1083–1090, quote p. 1083, doi:10.1080/00224499.2019.1568376.

13. L. Timmins, K. A. Rimes, & Q. Rahman, "Is being queer gay? Sexual attraction patterns, minority stressors, and psychological distress in non-traditional categories of sexual orientation," *Journal of Sex Research* (December 13, 2020), doi: 10.1080/00224499.2020.1849527; A. E. White, J. Moeller, Z. Ivcevic, & M. A. Brackett, "Gender identity and sexual identity labels used by U.S. high school students: A co-occurrence network analysis," *Psychology of Sexual Orientation and Gender Diversity, 5* (2018), 243–252, doi:10.1037/sgd0000266.

14. C. E. Flanders, M. E. LeBreton, M. Robinson, J. Bian, & J. A. Caravaca-Morera, "Defining bisexuality: Young bisexual and pansexual people's voices," *Journal of Bisexuality, 17* (2017), 39–57, doi:10.1080/15299716.2016.1227016; Flanders, "Under the bisexual umbrella"; Morandini, Blaszczynski, & Dar-Nimrod, "Who adopts queer and pansexual identities?"; Galupo, Ramirez, & Pulice-Farrow, "Regardless of their gender"; M. P. Galupo, R. C. Mitchell, & K. S. Davis, "Face validity ratings of sexual orientation scales by sexual minority adults: Effects of sexual orientation and gender identity," *Archives of Sexual Behavior, 47* (2018), 1241–1250, doi:10.1007/s10508-017-1037-y; Greaves et al., "Comparing pansexual and bisexual-identified participants"; White et al., "Gender identity and sexual identity labels."

15. Galupo, Ramirez, & Pulice-Farrow, "Regardless of their gender"; Galupo, Mitchell, & Davis, "Face validity ratings."

16. Belous & Bauman, "What's in a name?"

17. V. Papisova, "What is pansexual? A guide to pansexuality," *Teen Vogue* (April 21, 2020), www.teenvogue.com.

10. FLUIDITY

1. L. M. Diamond, "Sexual fluidity in males and females," *Current Sexual Health Reports, 8* (2016), 249–256, quote p. 255, doi:10.1007/s10508-017-0967-8.

2. L. M. Diamond, *Sexual Fluidity: Understanding Women's Love and Desire* (Cambridge, MA: Harvard University Press, 2008).

3. S. L. Katz-Wise, "Sexual fluidity in young adult women and men: Associations with sexual orientation and sexual identity development," *Psychology & Sexuality, 6* (2015), 189–208, doi:10.1080=19419899.2013.876445.

4. Diamond, "Sexual fluidity in males and females," 249.

5. See the Trevor Project, "About conversion therapy," www.thetrevorproject.org.

6. One of the first and most persistent conversion therapy organizations is the National Association for Research and Therapy of Homosexuality; see its statement on sexual orientation change in their *Journal of Human Sexuality, 4* (2012), 141–143. In 2010, George Rekers, a "scientific advisor," was photographed with a 20-year-old male prostitute (from Rentboy.com) who had accompanied him on a ten-day European vacation to "carry his luggage." Reported in J. Bryne, "Exposed: Christian leader caught with male escort says he needed help with his luggage," *Raw Story* (May 4, 2010), http://rawstory.com.

7. M. Bowman, *The Mormon People: The Making of an American Faith* (New York: Random House, 2012).

8. I. Stanley-Becker, "'I am proud to be a gay son of God': Mormon valedictorian comes out in graduation speech," *Washington Post* (April 29, 2019), www.washingtonpost.com.

9. E. Sasson, "Kristen Stewart, Miley Cyrus and the rise of sexual fluidity," *SpeakEasy* (blog), *Wall Street Journal* (August 17, 2015), http://blogs.wsj.com.

10. B. Ambrosino, "I wasn't born this way. I choose to be gay," *New Republic* (January 28, 2014), https://newrepublic.com.

11. G. Arana, "Macklemore is right. Being gay isn't a choice, it's a civil rights issue," *New Republic* (January 30, 2014), https://newrepublic.com.

12. C. P. Scheitle & J. K. Wolf, "Religion and sexual identity fluidity in a national three-wave panel of U.S. adults," *Archives of Sexual Behavior, 47* (2018), 1085–1094, doi:10.1007/s10508-017-0979-4; R. C. Savin-Williams, K. Joyner, & G. Rieger, "Prevalence and stability of self-reported sexual orientation identity during young adulthood," *Archives of Sexual Behavior, 41* (2012), 103–110, doi:10.1007/s10508-012-9913-y; A. Campbell, F. Perales, & J. Baxter, "Changes in sexual identity labels in a contemporary cohort of emerging adult women: Patterns, prevalence and a typology," *Journal of Sex Research* (2020), doi:10.1080/00224499.2020.1814092 (using the Australian Longitudinal Study on Women's Health).

13. L. Grossman, "Sexuality is fluid—it's time to get past 'born this way,'" *New Scientist* (July 22, 2015), www.newscientist.com; L. M. Diamond & C. J. Rosky, "Scrutinizing immutability: Research on sexual orientation and U.S. legal advocacy for sexual minorities," *Journal of Sex Research, 53* (2016), 363–391, doi:10.1080/00224499.

14. Grossman, "Sexuality is fluid."

15. This fascinating study deserves a good read: J. Berona, S. D. Stepp, A. E. Hipwell, & K. E. Keenan, "Trajectories of sexual orientation from adolescence to young adulthood: Results from a community-based urban sample of girls," *Journal of Adolescent Health, 63* (2018), 57–61, doi:10.1016/j.jadohealth.2018.01.015.

16. Scheitle & Wolf, "Religion and sexual identity fluidity."

17. Diamond, *Sexual Fluidity*, 3; Diamond, "Sexual fluidity in males and females."

18. For evidence and examples beyond Diamond, see R. F. Baumeister, "Gender differences in erotic plasticity: The female sex drive as socially flexible and responsive," *Psychological Bulletin, 126* (2000), 347–374, doi:10.1037/0033-2909.126.3.347; and L. A. Peplau, "Rethinking women's sexual orientation: An interdisciplinary, relationship-focused approach," *Personal Relationships, 8* (2001), 1–19, doi:10.1111/j.1475-6811.2001.tb00025.x.

19. J. M. Bailey, "What is sexual orientation and do women have one?," in D. A. Hope (Ed.), *Contemporary Perspectives on Lesbian, Gay, and Bisexual Identities* (Vol. 54, pp. 43–63). New York: Springer, 2009), 60–61.

20. E. Nagoski, *Come As You Are: The Surprising New Science That Will Transform Your Sex Life* (New York: Simon and Schuster, 2015).

21. M. L. Chivers, "The specificity of women's sexual response and its relationship with sexual orientations: A review and ten hypotheses," *Archives of Sexual Behavior, 46* (2017), 1161–1179, quote p. 1171, doi:10.1007/s10508-016-0897-x.

22. R. H. Farr, L. M. Diamond, & S. M. Boker, "Female same-sex sexuality from a dynamical systems perspective: Sexual desire, motivation, and behavior," *Archives of Sexual Behavior, 43* (2014), 1477–1490, quotes p. 1488, doi:10.1007/s10508-014-0378-z.

23. Diamond, "Sexual fluidity in males and females," 255.

24. D. Reynolds, "How Boy Erased helped unerase Lucas Hedges's attraction to men," *Advocate* (October 30, 2018), www.advocate.com.

25. Diamond, "Sexual fluidity in males and females"; Katz-Wise, "Sexual fluidity in young adult women and men"; Scheitle & Wolf, "Religion and sexual identity fluidity."

26. Diamond, "Sexual fluidity in males and females," 254; N. Cohen, I. Becker, & A. Štulhofer, "Stability versus fluidity of adolescent romantic and sexual attraction and the role of religiosity: A longitudinal assessment in two independent samples of Croatian adolescents," *Archives of Sexual Behavior, 49* (2020), 1477–1488, doi:10.1007/s10508-020-01713-y.

27. Savin-Williams, Joyner, & Rieger, "Prevalence and stability of self-reported sexual orientation identity."

28. M. Q. Ott, H. L. Corliss, D. Wypij, M. Rosario, & S. B. Austin, "Stability and change in self-reported sexual orientation identity in young people: Application of mobility metrics," *Archives of Sexual Behavior, 40* (2011), 519–532, doi:10.1007/s10508-010-9691-3.

29. L. Wignall & H. Driscoll, "Women's rationales and perspectives on 'mostly' as a nonexclusive sexual identity label," *Psychology of Sexual Orientation and Gender Diversity, 7* (2020), 366–374, quote p. 366, doi:10.1037/sgd0000385.

30. M. Sung, "Inside the online communities where straight guys help other straight guys get off," *Mashable* (May 19, 2019), https://mashable.com.

11. GENDERQUEER AND NONBINARY

1. M. Robertson, *Growing Up Queer: Kids and the Remaking of LGBTQ Identity* (New York: New York University Press, 2019).
2. C. Richards, W. P. Bouman, L. Seal, M. J. Barker, T. O. Nieder, & G. T'Sjoen, "Non-binary or genderqueer genders," *International Review of Psychiatry, 28* (2016), 95–102, quote p. 95, doi:10.3109/09540261.2015.1106446.
3. Additional resources at Trans Student Educational Resources, www.transstudent. org; County of Santa Clara, "The gender unicorn" (September 21, 2017), www. sccgov.org; C. Gillespie, "What does it mean to be gender fluid? Here's what experts say," *Health* (February 26, 2020), www.health.com.
4. E. Urquhart, "What the heck is genderqueer?," *Slate* (March 24, 2015), https://slate. com.
5. KC Clements, "What does it mean to identify as genderqueer?," *Healthline* (September 18, 2018), www.healthline.com.
6. J. M. Grant, L. A. Mottet, & J. Tanis, *Injustice at Every Turn: A Report of the National Transgender Discrimination Survey* (Washington, DC: National Center for Transgender Equality & National Gay and Lesbian Task Force, 2011), http:// transequality.org; Shondell, "10 celebrities you didn't know identify as gender-queer," *TheRichest* (January 2, 2016), www.therichest.com.
7. S. Killermann, *A Guide to Gender* (2nd ed.) (Austin, TX: Impetus Books, 2017).
8. Urquhart, "What the heck is genderqueer?"
9. J. S. Hyde, R. S. Bigler, D. Joel, C. C. Tate, & S. M. van Anders, "The future of sex and gender in psychology: Five challenges to the gender binary," *American Psychologist, 74* (July 18, 2018), 171–193, doi:10.1037/amp0000307.
10. H. Frohard-Dourlent, E. Saewyc, J. Veale, T. Peter, & M. MacAulay, "Conceptualizing gender: Lessons from the Canadian Trans Youth Health Survey," *Signs: Journal of Women in Culture and Society, 46* (2020), 151–176, quotes pp. 152, 166, 168, doi:10.1086/709302.
11. L. Kuyper & C. Wijsen, "Gender identities and gender dysphoria in the Netherlands," *Archives of Sexual Behavior, 43* (2014), 377–385, doi:10.1007/ s10508-013-0140-y.
12. E. Van Caenegem, K. Wierckx, E. Elaut, A. Buysse, A. Dewaele, F. Van Nieuwerburgh, et al., "Prevalence of gender nonconformity in Flanders, Belgium," *Archives of Sexual Behavior, 44* (2015), 1281–1287, doi:10.1007/s10508-014-0452-6.
13. A. Pollard, "How pop is starting a genderqueer dialogue," *Dazed* (May 25, 2015), www.dazeddigital.com.

12. GENDER VARIANCE AND GENDER TOXICITY

1. In order of presentation: K. P. Kochel, C. F. Miller, K. A. Updegraff, G. W. Ladd, & B. Kochenderfer-Ladd, "Associations between fifth graders' gender atypical problem behavior and peer relationships: A short-term longitudinal study," *Journal of Youth and Adolescence 41* (2012), 1022–1034, doi.10.1007/

s10964-011-9733-8; G. van Beusekom, K. L. Collier, H. M. W. Bos, T. G. M. Sandfort, & G. Overbeek, "Gender nonconformity and peer victimization: Sex and sexual attraction differences by age," *Journal of Sex Research, 57* (2020), 234–246, doi:10.1080/00224499.2019.1591334; G. Rieger & R. C. Savin-Williams, "Gender nonconformity, sexual orientation, and psychological well-being," *Archives of Sexual Behavior, 41* (2012), 611–621, doi:10.1007/s10508-011-9738-0; M. D. DiDonato & S. A. Berenbaum, "The benefits and drawbacks of gender typing: How different dimensions are related to psychological adjustment," *Archives of Sexual Behavior, 40* (2011), 457–463, doi:10.1007/s10508-010-9620-5.

2. Kochel et al., "Fifth graders' gender atypical problem behavior and peer relationships," 1022; H. Bos & T. Sandfort, "Gender nonconformity, sexual orientation, and Dutch adolescents' relationship with peers," *Archives of Sexual Behavior, 44* (2015), 1269–1279, doi:10.1007/s10508-014-0461-5.

3. F. Newport, "Gay and lesbian rights," *Gallup News* (May 22, 2018), https://news.gallup.com.

4. N. Koulogeoge, "P.S. Venus is uninhabitable: Toxic femininity & why it must be as discussed as toxic masculinity," *Fraternity Man* (July 22, 2018), https://fraternity-man.com.

5. American Psychological Association, Boys and Men Guidelines Group, *APA Guidelines for Psychological Practice with Boys and Men* (Washington, DC: Author, 2018), www.apa.org.

6. T. B. Edsall, "The fight over men is shaping our political future," *New York Times* (January 17, 2019), www.nytimes.com; see also N. Way, *Deep Secrets: Boys' Friendships and the Crisis of Connection* (Cambridge, MA: Harvard University Press, 2011).

7. M. Tapson, "Houston rescuers prove the lie of 'toxic masculinity,'" *National Review* (September 1, 2017), www.nationalreview.com.

8. Edsall, "Fight over men is shaping our political future."

9. E. A. Casey, N. T. Masters, B. Beadnell, E. A. Wells, D. M. Morrison, & M. J. Hoppe, "A latent class analysis of heterosexual young men's masculinities," *Archives of Sexual Behavior, 45* (2015), 1039–1050, doi:10.1007/s10508-015-0616-z.

10. Available at A. Robbins, "A frat boy and a gentleman," *New York Times* (January 26, 2019), www.nytimes.com.

11. Koulogeoge, "P.S. Venus is uninhabitable."

12. K. Anthony, "Is 'toxic femininity' a thing?," *Katykatikate* (December 19, 2018), www.katykatikate.com.

13. D. Price, "Toxic femininity holds all of us back," *Medium* (December 31, 2018), https://medium.com.

14. Quoted in Edsall, "Fight over men is shaping our political future."

15. S. E. Burke & M. LaFrance, "Lay conceptions of sexual minority groups," *Archives of Sexual Behavior, 45* (2016), 635–650, doi:10.1007/s10508-015-0655-5; S. E. Burke & M. LaFrance, "Stereotypes of bisexual people: What do bisexual people themselves think?," *Psychology of Sexual Orientation and Gender Diversity, 3*

(2016), 247–254, doi:10.1037/sgd0000168. See also K. M. Cohen, "Relationships among childhood sex-atypical behavior, spatial ability, handedness, and sexual orientation in men," *Archives of Sexual Behavior, 31* (2002), 129–143.

16. G. Rieger, L. Holmes, T. M. Watts, D. C. Gruia, J. M. Bailey, & R. C. Savin-Williams, "Gender nonconformity of bisexual men and women," *Archives of Sexual Behavior* (July 21, 2020); N. F. Kahn & C. T. Halpern, "Is developmental change in gender-typed behavior associated with adult sexual orientation?," *Developmental Psychology, 55* (2019), 855–865, doi:10.1037/dev0000662.

17. Van Beusekom et al., "Gender nonconformity and peer victimization."

18. M. I. Striepe & D. L. Tolman, "Mom, dad, I'm straight: The coming out of gender ideologies in adolescent sexual-identity development," *Journal of Clinical Child & Adolescent Psychology, 32* (2003), 523–530, doi:10.1207/S15374424JCCP3204_4; G. Rieger & R. C. Savin-Williams, "Gender nonconformity, sexual orientation, and psychological well-being," *Archives of Sexual Behavior, 41* (2012), 611–621, doi:10.1007/s10508-011-9738-0.

19. L. A. Spivey, D. M. Huebner, & L. M. Diamond, "Parent responses to childhood gender nonconformity: Effects of parent and child characteristics," *Psychology of Sexual Orientation and Gender Diversity, 5* (2018), 360–370, doi:10.1037/sgd0000279.

20. L. N. MacMullin, M. Aitken, A. N. Nabbijohn, & D. P. VanderLaan, "Self-harm and suicidality in gender-nonconforming children: A Canadian community-based parent-report study," *Psychology of Sexual Orientation and Gender Diversity, 7* (2020), 76–90, doi:10.1037/sgd0000353; S. W. Semenyna & P. L. Vasey, "Bullying, physical aggression, gender atypicality, and sexual orientation in Samoan males," *Archives of Sexual Behavior, 46* (2017), 1375–1381, doi:10.1007/s10508-015-0676-0; Rieger et al., "Gender nonconformity of bisexual men and women."

21. C. Brown, H. Frohard-Dourlent, B. A. Wood, E. Saewyc, M. Eisenberg, & C. Porta, "It makes such a difference," *Journal of the American Association of Nurse Practitioners, 32* (2020), 70–80, doi:10.1097/JXX.0000000000000217.

22. M. Li, "(Mis)matching: Journalistic uses of gender pronouns and names can influence implicit attitudes toward transgender people, perceived news content credibility, and perceived reporter professionalism," *Newspaper Research Journal, 40* (2019), 517–533, doi:10.1177/0739532919873083.

23. P. England, E. Mishel, & M. L. Caudillo, "Increases in sex with same-sex partners and bisexual identity across cohorts of women (but not men)," *Sociological Science, 3* (2016), 951–970, quotes pp. 951, 966, doi:10.15195/v3.a42; see also E. Mishel, "Intersections between sexual identity, sexual attraction, and sexual behavior among a nationally representative sample of American men and women," *Journal of Official Statistics, 35* (2019), 859–884, doi:10.2478/jos-2019-0036.

24. A. Vagianos, "Kyrsten Sinema makes history as first openly bisexual person sworn in to Senate," *HuffPost* (January 9, 2019), www.huffingtonpost.com; the Nicola Adams Obe story can be found on her website: https://nicola-adams.com.

25. B. Hochman, "He's the star running back at John Burroughs, team captain, Indiana State bound—and gay," *St. Louis Post-Dispatch* (December 22, 2017), www.stltoday.com.

13. RACE AND ETHNICITY MATTER

1. T. M. Haltom & S. Ratcliff, "Effects of sex, race, and education on the timing of coming out among lesbian, gay, and bisexual adults in the U.S.," *Archives of Sexual Behavior* (July 7, 2020), doi:10.1007/s10508-020-01776-x.
2. I. X. Kendi, *How to Be an Antiracist* (New York: One World, 2019), 18.
3. See Alberta Civil Liberties Research Centre, "Whiteness," www.aclrc.com.
4. A. Weinstein & the MOJO News Team, "The Trayvon Martin killing, explained," *Mother Jones* (March 18, 2012), www.motherjones.com.
5. The list could consume this chapter; see, for example, A. Arce, "It's long past time we recognized all the Latinos killed at the hands of police," *Time* (July 21, 2020), https://time.com.
6. D. Hartmann, J. Gerteis, & P. R. Croll, "An empirical assessment of whiteness theory: Hidden from how many?," *Social Problems, 56* (2009), 403–424, doi:10.1525/sp.2009.56.3.403.
7. Alberta Civil Liberties Research Centre, "Whiteness."
8. Kendi, *How to Be an Antiracist*, 18.
9. J. E. Pachankis, M. L. Hatzenbuehler, M. Mirandola, P. Weatherburn, R. C. Berg, U. Marcus, & A. J. Schmidt, "The geography of sexual orientation: Structural stigma and sexual attraction, behavior, and identity among men who have sex with men across 38 European countries," *Archives of Sexual Behavior, 46* (2017), 1491–1502, quote p. 1491, doi:10.1007/s10508-016-0819-y.
10. C. P. Scheitle & J. K. Wolf, "Religion and sexual identity fluidity in a national three-wave panel of U.S. adults," *Archives of Sexual Behavior, 47* (2018), 1085–1094, doi:10.1007/s10508-017-0979-4.
11. E. Patton, P. England, & A. Levine, "Sexual behavior and attitudes among White, Black, Latinx, and Asian college students," *Contexts: Sociology for the Public* (November 11, 2019), https://contexts.org/blog.
12. A. Morgan, B. Saunders, B. Dodge, G. Harper, & R. A. Sanders, "Exploring the sexual development experiences of Black bisexual male adolescents over time," *Archives of Sexual Behavior, 47* (2018), 1839–1851, doi:10.1007/s10508-017-1084-4.
13. Haltom & Ratcliff, "Effects of sex, race, and education."
14. At the time of the study, Dubé was a graduate student studying with me: E. M. Dubé & R. C. Savin-Williams, "Sexual identity development among ethnic sexual-minority male youths," *Developmental Psychology, 35* (1999), 1389–1399, quote p. 1396, doi:10.1037/0012-1649.35.6.1389; also see an earlier summary, M. F. Manalansan, "Double minorities: Latino, Black, and Asian men who have sex with men," in R. C. Savin-Williams & K. M. Cohen (Eds.), *The Lives of Lesbians, Gays, and Bisexuals: Children to Adults* (pp. 393–415) (Fort Worth, TX: Harcourt Brace, 1996).

15. "23% of young Black women now identify as bisexual," *The Conversation* (June 11, 2019), https://theconversation.com; T. Bridges & M. R. Moore, "Young women of color and shifting sexual identities," *Contexts, 17* (2018), 86–88, doi:10.1177/1536504218767125; P. England, E. Mishel, & M. L. Caudillo, "Increases in sex with same-sex partners and bisexual identity across cohorts of women (but not men)," *Sociological Science, 3* (2016), 951–970, doi:10.15195/v3.a42.

16. S. E. Rutledge, J. B. Jemmott, A. O'Leary, & L. D. Icard, "What's in an identity label? Correlates of sociodemographics, psychosocial characteristics, and sexual behavior among African American men who have sex with men," *Archives of Sexual Behavior, 47* (2018), 157–167, doi:10.1007/s10508-016-0776-5.

17. T. P. Duffin, "The lowdown on the down low: Why some bisexually active men choose to self-identify as straight," *Journal of Bisexuality, 16* (2016), 484–506, quotes pp. 488, 501–502, doi:10.1080/15299716.2016.1252301.

18. E. G. Ward, "Homophobia, hypermasculinity and the US Black church," *Culture, Health & Sexuality, 7* (2005), 493–504, quotes pp. 493–494, 496, doi:10.1080/13691050500151248.

19. Morgan et al., "Sexual development experiences of Black bisexual male adolescents," 1846, 1847.

20. "23% of young Black women now identify as bisexual."

21. T. Bridges & M. R. Moore, "Young women of color and shifting sexual identities," *Contexts, 17* (2018), 86–88, quote p. 86, doi:10.1177/1536504218767125; see also J. Bennett, "These teen girls are fighting for a more just future," *New York Times* (July 3, 2020), www.nytimes.com.

22. J. Carter, "Why are Black women increasingly identifying as bisexual?," *Gospel Coalition* (July 31, 2019), www.thegospelcoalition.org.

23. "23% of young Black women now identify as bisexual."

24. Bridges & Moore, "Young women of color and shifting sexual identities," 88; see also A. B. Helm, "Black women now the most educated group in US," *The Root* (June 5, 2016), www.theroot.com.

25. H. Carrillo, "How Latin culture got more gay," *New York Times* (May 16, 2013), www.nytimes.com; H. Carrillo & A. Hoffman, "'Straight with a pinch of bi': The construction of heterosexuality as an elastic category among adult US men," *Sexualities, 21* (2018), 90–108, doi:10.1177/1363460716678561.

26. Carrillo & Hoffman, "Straight with a pinch of bi"; E. H. Fankhanel, "The identity development and coming out process of gay youth in Puerto Rico," *Journal of LGBT Youth, 7* (2010), 262–283, doi:10.1080/19361653.2010.489330; W. L. Jeffries, "A comparative analysis of homosexual behaviors, sex role preferences, and anal sex proclivities in Latino and non-Latino men," *Archives of Sexual Behavior, 38* (2009), 765–778, doi:10.1007/s10508-007-9254-4.

27. Jeffries, "Comparative analysis of homosexual behaviors," 766.

28. Dubé & Savin-Williams, "Sexual identity development among ethnic sexual-minority male youths."

29. O. B. Jamil, G. W. Harper, M. I. Fernandez, "Sexual and ethnic identity development among gay-bisexual-questioning (GBQ) male ethnic minority adolescents,"
Cultural Diversity and Ethnic Minority Psychology, 15 (2009), 203–214, quote p.
203, doi:10.1037/a0014795.

30. Y. B. Chung & D. M. Szymanski, "Racial and sexual identities of Asian American
gay men," *Journal of LGBT Issues in Counseling, 1* (2006), 67–93, doi:10.1300/
J462v01n02_05; Y. Tong, "Acculturation, gender disparity, and the sexual behavior
of Asian American youth," *Journal of Sex Research, 50* (2013), 560–573, doi:10.1080
/00224499.2012.668976; N. Tang, L. Bensman, & E. Hatfield, "The impact of
culture and gender on sexual motives: Differences between Chinese and North
Americans," *International Journal of Intercultural Relations, 36* (2012), 286–294,
doi:10.1016/j.ijintrel.2011.12.013.

31. Dubé & Savin-Williams, "Sexual identity development among ethnic sexual-
minority male youths," 1396–1397.

14. BI IN THE COUNTRY

1. M. B. Thomeer & C. Reczek, "Happiness and sexual minority status," *Archives of
Sexual Behavior, 45* (2016), 1745–1758, quote p. 1756, doi:10.1007/s10508-016-0737-z.

2. R. Albelda, M. V. L. Badgett, A. Schneebaum, & G. J. Gates, *Poverty in the Lesbian,
Gay, and Bisexual Community* (Los Angeles: Williams Institute, 2009).

3. C. Wienke & G. J. Hill, "Does place of residence matter? Rural-urban differences
and the wellbeing of gay men and lesbians," *Journal of Homosexuality, 60* (2013),
1256–1279, quotes pp. 1271–1272, 1260, doi:10.1080/00918369.2013.806166.

4. J. S. Morandini, A. Blaszczynski, I. Dar-Nimrod, & M. W. Ross, "Minority stress
and community connectedness among gay, lesbian, and bisexual Australians: A
comparison of rural and metropolitan localities," *Australian and New Zealand
Journal of Public Health, 39* (2015), 260–266, quote p. 264,
doi:10.1111/1753-6405.12364.

5. M. L. Gray, *Out in the Country: Youth, Media, and Queer Visibility in Rural
America* (New York: New York University Press, 2009), 189; M. L. Gray, email
correspondence with the author (April 1, 2019).

6. Wienke & Hill, "Does place of residence matter?"

7. L. Moser, "In the Backwoods of Lost River, a gay retreat," *New York Times*
(October 30, 2013), www.nytimes.com; R. Ross, "Community makes itself known,
with discretion," *New York Times* (August 30, 2014), www.nytimes.com; K.
Severson, "Dollywood: A little bit country, a little bit gay," *New York Times*
(August 22, 2014), www.nytimes.com.

8. T. Silva, *Still Straight: Sexual Flexibility among White Men in Rural America* (New
York: New York University Press, 2021).

9. T. Silva, "Bud-sex: Constructing normative masculinity among rural straight men
that have sex with men," *Gender & Society, 31* (2017), 51–73, quote p. 69,
doi:10.1177/0891243216679934.

10. T. Silva, "'Helpin' a buddy out': Perceptions of identity and behaviour among rural straight men that have sex with each other," *Sexualities, 21* (2018), 68–89, quote p. 70, doi:10.1177/1363460716678564; also see Silva, "Bud-sex."

11. Silva, *Still Straight.*

12. J. Stroup, J. Glass, & T. J. Cohn, "The adjustment to U.S. rural college campuses for bisexual students in comparison to gay and lesbian students: An exploratory study," *Journal of Bisexuality, 14* (2014), 94–109, quote p. 103, doi:10.1080/15299716.2014.872482. See also Morandini et al., "Minority stress and community connectedness"; Thomeer & Reczek, "Happiness and sexual minority status."

13. Z. Zane, "Why bisexuals in the country experience higher rates of depression," *Pride* (December 5, 2016), www.pride.com.

14. S. Allen, "How 'real America' became queer America," *New York Times* (March 13, 2019), www.nytimes.com.

15. Gray, *Out in the Country*, 19.

15. BISEXUALITIES

1. P. C. R. Rodríguez Rust, "Bisexuality: The state of the union," *Annual Review of Sex Research, 13* (2002), 180–240, quote p. 224.

2. Major works of the pioneers: F. Klein, *The Bisexual Option: A Concept of One-Hundred Percent Intimacy* (New York: Arbor House, 1978); R. C. Fox, "Bisexuality in perspective: A review of theory and research," in B. A. Firestein (Ed.), *Bisexuality: The Psychology and Politics of an Invisible Minority* (pp. 3–50) (Thousand Oaks, CA: Sage, 1996); M. S. Weinberg, C. J. Williams, & D. W. Pryor, *Dual Attraction: Understanding Bisexuality* (New York: Oxford University Press, 1994); K. J. Taywaditep & J. P. Stokes, "Male bisexualities," *Journal of Psychology & Human Sexuality, 10* (1998), 15–41; J. D. Weinrich & F. Klein, "Bi-gay, bi-straight, and bi-bi: Three bisexual subgroups identified using cluster analysis of the Klein Sexual Orientation Grid," *Journal of Bisexuality, 2* (2002), 110–139. Later writers reinforced this perspective: A. Baldwin, B. Dodge, V. Schick, R. D. Hubach, J. Bowling, D. Malebranche, et al., "Sexual self-identification among behaviorally bisexual men in the midwestern United States," *Archives of Sexual Behavior, 44* (2015), 2015–2026, doi:10.1007/s10508-014-0376-1; B. Dodge & T. G. M. Sandfort, "A review of mental health research on bisexual individuals when compared to homosexual and heterosexual individuals," in B. A. Firestein (Ed.), *Becoming Visible: Counseling Bisexuals across the Lifespan* (pp. 28–51) (New York: Columbia University Press, 2007); J. Jabbour, L. Holmes, D. Sylva, K. J. Hsu, T. L. Semon, A. M. Rosenthal, A. Safron, E. Slettevold, T. M. Watts-Overall, R. C. Savin-Williams, J. Sylla, G. Rieger, & J. M. Bailey, "Robust evidence for bisexual orientation among men," *Proceedings of the National Academy of Sciences, 117* (2020), 18369–18377, doi:10.1073/pnas.2003631117; G. Rieger, L. Holmes, T. M. Watts, D. C. Gruia, J. M. Bailey, & R. C. Savin-Williams, "Gender nonconformity of bisexual men and women," *Archives of Sexual Behavior, 49* (2020), 2481–2495,

doi:10.1016/j.biopsycho.2019.107763; J. E. Rullo, D. S. Strassberg, & M. H. Miner, "Gender-specificity in sexual interest in bisexual men and women," *Archives of Sexual Behavior, 44* (2015), 1449–1457, doi:10.1007/s10508-014-0415-y; R. C. Savin-Williams & K. M. Cohen, "Prevalence, mental health, and heterogeneity of bisexual men," *Current Sexual Health Reports, 10* (2018), 196–202, doi:10.1007/s11930-018-0164-3; E. Slettevold, L. Holmes, D. Gruiaa, C. P. Nyssena, T. M. Watts-Overall, & G. Rieger, "Bisexual men with bisexual and monosexual genital arousal patterns," *Biological Psychology, 148* (November 2019), 107763; R. L. Worthington & A. L. Reynolds, "Within group differences in sexual orientation and identity," *Journal of Consulting Psychology, 56* (2009), 44–55, doi:10.1037/a0013498.

3. These and others are elaborated by Rodríguez Rust, "Bisexuality," 184 (first quote); S. E. Burke & M. LaFrance, "Stereotypes of bisexual people: What do bisexual people themselves think?," *Psychology of Sexual Orientation and Gender Diversity, 3* (2016), 247–254, second quote p. 247; S. E. Burke & M. LaFrance, "Lay conceptions of sexual minority groups," *Archives of Sexual Behavior, 45* (2016), 635–650, doi:10.1007/s10508-015-0655-5; B. Dodge, D. Herbenick, M. R. Friedman, V. Schick, T.-C. J. Fu, W. Bostwick, et al., "Attitudes toward bisexual men and women among a nationally representative probability sample of adults in the United States," *PLoS One, 11*(10) (2016), e0164430, doi:10.1371/journal.pone.0164430; M. R. Yost & G. D. Thomas, "Gender and binegativity: Men's and women's attitudes toward male and female bisexuals," *Archives of Sexual Behavior, 41* (2012), 691–702, doi:10.1007/s10508-011-9767-8; A. Zivony & T. Lobel, "The invisible stereotypes of bisexual men," *Archives of Sexual Behavior, 43* (2014), 1165–1176, doi:10.1007/s10508-014-0263-9

4. C. Dyar & B. A. Feinstein, "Binegativity: Attitudes toward and stereotypes about bisexual individuals," in D. Swan & S. Habibi (Eds.), *Bisexuality: Theories, Research, and Recommendations for the Invisible Sexuality* (pp. 95–111) (Cham, Switzerland: Springer International, 2018).

5. Yost & Thomas, "Gender and binegativity."

6. J. R. Sylla, email posted on Sexnet@listserv.it.northwestern.edu (May 15, 2020); K. Yoshino, "The epistemic contract of bisexual erasure," *Stanford Law Review, 52* (2000), 353–459, doi:10.2307/1229482.

7. Dodge et al., "Attitudes toward bisexual men and women," 13.

8. Burke & LaFrance, "Lay conceptions of sexual minority groups," 644; Burke & LaFrance, "Stereotypes of bisexual people," 252.

9. T. L. Semon, K. J. Hsu, A. M. Rosenthal, & J. M. Bailey, "Bisexual phenomena among gay identified men," *Archives of Sexual Behavior, 46* (2017), 237–245, quotes p. 240, doi:10.1007/s10508-016-0849-5. Also see R. C. Savin-Williams, *Becoming Who I Am: Young Men on Being Gay* (Cambridge, MA: Harvard University Press, 2016).

10. Dodge et al., "Attitudes toward bisexual men and women," 11.

11. M. King, J. Semlyen, S. S. Tai, H. Killaspy, D. Osborn, D. Popelyuk, & I. Nazareth, "A systematic review of mental disorder, suicide, and deliberate self harm in lesbian, gay and bisexual people," *BMC Psychiatry, 8* (2008), quote from abstract, doi:10.1186/1471-244X-8-70.

12. M. R. Friedman, B. Dodge, V. Schick, D. Herbenick, R. D. Hubach, J. Bowling, et al., "From bias to bisexual health disparities: Attitudes toward bisexual men and women in the United States," *LGBT Health, 1* (2014), 309–318, quote p. 310, doi:10.1089/lgbt.2014.0005.

13. L. E. Ross, T. Salway, L. A. Tarasoff, B. W. Hawkins, J. M. MacKay, & C. P. Fehr, "Prevalence of depression and anxiety among bisexual people compared to gay, lesbian, and heterosexual individuals: A systematic review and meta-analysis," *Journal of Sex Research, 55* (2018), 435–456, doi:10.1080/00224499.2017.1387755.

14. A. Költő, A. Cosma, H. Young, N. Moreau, D. Pavlova, R. Tesler, et al., "Romantic attraction and substance use in 15-year-old adolescents from eight European countries," *International Journal of Environmental Research and Public Health, 16* (2019), 3063, doi:10.3390/ijerph16173063.

15. Ross et al., "Prevalence of depression and anxiety among bisexual people," 435.

16. E. Steinman & B. Beemyn, "Introduction," *Journal of Bisexuality, 1* (2001), 1–14, quotes pp. 3–4, 7.

17. R. C. Savin-Williams, "A critique of research on sexual-minority youth," *Journal of Adolescence, 24* (2001), 5–13, doi:10.1006/jado.2000.0369; R. C. Savin-Williams, *The New Gay Teenager* (Cambridge, MA: Harvard University Press, 2005). Also see G. M. Russell, J. S. Bohan, & D. Lilly, "Queer youth: Old stories, new stories," in S. L. Jones (Ed.), *A Sea of Stories: The Shaping Power of Narrative in Gay and Lesbian Cultures* (pp. 69–92) (New York: Harrington Park, 2000); D. R. Arakawa, C. E. Flanders, E. Hatfield, & R. Heck, "Positive psychology: What impact has it had on sex research publication trends?," *Sexuality & Culture, 17* (2013), 305–320, doi:10.1007/s12119-012-9152-3.

18. A. Bryan, "Queer youth and mental health: What do educators need to know?," *Irish Educational Studies, 36* (2017), 73–89, quotes pp. 73, 77, 85, doi:10.1080/033233 15.2017.1300237.

19. Institute of Medicine, *The Health of Lesbian, Gay, Bisexual, and Transgender People: Building a Foundation for Better Understanding* (Washington, DC: National Academies Press, 2011). See also D. M. Doyle & L. Molix, "Disparities in social health by sexual orientation and the etiologic role of self-reported discrimination," *Archives of Sexual Behavior, 45* (2016), 1317–1327, doi:10.1007/s10508-015-0639-5; and W. B. Bostwick, C. J. Boyd, T. L. Hughes, & S. E. McCabe, "Dimensions of sexual orientation and the prevalence of mood and anxiety disorders in the United States," *American Journal of Public Health, 100* (2010), 468–475, quote p. 472, doi:10.2105/AJPH.2008.152942.

20. S. Šević, I. Ivanković, & A. Štulhofer, "Emotional intimacy among coupled heterosexual and gay/bisexual Croatian men: Assessing the role of minority

stress," *Archives of Sexual Behavior, 45* (2016), 1259–1268, doi:10.1007/s10508-015-0538-9; M. A. Busseri, T. Willoughby, H. Chalmers, & A. R. Bogaert, "Same-sex attraction and successful adolescent development," *Journal of Youth and Adolescence, 35* (2006), 563–575, doi:10.1007/s10964-006-9071-4; S. M. Horowitz, D. L. Weis, & M. T. Laflin, "Differences between sexual orientation behavior groups and social background, quality of life, and health behaviors," *Journal of Sex Research, 38* (2001), 205–218, doi:10.1080/00224490109552089; J. Konik & M. Crawford, "Exploring normative creativity: Testing the relationship between cognitive flexibility and sexual identity," *Sex Roles, 51* (2004), 249–253, doi:10.1023/B:SERS.0000; R. C. Savin-Williams, N. Antebi, & G. Rieger, "Psychological well-being of gay, lesbian, and bisexual youth: A matter of who and what is assessed," Brief Communication Abstract presented at the International Academy of Sex Research, Lisbon, Portugal (July 2012); S. B. Oswalt & T. J. Wyatt, "Sexual health behaviors and sexual orientation in U.S. national sample of college students," *Archives of Sexual Behavior, 42* (2013), 1561–1572, doi:10.1007/s10508-012-0066-9.

21. E. D. B. Riggle, J. S. Whitman, A. Olson, S. S. Rostosky, & S. Strong, "The positive aspects of being a lesbian or gay man," *Professional Psychology: Research and Practice, 39* (2008), 210–217, doi:10.1037/0735-7028.39.2.210.

22. These points are made by S. Salim, M. Robinson, & C. E. Flanders, "Bisexual women's experiences of microaggressions and microaffirmations and their relation to mental health," *Psychology of Sexual Orientation and Gender Diversity, 6* (2019), 336–346, doi:10.1037/sgd0000329; J. Taylor, J. Power, E. Smith, & M. Rathbone, "Bisexual mental health: Findings from the 'Who I Am' study," *Australian Journal of General Practice, 48* (2019), 138–144, quote p. 138; J. P. Robinson & D. L. Espelage, "Inequities in educational and psychological outcomes between LGBTQ and straight students in middle and high school," *Educational Researcher, 40* (2011), 315–330, doi:10.3102/0013189X11422112; R. C. Savin-Williams, *Gay and Lesbian Youth: Expressions of Identity* (Washington, DC: Hemisphere, 1990); Savin-Williams, *Becoming Who I Am.*

23. O. R. Phillips, A. K. Onopa, V. Hsu, H. M. Ollila, R. P. Hillary, J. Hallmayer, et al., "Beyond a binary classification of sex: An examination of brain sex differentiation, psychopathology, and genotype," *Journal of the American Academy of Child & Adolescent Psychiatry* (October 9, 2018), doi:10.1016/j.jaac.2018.09.425; R. C. Savin-Williams, K. M. Cohen, K. Joyner, & G. Rieger, "Depressive symptoms among same-sex oriented young men: Importance of reference group," *Archives of Sexual Behavior, 39* (2010), 1213–1215, doi:10.1007/s10508-010-9658 4; G. D. Wilson & Q. Rahman, *Born Gay? The Psychobiology of Sex Orientation* (London: Peter Owen, 2005).

24. J. E. Pachankis, "The psychological implications of concealing a stigma: A cognitive-affective-behavioral model," *Psychological Bulletin, 133* (2007), 328–345, quote p. 328, doi:10.1037/0033-2909.133.2.328.

25. These issues are discussed in T. S. Hottes, D. Gesink, O. Ferlatte, D. J. Brennan, A. E. Rhodes, R. Marchand, & T. Trussler, "Concealment of sexual minority identities in interviewer-administered government surveys and its impact on estimates of suicide ideation among bisexual and gay men," *Journal of Bisexuality, 16* (2016), 427–453, quote p. 441, doi:10.1080/15299716.2016.1225622. See also B. A. Feinstein, C. Dyar, D. H. Li, S. W. Whitton, M. E. Newcomb, & B. Mustanski, "The longitudinal associations between outness and health outcomes among gay/lesbian versus bisexual emerging adults," *Archives of Sexual Behavior, 48* (2019), 1111–1126, doi:10.1007/s10508-018-1221-8; Taylor et al., "Bisexual mental health"; G. van Beusekom, K. L. Collier, H. M. W. Bos, T. G. M. Sandfort, & G. Overbeek, "Gender nonconformity and peer victimization: Sex and sexual attraction differences by age," *Journal of Sex Research, 57* (2020), 234–246, doi:10.1080/00224 499.2019.1591334; B. A. Feinstein, B. C. Turner, L. B. Beach, A. K. Korpak, & G. Phillips II, "Racial/ethnic differences in mental health, substance use, and bullying victimization among self-identified bisexual high school-aged youth," *LGBT Health, 6* (2019), 174–183, doi:10.1089/lgbt.2018.0229.

26. Pachankis, "Psychological implications of concealing a stigma."

27. A. Caspi & T. E. Moffitt, "All for one and one for all: Mental disorders in one dimension," *American Journal of Psychiatry, 175* (2018), 831–844, doi:10.1176/appi. ajp.2018.17121383; A. Caspi, R. M. Houts, D. W. Belsky, S. J. Goldman-Mellor, H. Harrington, S. Israel, et al., "The *p* factor: One general psychopathology factor in the structure of psychiatric disorders?," *Clinical Psychological Science, 2* (2014), 119–137, doi:10.1177/2167702613497473.

28. Hottes et al., "Concealment of sexual minority identities," 429; J. E. Pachankis & R. Bränström, "How many sexual minorities are hidden? Projecting the size of the global closet with implications for policy and public health," *PLoS One, 14*(6) (2019), e0218084, doi:10.1371/journal.pone.0218084; J. Berona, S. D. Stepp, A. E. Hipwell, & K. E. Keenan, "Trajectories of sexual orientation from adolescence to young adulthood: Results from a community-based urban sample of girls," *Journal of Adolescent Health, 63* (2018), 57–61, doi:10.1016/j.jadohealth.2018.01.015.

29. S. Mukherjee, "What can odd, interesting medical case studies teach us?," *New York Times Magazine* (July 17, 2018), www.nytimes.com.

30. N. Way, *Deep Secrets: Boys' Friendships and the Crisis of Connection* (Cambridge, MA: Harvard University Press, 2011); N. Way, "Why 'boys will be boys' is a myth—and a harmful one at that," TEDMED Talk (2018), www.tedmed.com/talks/show?id=730069.

31. D. L. Tolman, "Female adolescents, sexual empowerment and desire: A missing discourse of gender inequity," *Sex Roles, 66* (2012), 746, doi:10.1007/s11199-012-0122-x; D. L. Tolman, *Dilemmas of Desire: Teenage Girls Talk about Sexuality* (Cambridge, MA: Harvard University Press, 2002); D. L. Tolman, R. Spencer, T. Harmon, M. Rosen-Reynose, & M. Striepe, "Getting close, staying cool: Early adolescent boys' experiences with romantic relationships," in N. Way & J. Y. Chu (Eds.), *Adolescent Boys: Exploring Diverse Cultures of Boyhood* (pp. 235–255) (New

York: New York University Press, 2004), 239. See also M. Fine, "Sexuality, schooling, and adolescent females: The missing discourse of desire," *Harvard Educational Review, 58* (1988), 29–53; and M. I. Striepe & D. L. Tolman, "Mom, dad, I'm straight: The coming out of gender ideologies in adolescent sexual-identity development," *Journal of Clinical Child & Adolescent Psychology, 32* (2003), 523–530, doi:10.1207/S15374424JCCP3204_4.

32. T. Bridges & M. R. Moore, "Young women of color and shifting sexual identities," *Contexts, 17* (2018), 86–88, quote p. 88, doi:10.1177/1536504218767125.

33. K. J. Hsu, A. M. Rosenthal, D. I. Miller, & J. M. Bailey, "Who are gynandro-morphophilic men? Characterizing men with sexual interest in transgender women," *Psychological Medicine, 46* (2016), 819–827, doi:10.1017/S0033291715002317; G. Rieger, A. M. Rosenthal, B. M. Cash, J. A. W. Linsenmeier, J. M. Bailey, & R. C. Savin-Williams, "Male bisexual arousal: A matter of curiosity?," *Biological Psychology, 94* (2013), 479–489, doi:10.1016/j.biopsycho.2013.09.007; M. L. Chivers, "The specificity of women's sexual response and its relationship with sexual orientations: A review and ten hypotheses," *Archives of Sexual Behavior, 46* (2017), 1161–1179, doi:10.1007/s10508-016-0897-x.

34. M. Morris, "'Gay capital' in gay student friendship networks: An intersectional analysis of class, masculinity, and decreased homophobia," *Journal of Social and Personal Relationships, 35* (2018), 1183–1204, quotes p. 1194, doi:10.1177/026540751770573. Also see M. McCormack, E. Anderson, & A. Adams, "Cohort effect on the coming out experiences of bisexual men," *Sociology, 48* (2014), 1207–1223, doi:10.1177/0038038513518851; E. Anderson & M. McCormack, *The Changing Experiences of Bisexual Men's Lives: Social Research Perspectives* (New York: Springer, 2016).

16. POSTIDENTITY REVOLUTION

1. C. Harris, "Son of the beach," featuring Woody Cook at PRM Models, *Boys by Girls* (January 28, 2019), www.boysbygirls.co.uk.

2. C. M. Blow, "Up from pain," *New York Times* (September 19, 2014), www.nytimes.com; C. M. Blow, *Fire Shut Up in My Bones: A Memoir* (Boston: Houghton Mifflin Harcourt, 2014).

3. C. Cauterucci, "Will America accept Andrew Gillum?," *Slate* (September 15, 2020), https://slate.com.

4. C. Eller, "Emma Gonzalez opens up about how her life has changed since Parkland tragedy," *Variety* (October 9, 2018), https://variety.com.

5. Harris, "Son of the beach."

6. B. Alfonso, *A Voice of the Warm: The Life of Rod McKuen* (Lanham, MD: Backbeat Books, 1979), 128.

7. The 2020 National College Student Sexual and Reproductive Health Survey of China: "Over 20% of Chinese university students say they are not straight," *Gay Star News* (May 19, 2020), www.gaystarnews.com.

8. A. Hoyle, "Why do so many young people say they're bisexual? Honest? Confused? Influenced by celebrities? We talk to three youngsters—and their (somewhat bemused) parents," *Daily Mail* (UK) (October 31, 2016), www. dailymail.co.uk.

9. M. Morris, M. McCormack, & E. Anderson, "The changing experiences of bisexual male adolescents," *Gender and Education, 26* (2014), 397–413, quote p. 408, doi:10.1080/09540253.2014.927834.

10. A. Hawgood, "Everyone is gay on TikTok," *New York Times* (October 24, 2020), www.nytimes.com; N. Way, *Deep Secrets: Boys' Friendships and the Crisis of Connection* (Cambridge, MA: Harvard University Press, 2011).

11. M. McCormack & E. Anderson, "The influence of declining homophobia on men's gender in the United States: An argument for the study of homohysteria," *Sex Roles, 71* (2014), 109–120, quote p. 109, doi:10.1007/s11199-014-0358-8; M. McCormack, *The Declining Significance of Homophobia: How Teenage Boys Are Redefining Masculinity and Heterosexuality* (New York: Oxford University Press, 2012).

12. K. Parker, N. Graf, & R. Igielnik, "Generation Z looks a lot like Millennials on key social and political issues," Pew Research Center (January 17, 2019), www. pewsocialtrends.org; A. Taylor, "Out with the old, in with the young," *New York Times* (October 18, 2019), www.nytimes.com.

13. For more about this scholarship, see the website: https://thepinnaclefoundation. org.

14. A. E. White, J. Moeller, Z. Ivcevic, & M. A. Brackett, "Gender identity and sexual identity labels used by U.S. high school students: A co-occurrence network analysis," *Psychology of Sexual Orientation and Gender Diversity, 5* (2018), 243–252, doi:10.1037/sgd0000266.

15. C. L. Muehlenhard, "Categories and sexuality," *Journal of Sex Research, 37* (2000), 101–107; A. C. Salomaa & J. L. Matsick, "Carving sexuality at its joints: Defining sexual orientation in research and clinical practice," *Psychological Assessment, 31* (2019), 167–180, doi:10.1037/pas0000656.

16. J. Nelson, "Rita Ora respond to 'Girls' backlash: 'I have had romantic relationship with women and men,'" *People* (May 14, 2018), http://people.com.

17. R. C. Savin-Williams, *The New Gay Teenager* (Cambridge, MA: Harvard University Press, 2005), 1, 222.

18. P. L. Hammack, D. M. Frost, & S. D. Hughes, "Queer intimacies: A new paradigm for the study of relationship diversity," *Journal of Sex Research, 56* (2019), 556–592, doi:10.1080/00224499.2018.1531281; S. T. Russell, T. J. Clarke, & J. Clary, "Are teens 'post-gay'? Contemporary adolescents' sexual identity labels," *Journal of Youth and Adolescence, 38* (2009), 884–890, doi:10.1007/s10964-008-9388-2; S. T. Russell, R. B. Toomey, C. Ryan, & R. M. Diaz, "Being out at school: The implications for school victimization and young adult adjustment," *American Journal of Orthopsychiatry, 84* (2014), 635–643, quote p. 636, doi:10.1037/ort0000037.

19. Q. Rahman, Y. Xu, R. A. Lippa, & P. L. Vasey, "Prevalence of sexual orientation across 28 nations and its association with gender equality, economic development, and individualism," *Archives of Sexual Behavior, 49* (2020), 595–606, quote p. 595, doi:10.1007/s10508-019-01590-0. See also A. Ganna, K. J. H. Verweij, M. G. Nivard, R. Maier, R. Wedow, A. S. Busch, et al., "Large-scale GWAS reveals insights into the genetic architecture of same-sex sexual behavior," *Science* 365 (2019): eaat7693, doi:10.1126/science.aat7693.

20. S. Abramovitch, "'Westworld' star Evan Rachel Wood shares details of her bisexuality at LGBT gala," *Hollywood Reporter* (February 7, 2017), www.hollywoodreporter.com.

21. T. Henderson, "'Atypical's' Brigette Lundy-Paine comes out as queer," *Pride* (September 14, 2018), www.pride.com.

22. R. Gajewski, "The star of the CW's 'Roswell' reboot isn't a poster child of anything but his own path," *Playboy* (June 12, 2019), www.playboy.com; D. Artavia, "Do you think you really know Tyler Blackburn?," *Advocate* (April 19, 2019), www.advocate.com.

23. R. Ermac, "Paris Jackson doesn't want anyone to label her sexuality," *Pride* (August 5, 2020), www.pride.com; D. Artavia, "Ronan Farrow confirms rumors he's part of LGBT community," *Advocate* (April 10, 2018), www.advocate.com; A. Stoner, "I, Alyson, am attracted to men, women, and people who identify in other ways," BuzzFeed Facebook page (April 1, 2018), www.facebook.com/BuzzFeed/posts/i-alyson-am-attracted-to-men-women-and-people-who-identify-in-other-ways/10157620727665329/; R. Lynch, "Popular DJ comes out as bisexual," *South Florida Gay News* (March 2, 2018), https://southfloridagaynews.com; *Out* Editors, "'Boy Erased' star Lucas Hedges comes out as 'not totally straight,'" *Out* (September 5, 2018), www.out.com; B. Spanos, "Janelle Monáe frees herself," *Rolling Stone* (May 17–30, 2018), www.rollingstone.com; A. Iasimone, "Kehlani answers questions about her sexuality on Twitter: 'I'm queer,'" *Billboard* (April 22, 2018), www.billboard.com.

24. B. Moylan, "Lee Pace is barnstorming back to Broadway with the first revival of 'Angels in America,'" *W* (February 28, 2018), www.wmagazine.com.

25. Harris, "Son of the beach."

26. "Introducing 2019 Connecticut's Kid Governor®-Elect Ella Briggs," Connecticut's Kid Governor (2019), http://ct.kidgovernor.org.

INDEX

ABOUT THE AUTHOR

Ritch C. Savin-Williams, Professor Emeritus of Developmental Psychology at Cornell University, received his PhD from the University of Chicago. This is his tenth book on adolescent development, including *Mostly Straight: Sexual Fluidity among Men* (2017), *Becoming Who I Am: Young Men on Being Gay* (2016), *The New Gay Teenager* (2005), and *"Mom, Dad. I'm Gay.": How Families Negotiate Coming Out* (2001). Dr. Savin-Williams writes about the sexual and romantic development of young men and women, regardless of their sexuality. He is also a licensed clinical psychologist and has served as an expert witness on same-sex marriage, gay adoption, gender discrimination, and Boy Scout court cases. Dr. Savin-Williams has consulted for media outlets such as MTV, *20/20*, *The Oprah Winfrey Show*, *Good Morning America*, *The Today Show*, *National Geographic*, National Public Radio, *Rolling Stone*, *Time*, the *New York Times*, and the *Washington Post*. He has also written a junior high curriculum for the Unitarian Universalist Association, *Beyond Pink and Blue: Exploring Our Stereotypes of Sexuality and Gender*. Dr. Savin-Williams blogs on sex and romance for *Psychology Today*: www.psychologytoday.com/experts/ritch-c-savin-williams-phd.